Discourses of Hope and Reconciliation

Also available from Bloomsbury

Applying Systemic Functional Linguistics, edited by
Jonathan J. Webster and Xuanwei Peng
Halliday in the 21st Century, edited by Jonathan J. Webster
Interviews with M.A.K. Halliday, edited by J. R. Martin
The Bloomsbury Companion to M. A. K. Halliday, edited by Jonathan J. Webster
The Essential Hyland, by Ken Hyland

Discourses of Hope and Reconciliation

On J. R. Martin's Contribution to Systemic Functional Linguistics

Edited by
Michele Zappavigna and Shoshana Dreyfus

BLOOMSBURY ACADEMIC
LONDON • NEW YORK • OXFORD • NEW DELHI • SYDNEY

BLOOMSBURY ACADEMIC
Bloomsbury Publishing Plc
50 Bedford Square, London, WC1B 3DP, UK
1385 Broadway, New York, NY 10018, USA
29 Earlsfort Terrace, Dublin 2, Ireland

BLOOMSBURY, BLOOMSBURY ACADEMIC and the Diana logo are
trademarks of Bloomsbury Publishing Plc

First published in Great Britain 2020
This paperback edition published 2022

Copyright © Michele Zappavigna, Shoshana Dreyfus and Contributors, 2020

Michele Zappavigna and Shoshana Dreyfus have asserted their right
under the Copyright, Designs and Patents Act, 1988, to be identified
as Editors of this work.

For legal purposes the Acknowledgements on p. xiv constitute an
extension of this copyright page.

Cover design: Ben Anslow
Cover image: © Colonel / Getty Images

All rights reserved. No part of this publication may be reproduced or
transmitted in any form or by any means, electronic or mechanical,
including photocopying, recording, or any information storage or retrieval
system, without prior permission in writing from the publishers.

Bloomsbury Publishing Plc does not have any control over, or
responsibility for, any third-party websites referred to or in this book.
All internet addresses given in this book were correct at the time of
going to press. The author and publisher regret any inconvenience
caused if addresses have changed or sites have ceased to exist,
but can accept no responsibility for any such changes.

A catalogue record for this book is available from the British Library.

Library of Congress Cataloging-in-Publication Data
Names: Zappavigna, Michele, editor. | Dreyfus, Shoshana, editor. |
Martin, J. R., 1950-Honouree.
Title: Discourses of hope and reconciliation: J. R. Martin's contribution to systemic
functional linguistics / edited by Michele Zappavigna and Shoshana Dreyfus.
Description: London; New York: Bloomsbury Academic, 2020. | Includes bibliographical
references and index. |
Identifiers: LCCN 2020019582 (print) | LCCN 2020019583 (ebook) | ISBN 9781350116061
(hardback) | ISBN 9781350116078 (ebook) | ISBN 9781350116085 (epub)
Subjects: LCSH: Systemic grammar. | Functionalism (Linguistics) | Discourse analysis.
Classification: LCC P149 .D57 2020 (print) | LCC P149 (ebook) | DDC 410.1/833–dc23
LC record available at https://lccn.loc.gov/2020019582
LC ebook record available at https://lccn.loc.gov/2020019583

ISBN:	HB:	978-1-3501-1606-1
	PB:	978-1-3502-0259-7
	ePDF:	978-1-3501-1607-8
	ePUB:	978-1-3501-1608-5

Typeset by Integra Software Services Pvt. Ltd.

To find out more about our authors and books visit www.bloomsbury.com
and sign up for our newsletters.

Contents

List of figures	vi
List of tables	viii
Notes on contributors	ix
Preface	xii
Acknowledgements	xiv

1	J. R. Martin, language and linguistics *Y. J. Doran*	1
2	Attitudinal alignments in journalistic commentary and social-media argumentation: The construction of values-based group identities in the online comments of newspaper readers *Peter R. R. White*	21
3	The foundational role of discourse semantics beyond language *John A. Bateman*	39
4	Construing entities through nominal groups in Chinese *Pin Wang*	57
5	Launching research: A Martinian perspective on science pedagogy *Sally Humphrey, Jing Hao and David Rose*	85
6	Familiarity for the unfamiliar: Thailand, kinship, culture and language *John S. Knox*	109
7	Intermodal relations, mass and presence in school science explanation genres *Len Unsworth*	131
8	Engaging readers and institutionalizing attitude: A social semiotic perspective on multimodal EFL pedagogic materials *Yumin Chen*	153
9	Uncovering 'The Story' behind meaningful texts: Bilingual students' intentions and linguistic choices *María Estela Brisk and Jasmine Alvarado*	167
10	We are all one: Shifting reference in reconciliation talk *Lise Fontaine and Katy Jones*	185
11	A nation remembers: Discourses of change, mourning and reconciliation on Australia Day *Helen Caple and Monika Bednarek*	205

Name index	221
Subject index	223

Figures

0.1	J. R. Martin	xiii
2.1	Strategies of dialogic affiliation, adapted from Zappavigna (2019, p. 58), and Zappavigna and Martin offer the following framework for the analysis of 'ambient affiliation'. (see Figure 2.2 below)	24
2.2	System of communing affiliation, adapted from Zappavigna and Martin (2018, p. 8)	25
4.1	SFL model of stratification (with stratified context), based on Martin (2014, pp. 35–7)	59
4.2	Systemic representation of field, based on Doran and Martin (2020)	59
4.3	Types of entity	60
4.4	Basic IDENTIFICATION system	69
4.5	General Chinese nominal group systems	75
4.6	The CLASSIFICATION system of Chinese nominal group	76
4.7	The DESCRIPTION system of Chinese nominal group	77
4.8	The QUANTIFICATION system of Chinese nominal group	77
4.9	The DETERMINATION system of Chinese nominal group	78
4.10	The QUALIFICATION system of Chinese nominal group	79
4.11	Delicate specifying nominal groups in Chinese	79
5.1	Year 12 Biology Poster. Alden	87
5.2	Pre-intervention scores	103
5.3	Post-intervention scores	103
6.1	Subsystems of tenor: Detail of Poynton's (1989) subsystem of power (top) and detail of Hasan's (2014) subsystem of status (bottom)	113
6.2	System English G+2	116
6.3	Systems for Thai G+2 (left) and Teochew G+2 (right)	116
6.4	Direct G+1 kinship terms across the three languages	119
6.5	System network of English indirect G+1 kinship terms	121
6.6	System network of Thai indirect G+1 kinship terms	121
6.7	System network for Teochew G+1 indirect female kinship terms as commonly used in Thailand	123
6.8	System network for Teochew G+1 indirect male kinship terms as commonly used in Thailand	123

7.1	Mulga tree text (Scott & Robinson, 1993)	133
7.2	Infographic explanation of mitosis – Nelson (Chidrawi et al., 2013, p. 19)	135
7.3	Infographic explanation of mitosis – Oxford (Silvester, 2016, p. 10)	135
7.4	Stages of mitosis – Oxford (Silvester, 2016, p. 11)	136
7.5	Diagram of mitosis – Jacaranda (Lofts, 2015, p. 28)	136
7.6	Image of unicellular organisms undergoing mitosis (Lofts, 2015, p. 28)	137
7.7	Multimodal explanation of mitosis – Pearson (Linstead et al., 2012, p. 12)	137
7.8	Composition taxonomy for the cell derived from the eight-textbook corpus	138
7.9	Momenting and tiering of activity in the cell cycle	139
7.10	Image only depiction of mitosis from the Nelson infographic	145
8.1	Explaining rules of games by demonstration. Excerpted from PEP *Primary English Students' Book I for Year 3*, 2003, p. 53. Reproduced with permission	156
8.2	Explaining rules of games by demonstration. Excerpted from PEP *Primary English Students' Book I for Year 6*, 2003, p. 12. Reproduced with permission	157
8.3	Jointly constructed text. Excerpted from PEP *Primary English Students' Book I for Year 3*, 2003, p. 16. Reproduced with permission	158
8.4	Inscribed happiness of English-learning. Excerpted from *PEP Primary English Students' Book I for Year 6*, 2003, p. 5. Reproduced with permission	160
8.5	Logogenetic recontextualization. Excerpted from *PEP Primary English Students' Book II for Year 3*, 2003, p. 15. Reproduced with permission	162
8.6	Recontextualizing feeling in Figure 8.5. Adapted from Martin, 2002, p. 199; Chen, 2010b	162
10.1	Martin's IDENTIFICATION System (adapted from Martin, 1992, p. 112)	193
10.2	Experiential representation for the three main reference chains: #ChiefJoseph, #Church and #aboriginalpeople	196
11.1	The national flag of Australia and the Aboriginal flag (Used in conjunction with © Commonwealth of Australia 2006 protocols)	207
11.2	Instagram posts using #invasionday, collected over five days between 24 to 28 January 2017	210
11.3	*Invasion Day* in the AusDay corpus	214

Tables

4.1	Realization statements for general Chinese nominal group features	76
4.2	Realization statements for specifying Chinese nominal group features	80
5.1	Extract from investigation report (Figure 5.1)	89
5.2	Sequence of reasoning in the Discussion stage	95
5.3	Positions launching phenomena	96
5.4	Detailed reading of the confirming prior research phase	99
5.5	Elaboration of launching structure	99
5.6	Elaboration by unpacking grammatical metaphor	100
5.7	Explaining evaluative function	100
6.1	Kinship terms in three languages: second generation above ego, direct (G+2)	115
6.2	First generation above ego (G+1), direct	118
6.3	First generation above ego (G+1), indirect	120
7.1	Composite representation of the tiered activity of mitosis	140
7.2	Composition in the year 10 textbook infographics on mitosis	140
7.3	The contribution of the images and the different forms of verbiage to the construal of compositional relations in the four infographics	143
7.4	Summary of the distribution across image and verbiage of the construal of composition	144
7.5	The construal of momented activity in mitosis in four year 10 infographics	146
7.6	Summary of the distribution across image and verbiage of the construal of activity	147
8.1	The distribution of different visual styles in EFL textbooks	163
10.1	List of reference chains and associated referents	190
10.2	Chain length for each chain (number of references), in order of length	192
10.3	Types of phoricity in all reference chains	195
10.4	Frequency of experiential roles in the Chief Joseph text	195
11.1	Frequency and distribution of word forms (separately)	212
11.2	Frequency and distribution of word forms (combined)	213
11.3	Competing labels, their frequencies and distribution	213

Notes on contributors

Jasmine Alvarado is Doctoral Candidate in Curriculum and Instruction at Boston College Lynch School of Education and Human Development. Her research interests include language and literacy development of bilingual students, bilingual teacher education and the relation between urban schooling and housing policies.

John A. Bateman, Professor of Applied Linguistics, Bremen University, Germany, specializes in functional, computational and multimodal linguistics. His research interests include functional linguistic approaches to multilingual and multimodal document design, semiotics and theories of discourse.

Monika Bednarek is Associate Professor in Linguistics at the University of Sydney. She has published widely in the fields of corpus linguistics and media linguistics, including most recently *The Discourse of News Values* (2017, OUP), *Language and Television Series* (2018, CUP) and *Creating Dialogue for TV* (2019, Routledge Focus).

Maria Estela Brisk is Professor of Education, Boston College. Her research and teaching interests include writing instruction, genre pedagogy, bilingual education, bilingual language and literacy acquisition, and preparation of mainstream teachers to work with bilingual learners. Author of numerous articles, book chapters and six books, Professor Brisk is a native of Argentina.

Helen Caple is Associate Professor in Journalism at the University of New South Wales, Australia. Her research interests centre on news photography, text–image relations and discursive news values analysis. Helen has published in the area of photojournalism and social semiotics. Her latest monograph with Routledge is *Photojournalism Disrupted: The View from Australia* (2019).

Shoshana Dreyfus is Senior Lecturer in Linguistics at the University of Wollongong, specializing in systemic functional linguistics and discourse analysis. Her research has mostly focused on non-verbal communication and language disorder in intellectual disability, discipline-specific academic literacy as well as developments in systemic functional linguistic theory and discourse semantics.

Yumin Chen received her PhD degree in linguistics from the University of Sydney in 2009 (Cotelle Program with Sun Yat-sen University) and is currently a Professor of Linguistics in School of Foreign Languages, Sun Yat-sen University. Her research interests include functional linguistics, discourse analysis and social semiotics.

Y. J. Doran is Lecturer in the Department of Linguistics at the University of Sydney. His research focuses on language, semiosis, knowledge and education from the perspectives of Systemic Functional Linguistics and Legitimation Code Theory, spanning the interdisciplinary fields of educational linguistics, language description, multimodality, and language and identity.

Lise Fontaine is Reader at Cardiff University (Wales). She lectures mainly on functional grammar, word meaning, corpus linguistics and introductory psycholinguistics. Her research interests include functional grammar theory and, more specifically, the study of referring expressions. She is the author of *Analysing English Grammar: A Systemic-functional Introduction* (Cambridge University Press, 2012).

Jing Hao is Postdoctoral Research Fellow at the Pontificia Universidad Católica de Chile, following her previous postdoctoral fellowship at The Hong Kong Polytechnic University, and her doctorate in Linguistics at the University of Sydney. Her research explores knowledge building through English and Mandarin Chinese and its interaction with other semiotic modes.

Sally Humphrey has worked for many years in language and literacy education, using systemic functional linguistics and genre theory. She has drawn particularly on understandings of discourse semantics and more recently multimodal literacies to support learners to develop the literacies needed for participation in academic and civic life.

Katy Jones is Lecturer at Cardiff University. She lectures mainly on second language development and discourse related modules such as Communication in Relationships. Her research interests concentrate on approaching the study of language (in particular, referring expressions) from a multi-disciplinary perspective, combining areas such as discourse analysis, cognitive linguistics, psycholinguistics, pragmatics and grammar.

John S. Knox is Senior Lecturer at Macquarie University. Language in education, mediated discourse, and multimodality are among his teaching, research supervision, and research interests.

David Rose is Director of Reading to Learn, an international literacy program that trains teachers across school and university sectors (www.readingtolearn.com.au). He is an Honorary Associate of the University of Sydney. His research interests include literacy teaching practices, teacher professional learning, analysis and design of classroom discourse, language typology and social semiotic theory.

Len Unsworth is Professor in English and Literacies Education and Research Director of educational semiotics in English and literacy pedagogy at the Institute for Learning Sciences and Teacher Education (ILSTE), at the Australian Catholic University in Sydney, Australia. Len's current research interests include systemic functional semiotic perspectives on multimodal and digital literacies in English and in curriculum area teaching and learning in primary and secondary schools.

Peter R. R. White teaches linguistics with a socio-semiotic orientation and journalism studies at the University of New South Wales. He was formerly a journalist with several Australian newspapers. He currently performs on saxophone and keyboards with the Travelling Circumstances, a jazz and blues combo of (mostly) linguists.

Pin Wang is Lecturer and Researcher at the Martin Centre for Appliable Linguistics of the School of Foreign Languages, Shanghai Jiao Tong University, China. His chief research interests are: Systemic Theory, Functional Grammar, and Functional Language Typology, with particular focus on classical languages, Mandarin and minority languages of China.

Michele Zappavigna is Senior Lecturer in the School of Arts and Media at the University of New South Wales. Her major research interest is the discourse of social media and ambient affiliation. Recent books include: *Searchable Talk: Hashtags and Social Media Metadiscourse* (2018) and *Diversionary Justice: An Analysis of Ceremonial Redress in Youth Justice Conferencing* (2018, with J. R. Martin).

Preface

J. R. Martin is a leading light in the development of Systemic Functional Linguistics (SFL). For over forty years, he has advocated the advancement of SFL theory and application around the world, with a profound impact on the lives and research of so many scholars. To celebrate his illustrious career, this book brings together some of these scholars, both established and emerging, to review, explore, and push forward the theoretical agenda Martin has set out, and continues to set out, in his momentous body of work.

This book celebrates, on the occasion of his seventieth birthday, Martin's distinguished career and the major contributions he had made to SFL, focusing on four themes – SFL theory, linguistic typology, educational linguistics, and positive discourse analysis. It opens with a biographic account of the development of his linguistic thinking, followed by a series of chapters debating and developing key concepts across genre, discourse semantics, lexicogrammar, and affiliation. The book concludes with chapters exploring the role analysing discourse can play in bringing about positive social change, a theme at the heart of Martin's linguistics.

There are so many of us who would not be working as linguists if it were not for Jim. He is a generous and kind mentor, and a true leader. His ability to inspire and guide so many different projects and aspects of the theory, to work with so many different people in so many contexts around the world, and the level of support he has given to all of us are the reasons we decided to put together this festschrift.

To Jim, we thank you for all your hard work with all of us. We honour your contribution to our field. Long may it last!

Michele Zappavigna and Shoshana Dreyfus, editors
Sydney, September 2020

Figure 0.1 J. R. Martin.

Acknowledgements

Permission to reproduce copyright-protected material is included for all the figures displayed in Chapters 7 and 8. Figures 7.1 and 7.7 have been granted permission by Pearson; Figure 7.2 has been granted permission by Nelson; Figures 7.3 and 7.4 have been granted permission by Oxford and rights have been paid to the Science Photo Library; Figures 7.5 and 7.6 have been granted permission by Wiley; and Figures 8.1–8.5 have been granted permission by the People's Education Press Copyright Department of China.

1

J. R. Martin, language and linguistics

Y. J. Doran
The University of Sydney

By any measure, J. R. Martin is a major figure in linguistics. A brief look at Martin's impact quickly shows this. If quantitative measures are anything to go by, at the time of writing, his Google Scholar citation count is 46,579 with an h-index of 85, which puts him eighth in the world in terms of citations for the tag 'Linguistics' and third in the world for 'Literacy', with a number of those above him no longer active (or alive). This numerical impact is accompanied by the fifty-six and growing PhD students he has supervised (plus innumerable Masters and undergraduate honours students), his forty-odd authored and edited books (or more, depending on when you are reading this), his eight volumes of collected works, plus the twenty-odd books of school-teaching materials he has co-produced, and the roughly 250 journal articles, book chapters, special issues, working papers and the like he has written. Couple this with the fact that research he has driven strongly underpins literacy curricula and pedagogy in both Australia and worldwide and that this festschrift has appeared while he is in his prime with many years of major contributions to come, and the significance of Martin's work becomes clear.

The role of this chapter is to give some account of Martin's work and influence. An obvious way of coming at this is by overviewing the enormously broad and varied work he has engaged in thus far and the descriptive, theoretical and applied models and interventions he has developed. This would highlight the range of Martin's work, from Systemic Functional theory and metatheory to description and application across language and semiosis, from educational linguistics to clinical and forensic linguistics, from critical discourse analysis to positive discourse analysis, from language variation and development to identity and affiliation, from genre to register to discourse semantics to lexicogrammar to phonology, from language description and typology involving English, Tagalog, Korean and Spanish, to multimodality of images and body language and Powerpoint and space, from the language of science to that of history and literature and music and administration and news and opinion and tragedy and hope and activism and schizophrenia, from classrooms to conversations, from written language to spoken language and a wealth of interdisciplinary ventures throughout. Such an overview would emphasize the diversity of objects of study and give a sense of the richness and detail for which Martin is renowned. But to give such an overview would give little sense as to why these objects occurred and what we can learn from them; it would tell us little about how these come together or the unity in diversity of Martin's work. More practically, if this chapter were written ten years ago, a number of these objects would be missed; or by writing it today, I am surely missing the new focuses and developments of the years to come. To give an overview of the objects of Martin's work is to give a list. But it says little about how the list holds together, how it came to be or the principles upon which new things are added to it. Put simply, we learn little from such an overview that can help us reflect on our own work.[1]

Another point of departure is to emphasize not the breadth and diversity of Martin's work, but its stability. From this perspective we may say that Martin has firmly positioned his work within the framework of Systemic Functional Linguistics (SFL). This gives a good insight into the unity of his work and a sense that he has developed the tradition pushed forward by his teacher Halliday and by Firth before him. But again, this would miss the enormous change that this field has had during his lifetime. For one, the name of this approach has continually changed from its earliest days, from neo-Firthian linguistics, to scale and category grammar, to systemic grammar to systemic functional grammar, to systemic functional linguistics to social semiotics and systemic functional semiotics. This name change of course reflects the continuous change that has marked the field. For a student of current Systemic Functional Linguistics to read Gregory's scale and category grammar of English that Martin was trained on in his undergraduate years (Gregory, 1966–72) would be like a modern English speaker reading Middle English; although there is some vague semblance for those who understand the relation, for other than historical reasons, it would be best to consider it a different linguistic approach.

But this constant change and diversity holds the key to understanding Martin's work. It has been said that Chomsky has consistently been the first post-Chomskyan (Gregory, 1998). Such a description could also be applied to Martin (and to Halliday before him). This pithy remark holds the insight that the wavelength of academic change is often larger than can be noticed if one is engaging in detail with a field's development for only a few years (as, say, a PhD student would be), while short enough for the field to be a little unrecognizable if one is away from the coal-face for a while (as, say, for a post-PhD scholar forced to move away and focus on securing a job for a number of years rather than on keeping up with and developing their field). In this continual but at a glance unnoticeable change, it becomes easy to take the principles of one's field when one is trained as the principles forever more, and to then be frustrated and angered when the field seems to increasingly and irrevocably move away from its 'true' essence. It is in this sense that many look to the key books and the key knowers for answers – in the field of SFL/Social Semiotics these tend to be either Firth, Halliday, Hasan, Martin, Matthiessen, Kress and/or van Leeuwen, depending on when and where you were trained – and to shun new developments as vulgar. If Martin is regularly the first post-Martinian just as Halliday was consistently the first post-Hallidayan, then the question is what drives this change. What are the principles upon which Martin's work has developed, and how can we understand its unity and diversity in a way that can enable a more sober understanding of the development of academic knowledge in general. It is these questions that this chapter will explore.

Linguistics and other things

In his 1992 *English Text*, Martin describes his linguistic upbringing as follows:

> I first became interested in discourse analysis in 1968. I was a first year student at the time, in Michael Gregory's English department at Glendon College in Toronto. Gregory began our course by introducing us to Hallidayan linguistics (grammar, register theory and stylistics) and hired Waldemar Gutwinski to join the department to teach 'American' linguistics. It was Gutwinski who first introduced me to discourse structure, and I have been shunting between clause grammar and cohesion analysis ever since.
>
> Gutwinski was a student of Al Gleason's, and after finishing my BA at Glendon I enrolled in an MA at the University of Toronto to study discourse analysis with him. After my MA I went to Essex to begin a PhD with Michael Halliday, returning to Toronto for 18 months to work with Gleason before finishing my degree in Sydney in 1977 ... My debt to Al Gleason, and to Michael Halliday and Ruqaiya Hasan will be more than obvious to readers of this book. Readers familiar with systemic grammar will perhaps forgive me if I refer to Gleason as my meta-Theme and Halliday and Hasan as my meta-New. (1992, p. xiii)

There are a number of things striking about this training in linguistics. The first is the unusual scope this training would have been at the time, especially in North America, bridging scale and category grammar, register, stylistics and cohesion (in undergraduate at Glendon), stratificational linguistics, fieldwork-based language description and discourse structure (with Gleason in both his MA and during his PhD), and the enormously expansive socially, theoretically, descriptively and appliably oriented focuses of Halliday and Hasan that developed through the 1970s, which pushed much further than linguistics was generally assumed to cover at the time.

But there is another set of striking similarities between each of the people Martin notes in his training that he has carried through in his work. This is the openness in which linguistics, however it is defined, is conceptualized in relation to other things – other academic fields (e.g. sociology, literature, education), other arenas (e.g. non-research institutions such as schools, legal systems, family and healthcare contexts) and things typically considered 'other than language' (context, broader semiosis, society, etc.). Although at times, especially in the early 1960s, nods were made by a number of these teachers – especially Gregory (e.g. 1966-72) – to linguistics being the study of language for its own sake, each of these teachers all made regular reference to the need for linguistics to be useful for things outside of linguistics.

In the preface to the grammar of English that Martin was initially trained in, for example, Gregory (1966-72, p. 14) notes that:

> to make statements about language in its own terms is not, nor should it be, the sole purpose for any linguist's study. Unless his statements about language are useful, useful not only to other linguists, but also to other men, this has essentially been a trivial study. Inevitably the statements of the majority of linguists do have such value.

Similar sentiments, often arising from the problematics of various applied research goals, can be found in the work of Gleason (particularly in relation to translation, second language teaching and school education, e.g. 1965, 1968), Gutwinski (in relation to stylistics and literature, 1976), Hasan (across a range of areas associated with education, social transmission and verbal art, e.g. 1985, 2009, 2011) and, of course, Halliday who famously emphasized his commitment that 'linguistics cannot be other than an ideologically committed form of social action' (1985, p. 5).[2] This type of linguistics is one that involves a dialectic between theory and practice, where the theory is both developed to be appliable to any problem that arises in the real world and in research, and flexible enough for problems to drive its expansion and development.

This concern for an appliable linguistics has run deep in Martin's work as well as those of his students and close colleagues (as strongly exemplified by the chapters in this volume; see also Caldwell et al. in press). As he describes:

> I have tried to practice linguistics as a form of social action, a practice which Halliday (e.g. 1985) has suggested cannot be other than ideologically committed. This practice dissolves the linguistics vs applied linguistic opposition which has evolved in response to the hegemony of American formalism – whose idealizing reductivity comes nowhere near serving the need of language users and their aids around the world. In its stead, linguistics as social action engages theory with practice in a dialectic whereby theory informs practice which, in turn, rebounds on theory, recursively, as more effective ways of intervening in various processes of semogenesis are designed. (Martin, 2000, p. 116)

As Martin's work has shown, practising linguistics in this way is not a simple task. It implicates a wide range of principles and practices that at times can be in tension with each other. We will explore these here.

Linguistics and practice

The most obvious feature of an appliable linguistics is its use in solving problems outside linguistics. Importantly, this is not a one-way street; an appliable linguistics in Halliday's sense is one where outside problems in turn drive the development of linguistics (2008).[3] As far as Martin's work is concerned, the area in which he has worked most deeply in this sense is his concern for designing and implementing literacy pedagogy. This pedagogy has become known as 'Sydney school pedagogy' or 'genre pedagogy'. Twenty years ago Martin (2000, p. 116) described the ongoing development of pedagogical work in the 'Sydney school' as follows:

> The transdisciplinary literacy research to which I am referring evolved as an action research project in and around Sydney from 1979 ... involving at key stages the Linguistics Department at the University of Sydney and the Metropolitan East Region of the New South Wales Disadvantaged Schools program. Our goal, as educational linguists, was to intervene in the process of writing development in

primary and secondary school across various depths of time. As far as logogenesis was concerned, we attempted to provide students with knowledge about language ... that they could use in reading, writing and editing. As for ontogenesis, we worked with teachers on the design of curriculum (learner pathways) and pedagogy (classroom activity). Finally, with respect to phylogenesis, we were committed to a redistribution of literacy resources and critical language awareness ... which we hoped would emancipate the meaning potential of the students we were working with, with a view to giving them ways of redesigning their world. To date, we have had some impact on the first two of these frames for intervention; only time will tell the extent to which the work been socially empowering for the non-mainstream students involved.

This description gives a sense of the multifaceted pedagogy that has been developed, concerned not only with what students write, but with what they can know to help them write; not just what the curriculum should be, but how teachers can effectively teach this curriculum at every level of granularity, from the largest-scale lesson-sequences down to the small-scale exchanges that take place in the classroom; and not just an individualist perspective where each student can 'attain their potential' but an explicitly social and political one, concerned with the redistribution of cultural capital traditionally horded by the ruling classes in a way that enables students not just to succeed in their world, but to change it.

As far as the role of linguistics is concerned, this quote makes clear that Martin and colleagues' work in this area does not begin from the perspective of linguistics, per se. Rather, it begins with educational, social and political issues at stake and, in a sense, 'works back' to linguistics. It does not ask 'what can linguistics do to help education?', which is likely to lead to the help being limited to what linguistics can do at the time, but rather begins with questions of education and asks 'how can we develop a linguistics that can help solve this problem?' This is a profoundly different question that puts the onus back on linguistics to develop itself in a way that can be useful – not just develop a linguistics on its own terms and then find a use for it once it has been developed.

In this chapter we will not go into detail into the various components of the Sydney School pedagogy that has developed (and is still developing), other than to indicate that coming at the issue from the perspective of education implicates a highly multifaceted understanding of education as a social practice and a highly intricate design of pedagogy (see also Humphrey, Hao and Rose this volume for a cutting-edge view of this in science education). Rose and Martin (2012) and Martin (1999a, 2012e) give extensive overviews of the programme as it developed at various points. Here we shall simply exemplify the dialectic of theory and practice by giving a small overview of the role of genre in this pedagogy and how it fits within Martin's framework. This overview is necessarily simplified but should hopefully give a taste as to what it means to develop an appliable linguistics.

The first thing to say about the notion of genre in SFL is that, in contrast to the oft-repeated story of its development, it did not arise purely from educational work. In Martin's conception, genre has its roots in, amongst other things, the interplay between

Gregory's functional tenor in a four-variable understanding of register (Gregory, 1967), in relation to Halliday's three-variable understanding of register (1978); Hasan's work on text structure (1979); Mitchell's Firthian account of the staging and options in service exchanges in Cyrenaica (1957); Labov and Waletsky's work on narrative (1967); Gleason and the Hartford Stratificationalists' concern for text schematic structure (1968); and, a little later, Bakhtin's speech genres (1986) and ongoing work of Kress (1985). More directly, however, seminal work driving the development of the SFL notion of genre came from a number of students working in a research group with Martin from 1980 to 1985, which

> included Plum, who worked on a variety of spoken genres elicited from dog breeders (Plum, 1998), Ventola, who studied Finnish migrants' interactions with Australian staff in post office and travel agency service encounters (Ventola, 1987), Eggins, who examined dinner table conversations among her housemates and friends (Eggins & Slade, 1997), Rothery, who was interested in doctor/patient consultations as well as primary school writing (Rothery, 1996) and myself a would-be critical linguist, who was working on environmental and administrative discourse. (Martin, 2015, p. 34)

The roots of genre, then, came from a diverse range of influences and impetuses. But it is true that it has gained it most significant foothold in relation to work concerned with educational issues. A significant reason for this is that, as Martin, Rothery and others quickly realized, genre – in its recontextualized form for teachers and educationalists as a 'text type' described as a 'staged, goal-oriented social process' – was a relatively easy and unobtrusive starting point for teachers to understand and teach the texts that students need to write. This is in contrast to a starting point from grammar in an Australian context where grammar had been systematically removed from the curriculum for decades, and so could not be reliably assumed to be known by teachers (Rose & Martin, 2012, pp. 1–4).

As this 'way in' through genre was developing, the question naturally arose as to how to teach it in a way that ensured access for everyone – particularly those from marginalized backgrounds who were (are) consistently left aside by both 'traditional' and 'progressivist' pedagogies, such as students from working class, migrant or Indigenous backgrounds. An early and well-known response to this came in the form of the 'Teaching-Learning Cycle', a designed curriculum genre that aimed to make explicit the nature of the particular literacy tasks students need to master and give them gradual and aided experience in succeeding in this task. Martin (1999a, pp. 126–7) explains this pedagogy as follows:

> It comprises three main phases: Modelling, Joint Construction and Independent Construction. Modelling involves introducing students to an example of the text type in focus, discussing the function of the genre, and examining its structure, including relevant language features. Joint construction involves preparing for work on another example of the genre, which will be jointly constructed by the teacher and students (with the teacher developing a text on the board, on large sheets

of paper or on the overhead projector in response to suggestions from students). Independent construction involves students preparing for another instantiation of the genre, which they will write on their own; it explicitly encourages creative exploration of the genre and its possibilities ... teaching can begin at any point, depending on the needs of the students. For example, some teachers found the Joint Construction stage unnecessary for some students, whereas for others, this stage needed to be worked through more than once before students were ready to write on their own.

This curriculum genre has been elaborated significantly since the 1980s, encompassing a much wider range of practices (including reading, writing and listening), year levels (from primary through to tertiary and education outside of schooling contexts), subjects across the disciplinary map and degrees of detail in teaching (from whole curriculum and assessment to highly detailed design of teacher–student interaction).

But the needs of the pedagogy did not just emphasize the design of teaching practices, it also involved questioning both what students need to write to succeed and what they actually do write. This required a significant descriptive effort in a way that 'handed back' a problem from education to linguistics. This descriptive effort has dramatically expanded the horizons of text linguistics, both in SFL and beyond. This is first by broadening the models and mapping of genres that occur across our social lives. But second, this is because, despite its name, 'Sydney School genre pedagogy' and the descriptive and theoretical research programmes it has driven by no means only involve genre. Genre is, in one sense, just a useful way in. The pedagogy more broadly aims to target all language and literacy issues needed for success in any area. In this sense, the expansion of studies of genre raised their own issues surrounding linguistic features of texts that were not yet understood. Factual genres often used in science, for example, highlighted key issues associated with ideational meaning in lexicogrammar, discourse semantics and field, amongst other things (see Humphrey, Hao and Rose this volume). Similarly work on various story genres helped spark various concerns about evaluative language, including distinguishing the different types of evaluation used in anecdotes, exemplums and observations. This helped develop the categories of affect, judgement and appreciation within the system of attitude, while a concern for understanding the reader positioning that occurs in various journalistic texts drove the development of the system of engagement, all contributing to the now highly influential model of appraisal given in Martin and White (2005) (see also White this volume and Chen this volume). These descriptions have in turn been recontextualized as pedagogical tools in a wide range of teacher-oriented resources and embedded into curricula around the world (see Brisk and Alvarado this volume for a US perspective in this regard).

It is this back and forth between theory and application shown by Martin and colleagues' work that illustrates an appliable linguistics. A problem in the outside world drives an expansion in linguistic modelling which in turn is used to solve the problem in the outside world, which leads to further problems for linguistics to help solve and back and forth and so on. Of course, this account is highly simplified. Such a programme is not a simple case of clean transitions from education to linguistics and back; nor is it a case that the two fields are perfectly siphoned off from each other; the dynamics are such that they co-develop at various degrees of intensity, in relation to various other programmes and issues both inside and outside of education or linguistics.[4]

Linguistics for understanding language

To stop at this point and suggest that Martin's work has been entirely driven by external concerns would do injustice to it. The interplay between theory and practice has been a key driver through Martin's career, but throughout, it has been doubled with a concern for developing a linguistics for understanding the enormous and multifaceted nature of language and semiosis itself (or, in a Hallidayan vein, the 'social semiotic').[5]

This is most obvious in Martin's long-term descriptive and typological programmes focusing on Tagalog and English, and more recently with Mira Kim and Gi-Hyun Shin on Korean and Beatriz Quiroz on Spanish (see also Wang this volume on Chinese entities and nominal groups, and Knox this volume on interpersonal meaning in Thai, Teochew and Australian English for descriptions heavily influenced by this work). Beginning with Tagalog, Martin first encountered this language during his MA field-methods course run by Gleason at Toronto before enrolling in a six-week intensive Tagalog course in Hawaii associated with a Linguistic Society of America Institute during his PhD and eventually undertaking three field-work trips in Manilla once working in Sydney. More recently, he has worked with Prixie Cruz, a Tagalog speaker and linguist living in Manilla, as well as supervising a doctoral student working on Tagalog, Kent Ramos. From the perspective of general descriptive linguistics, as with much discussion about Tagalog, Martin has unpicked its well-known and extensively discussed case and alignment features from an SFL perspective (in terms of TRANSITIVITY, Martin, 1996a). But importantly, Martin's work does not stop at these well-known features. He has also put forward detailed descriptions of the interpersonal systems of MOOD and MODALITY (1990), and POLARITY, TAGGING, VOCATION, COMMENT and ENGAGEMENT (2018), logical meanings across a range of grammatical environments (1995), the discourse semantic systems of CONJUNCTION and CONTINUITY (1981) and PARTICIPANT IDENTIFICATION (1983), and a brief discussion of textual meaning and THEME (2004a).

A crucial feature of Martin's work in this area is the use of descriptions to make broader arguments about language and linguistics. This is seen, for example, through his work on the Tagalog logical linker *na-/ng-*. This linker is a generally productive linker for hypotaxis across ranks and systems throughout the grammar, shown by examples (1) and (2) (both from Martin, 1995) where it links elements in the nominal group and the clause complex respectively (linker in bold, with the examples glossed for morpheme and word in (1) and clause and complex in (2)).[6] In these situations, they follow Halliday's (Halliday & Matthiessen, 2014) interpretation of hypotaxis fairly closely, showing an iterative structure organized through dependency.

(1) | iyo-**ng** | marami-**ng** | masama-**ng** | bata
| that-LK | many-LK | bad-LK | child
| δ | γ | β | α
| that | many | bad | child

'those naughty children'

(2) | Ewan niya kung | natatakot dom so Raffy **na** | makakita ng damdamin sa mata niya
| α | β | γ
| She didn't know | Raffy was also afraid | he'd be able to see the feeling in her eyes

'She didn't know if Raffy was also afraid he'd be able to see the feeling in her eyes'

In certain situations, however, Martin argues that these linkers are 'co-opted' for interpersonal purposes where they appear to mark the scope across which various interpersonal meanings are covered. In (3), for example, the linker marks off the attitudinal meaning exclaiming her speed, positioned at the front of the clause, from the running which is the target of the attitude.

(3) | ang | bilis | niya-**ng** | t<um>akbo
| T | fast | 3SG-LK | run<COMPL>
| α | | | β

'How fast she ran'

In an instance like this, the linker does not necessarily relate two similar units, as occurs in prototypical hypotactic structures, nor is it particularly iterative. In fact, it is relatively variable as to what units may come before or after the linker and it typically only relates two elements. This poses a problem for descriptions that take constituency as its primary means of structure. Without relatively distinct units, it is difficult to parse the clause in a consistent manner; moreover, a purely constituency representation would not be able to account for the scoping that occurs between the fronted interpersonal elements and their domain after the linker. Martin uses this and other descriptions to argue for the importance of recognizing both multiple tiers and distinct types of structure in grammatical description – in this case, the interaction between constituency, interdependency and scoping (or prosody). In conjunction with his work on Tagalog transitivity and various areas of English, this contributed to Martin's reinterpretation of Halliday's particulate structures in terms of orbital and serial structures (1996c) and clearly resonates with his emphasis on prosodic structure in interpersonal domains such as appraisal (Martin & White, 2005).

In this sense, Martin's work on Tagalog has opened the way for him to make significant contributions to broader theoretical, metatheoretical and descriptive issues in linguistics. In addition to the need for a plurality of types of structure in description rather than just constituency, he has shown the need for cryptotypic description, rather than just phenotypic description (e.g. 1990, 1996a), the need for metafunctionally (2004a) and stratally diverse (1981, 1983) perspectives on description, rather than just ideational meaning within the grammar, the constant interplay between a structural (syntagmatic) perspective and a paradigmatic perspective (Martin & Cruz, 2018), not just a focus on syntagms of classes, and the need for recognizing, accepting and celebrating metalinguistic diversity (in terms of approaches to linguistics), not just linguistic diversity (1996b).

In terms of typology proper – the comparison and categorizing of languages, rather than just their description – Martin's work has evolved over the years from emphasizing an interpretation of grammar from the perspective of discourse (1983) to a more generalized 'defeasible' typology (Martin & Quiroz, 2020). In such a typology, all typological statements are necessarily tentative, being made with reference to the particular stratum, rank, metafunction, level of delicacy and axial perspective from which things are said to look 'the same' or 'different'. Throughout, Martin has emphasized a constant reflexivity about the ways of describing language, not just the descriptions or typologies themselves.

Although his descriptive work on Tagalog has developed from the earliest years of his career, more well-known is Martin's descriptive work on English. This work began during his PhD, focusing on children's storytelling (1977), and has continued to develop since. The key feature of this work is its broadening focus; Martin has continually worked with a view that expands what can be studied by linguistics. Given Martin's (and SFL's in general) concern for a linguistics that can help the world, this makes sense. When one's research is driven largely by a field's internal problems, these internal problems tend to bound what the research can find. In the case of linguistics, this tends to mean that if one's research is driven by trying to see what types of phonetic, phonological, morphological or syntactic patterns occur around the world, research in this area will inevitably tend to remain focused on phonetics, phonology, morphology or syntax. However if one's research is driven not by internal issues only but also by problems external to the field, this has the potential to significantly expand what the field focuses on. A linguistics that looks to a world outside linguistics is a linguistics that expands what it can be. Martin's work very definitely shows this trajectory.

Starting in the 1970s, Martin interpreted Gleason's stratificational linguistic concern for discourse structure through a Systemic Functional lens. His PhD thesis used the systems of reference and conjunction to force the issue of stratification in SFL. In particular, he worked to establish space in the theory for the cohesive resources identified by Halliday and Hasan (1976) to be interpreted as discourse systems and structures rather than as non-structural elements within the grammar. This was followed by a gradual expansion of discourse semantic systems, such as negotiation and speech function, appraisal, the discourse structure of periodicity, and ideation (see Martin 1992; Martin & White 2005; see Bateman this volume for the significance of this discourse semantic model for multimodality). As these systems developed, this broadening focus expanded into exploring patterns of register and genre, as well as issues surrounding identity, community, ideology, individuation, allocation and affiliation (Martin, 2010; see also Caple and Bednarek this volume), and, following the multimodal revolution heralded by Kress and van Leeuwen (1990), detailed descriptions of non-linguistic semiosis such as image–text relations in children's picture books (Painter, Martin and Unsworth, 2013), body language, gesture and paralanguage (Martin & Zappavigna, 2019; Ngo et al., forthcoming), and highly technical infographics and other semiotic resources used in school science (Martin et al., 2020; Doran & Martin, 2020; see Unsworth this volume).

Coupled with this expansion is Martin's insistence not to privilege one particular register, such as casual conversation, over any other (as reflected in the list of focuses given at the beginning of this chapter). A useable theory of language and semiosis in this conception must be able to account for the variability of use in both 'everyday' language and language across various institutional and academic arenas, as well as the variability in users of language (and not just in terms of surface-level dialect features). This was shown right from the very beginning of Martin's work, with his first book, written with Sherry Rochester, exploring the discourse of people with various forms of schizophrenia (focusing in particular on their means of participant tracking; Rochester & Martin 1979), while his PhD tracked the storytelling and discourse patterns of children at six/seven years old, eight/nine years old and ten/eleven years old (1977). This breadth of focus has continued to this day, exemplified through his recent work with Michele Zappavigna and Paul Dwyer in the legal setting, where they explored the language and paralanguage of people engaging with Youth Justice Conferencing – a form of restorative justice that aims to divert young people away from a long engagement with the court and prison system (Zappavigna & Martin, 2018 and Volume 8 of his collected works, Martin, 2012f). As with previous work, this research developed a rich picture of the language and body language that organize this institutional setting *and* the way people used this to perform a range of identities.

To intervene in the contexts of schooling or law or medicine or any other field requires an understanding of how these fields work and how people differentially engage with them – a linguistic theory that takes unconscious, everyday chat as the most 'pure' of language will struggle to do anything in this area.

Theory, description and instance

Through this expansion, Martin has extended Halliday's 'extravagant' approach by pushing for a model that can integrate an increasingly large range of semiosis (or, as he has put it in personal conversation, a model that can bring more of the etic into the emic). The effect of this integrative approach is that every area of language resonates out to all others, and parallels, similarities and complementarities can occur across all levels, metafunctions and objects of language and linguistics. An illustration of this is given by the opening paragraph of Martin and White's Preface in their (2005) *Language of Evaluation*, the key text for the influential description of English APPRAISAL. APPRAISAL is often used in isolation to the rest of SFL, but, as Martin and White emphasize, it arose from concerns about other features of language and so resonates strongly across SFL theory:

The impetus for this book grew out of work on narrative genres, principally undertaken by Gunther Plum and Joan Rothery at the University of Sydney through the 1980s. Their point was that interpersonal meaning was critical both to the point of these genres (as emphasised by Labov) and also to how we classified them. This encouraged us to extend the model of interpersonal meaning that we had available at the time (based largely on work by Cate Poynton on language and gender), especially in the direction of one that could handle affect alongside modality and mood. (2005, p. xi)

This brief overview makes clear that the work of APPRAISAL inherently impinges on the SFL descriptions of genre, as its systems map key variables that occur across different story genres (Martin & Rose, 2008). It also indicates APPRAISAL's importance for understanding register, in terms of the variation in tenor shown through the model proposed by Poynton (1990), and grammar, shown through the nod to mood and modality and Poynton's work on vocation and naming (which, in turn, all impinge on into national and rhythmic phonology). Although not developed by 2005, APPRAISAL is also key to the growing models of affiliation and individuation (see chapters collected in Bednarek & Martin, 2010, and White this volume), which in turn resonates out to Hasan's work on semantic variation, class and gender (2009). When looked at from this perspective, it becomes clear that appraisal is situated not as an isolated system in itself but in relation to a wider context of linguistic and social variables. This is illustrated further by the next two paragraphs of the preface which overview the range of research projects, researchers, objects of study and external interventions that influenced the development of the system:

The appraisal framework we're presenting here was developed in response to this need as part of the Disadvantaged Schools Program's Write it Right literacy project, which looked intensively at writing in the workplace and secondary school (from about 1990 to 1995). Jim was academic adviser to this project, in which Joan Rothery focused on secondary school English and Creative Arts (working closely with Mary Macken-Horarik and Maree Stenglin). Peter [White] joined the team, and drew on his background as a journalist to focus on media discourse (working closely with Rick Iedema and Susan Feez). Appraisal theory developed as we moved from one register to another, and shuttled among theory, description and applications to school-based literacy initiatives. Caroline Coffin focused on secondary school history in this project, and adapted appraisal analysis to this subject area. The main innovation in this period involved moving beyond affect to consider lexical resources for judging behaviour and appreciating the value of things, and the recognition of syndromes of appraisal associated with different voices in the media and discourses of history.

During the 1990s Jim was also supervising influential PhD work by Gillian Fuller, Mary Macken-Horarik and Henrike Körner. Fuller's heteroglossic perspective on evaluation in popular science, drawing on Bakhtin, was a major influence on the development of engagement as a resource for managing the play of voices in discourse. Körner specialised in legal discourse, and her work on graduation, especially the distinction between force and focus, was also foundational. Macken-Horarik's study of appraisal in secondary school narrative drew attention to the need for a more dynamic perspective on evaluation as it unfolded prosodically in discourse. More recently Sue Hood's application of appraisal theory to academic discourse led to further developments with respect to graduation, some of which we have incorporated here. (2005, pp. xi–xii)

This preface gives a sense of the integrative scope of SFL theory and its concern with coherently 'importing' what it needs into the theory, rather than leaving difficult questions to other approaches. But to emphasize the integrative and expansive nature of SFL under Martin's influence is not to suggest that he has isolated himself from other approaches or fields. Throughout his entire career Martin has engaged deeply with other approaches and theories for insights that SFL and linguistics in general could not at the time see. Indeed this interaction has sewn some of the most 'creative tensions', to use Bernstein's words (1995, p. 398), that have pushed Martin to new thinking and expanded SFL. In addition to the major synthesis of systemic functional and stratificational concerns from the earliest days of Martin's work, the approaches Martin has engaged with have ranged from speech act theory and interactional linguistics to case grammar, cognitive grammar and a wide range of traditions that have explored Tagalog, to corpus linguistics and critical linguistics, approaches derived from Bakhtin, Vygotsky, Labov and Hjelsmlev, and a range of progressivist educational frameworks.

But the most long-standing and intense engagement has been the sociological approach of code theory, progenating from the work of Bernstein and the long engagement with this by Halliday and Hasan, and most recently taking the form of Legitimation Code Theory (LCT) (Maton, 2014; see Maton & Doran, 2017). Martin's deep interaction with Bernstein's code theory and LCT has regularly offered a complementary perspective on phenomena and has posed questions not readily available to linguistics at the time. Often this has led to developments in Martin's model of linguistics itself in the form of 'responses' or SFL interpretations of what code theory has seen.

A recent example of this is his development of 'mass' and 'presence' (Martin, 2020; Martin & Matruglio, 2020; see Unsworth this volume). These concepts have been provoked by the LCT concepts of 'semantic density', described as the degree of complexity of meaning, and 'semantic gravity', the degree of context dependence of meaning (Maton, 2014). As LCT increasingly engaged with text analysis, it became clear that these analyses were generating insights that did not have obvious corollaries in linguistics. In particular, Martin realized that there was a wide range of linguistic features that tended to be implicated by shifts in semantic gravity and semantic density that were not tied to any particular metafunction, rank or stratum. In terms of the context dependence of meaning implicated by semantic gravity, this had tended to be considered to that point as an aspect of the register variable mode, associated with the degree to which language is constitutive of or ancillary to what is going on (Halliday & Hasan, 1985; Martin, 1992). Under standard SFL modelling, then, context dependence should primarily impact on features within the textual metafunction. However, Martin and Matruglio (2020) showed that this was not the case, with context dependence affecting features across all metafunctions. To account for this, they proposed the concept of 'presence' as the linguistic conception of context dependence and detailed a range of variables and linguistic features associated with it (a similar process happened for mass in relation to field, Martin, 2020). Importantly for this chapter, this example illustrates how insights generated by another approach, used in close proximity to Martin's work in SFL, led to the development of concepts in SFL itself. But this is not the end of the story. A big question still remains about where mass and presence 'fit' in the theory. They do not fit within strata, ranks or metafunctions within the realization hierarchy but rather appear to organize the selection of features across the realization hierarchy. In this sense, they appear more associated with the dimension of instantiation. But at the time of writing, what this actually means for the theory and how it conceptualizes semiosis is not yet clear. This is worth noting, as it illustrates the flow-on effect that a development in one area can have on the rest of the theory; the insights developed by LCT have led to developments in SFL, which in turn are likely to drive serious exploration of the theoretical dimensions of instantiation and realization. An integrative and relational theory means that all its components resonate with all the others, and so changes in one lead to changes in all others.

To manage this ever-growing theoretical and descriptive apparatus, the constant interplay between theory and practice, and the various creative tensions that arise through interaction with other approaches, Martin has regularly reflected on the nature of SFL theory itself. Such metatheoretical explorations, taking their lead from similar concerns by his teachers Halliday (2003), Hasan (2009) and Gleason (1965, 1973), have enabled a continually reflexive understanding of how approaches develop, and, perhaps more importantly, how approaches *should* develop if they are to achieve the broad goal of being socially responsible. But as anyone who has read Martin's work will testify, he does not spend his time in purely abstract space; all concepts are continually put at risk through engagement with actual instances of language. It is a rare publication of Martin's that does not centre on a very close analysis of an instance of language or semiosis.

Community and values

As we have seen, throughout his career, Martin has emphasized a socially responsible linguistics. In addition to the interventions noted above, his work has insisted on thinking through the implications of research. A key example of this is his call and development in the late 1990s and early 2000s for a positive discourse analysis (see volume 6 of his collected works, Martin, 2012d). This arose, in part, from a frustration that multiple decades of critical discourse analysis had had little effect on the world, seemingly partly due to the assumption that by exposing a discourse's underlying power structures, this would somehow change them. In response, and through his long engagement with interventionist programmes, he emphasized that it is not enough to simply expose and critique. One must also model, design and intervene:

> I sometimes get the feeling that modernity has mesmerized critique, to the point where an obsession with hegemony rules virtually all critical inquiry; as a result, all we end up doing is exposing power and showing why the world is a terrible place. This is not only depressing but frustrating, since it doesn't tell us what we need to know about change for the better. There is more to challenging power than critiquing it; in addition we need to know how people commune in ways that rework its circulation (Gore, 1993) – personally, locally, nationally and globally. I think it is time to get off the high moral ground and take a look at people we admire and how they get on with what they do. We can learn some things from them that we need to know if we are going to intervene effectively as discourse analysts in the sites that motivate us. (Martin, 2002, p. 187)

It was in this sense that positive discourse analysis was born: an approach to discourse that did not simply criticize the bad but looked for the good in the world in order to understand how it works and how it came about, and to use this as a model for the design of interventions to change the world. A significant focus in this regard has been Martin's work on discourses of reconciliation, in particular with respect to Indigenous Australia and South Africa (e.g. Martin 1999b, 2002, 2004b; Martin & Rose, 2007; aptly, Fontaine and Jones' and Caple and Bednarek's chapters in this volume explore this reconciliation in Martin's two homelands Canada and Australia).

Critical Discourse Analysis still dominates the broader field of discourse analysis – it is, of course, easier in academia to critique than to celebrate, to expose than to design, to write than to intervene. But this will change. And such an emphasis on Martin's part shows the seriousness with which he takes the social responsibility of theory.

This seriousness of responsibility plays out in other ways. No single person can change the world from the academy. To have any hope of a lasting influence requires a committed and thoughtful community who are constantly developing and adapting to the world around them, while also keeping an unwavering eye on social changes they want to make. Throughout his career Martin has enacted community, working with others to build infrastructure to support young scholars and keep discussion pushing forward. To be an SFL doctoral student in Sydney is to have constant support – a weekly doctoral seminar, a weekly SFL seminar, weekly masterclasses, ad hoc workshops and regular supervisions, annual national conferences combined with annual international conferences, and a constant interaction of junior and senior scholars across all possible objects of study. At an international level, Martin has regularly travelled and worked with scholars across the world, with a particular emphasis on the 'global south' of Latin America and Asia (or more broadly, areas traditionally marginalized by Euro- and Americo-centric academia), and is regularly worrying about how to ensure knowledge is shared and community developed. Although intellectual achievement is the general focus of academic biography, it means nothing without a community engaging, pushing and extending it. Martin understands this well and has practised it throughout his career.

Envoi

Festschrifts can be double-edged swords. Some are there to celebrate a scholar. Others can be a capstone, concluding a career. This is most definitely the former (and only the former) – Martin is continually expanding the horizons of linguistics and will do so for a long time yet. The principles discussed in this chapter continue to drive and expand his work, and to be away from his office for even a few months is to miss much theoretical and descriptive development (by him, his students, those engaging with them and those in the broader SFL community). For this reason, this chapter is a summary, not a summation. We have taken only a moment here to rest, to steal a view of an intellectual career that is ongoing, to look back on the distance Martin and the field has come, and to look toward its future. In the spirit of positive discourse analysis, it is a celebration and an analysis, so we can use its object as a model to design and improve.

That is to say, keep pushing us all along, Jim.

Notes

1. In lieu of a complete referencing of Martin's work, the reader is directed to the list of his collected works at the end of this chapter. At the time of writing, a full list of his publications could be found via his university staff page: https://sydney.edu.au/arts/about/our-people/academic-staff/james-martin.html. Last accessed 14 April 2020.
2. The *cannot* in this now aphorism is a beautiful ambiguity in modality, interpretable in Halliday's terms (Halliday & Matthiessen, 2014) as either probability or obligation.
3. In this sense, we can make a crude distinction between 'applied linguistics', where an already-established linguistics is applied to outside problems, and an appliable linguistics that aims to develop a linguistics to be applied and so bounces back and forth between theory, description and application.
4. This account is also highly simplified in awkwardly attributing the development of genre pedagogy almost entirely to Martin. It was very much a social enterprise encompassing an enormous range of people. This is made clear, for example, in the acknowledgements section of Rose and Martin (2012). See also Cope et al. (1993) who detail the development of this pedagogy through the late 1970s and 1980s.
5. Here I am avoiding using the phrase 'linguistics for linguistics' sake' as it sits uncomfortably with me as suggesting what Martin has (in personal conversation) called a 'dilettante' linguistics – an interest in the linguistic world without a commitment to changing the world. This section should be read in the context of his commitment to an appliable linguistics that 'cannot be other than ideologically committed'.
6. These examples are glossed using the Systemic Functional glossing conventions developed by the Systemic Language Modelling Network, to which Martin himself contributed. https://systemiclanguagemodelling.com/glossing/. Last accessed 12 April 2020.

References

Bakhtin, M. M. (1986). The problem of speech genres. In C. Emerson & M. Holquist (Eds.), V. W. McGee (Trans.), *Speech Genres and Other Late Essays* (pp. 60–102). Austin, TX: University of Texas Press.
Bednarek, M. & Martin, J. R. (Eds.) (2010). *New Discourse on Language: Functional Perspectives on Multimodality, Identity and Affiliation*. London: Continuum.
Bernstein, B. (1995). A response. In A. Sadovnik (Ed.), *Knowledge and Pedagogy: The Sociology of Basil Bernstein* (pp. 385–424). Norwood: Ablex.
Caldwell, D., Knox, J., & Martin, J. R. (Eds.) (in press). *Appliable Linguistics and Social Semiotics: Developing Theory*. London: Bloomsbury.
Cope, B., Kalantzis, M., Kress, G., Martin, J. R., & Murphy, L. (1993). Bibliographical essay: Developing the theory and practice of genre-based literacy. In B. Cope & M. Kalantzis (Eds.), *The Powers of Literacy: A Genre Approach to Teaching Writing* (pp. 231–47). London: Falmer.
Doran, Y. J., & Martin, J. R. (2020). Field relations: Understanding scientific explanations. In K. Maton, J. R. Martin, & Y. J. Doran (Eds.), *Studying Science: Knowledge, Language, Pedagogy*. London: Routledge.
Eggins, S., & Slade, D. (1997). *Analysing Casual Conversation*. London: Cassell.
Gleason, H. A. (1965). *Linguistics and English Grammar*. New York: Holt, Rinehart and Winston.
Gleason, H. A. (1968). Contrastive analysis in discourse structure. In J. E. Alatis (Ed.), *Contrastive Linguistics and Its Pedagogical Implications* (pp. 39–64). Washington, DC: Georgetown University Press.
Gleason, H. A. (1973). *The Architecture of Language and the Strategy of Description*. Unpublished Draft Manuscript.
Gore, J. (1993). *The Struggle for Pedagogies: Critical and Feminist Discourses as Regimes of Truth*. London: Routledge.
Gregory, M. (1966–72). English patterns: Perspectives for a description of English. In J. De Villiers & R. Stainton (2009) (Eds.), *Michael Gregory's Proposals for a Communication Linguistics: Volume II of Communication in Linguistics* (pp. 1–142). Toronto: Gref.
Gregory, M. (1967). Aspects of varieties differentiation. *Journal of Linguistics*, 3(2), 177–98.
Gregory, M. (1998). Systemic functional linguistics and other schools: Prospectives and retrospectives. In J. De Villiers & R. Stainton (2009) (Eds.), *Michael Gregory's Proposals for a Communication Linguistics: Volume II of Communication in Linguistics* (pp. 312–29). Toronto: Gref.
Gutwinski, W. (1976). *Cohesion in Literary Texts*. The Hague: Mouton.
Halliday, M. A. K. (1978). *Language as Social Semiotic: The Social Interpretation of Language and Meaning*. London: Edward Arnold.
Halliday, M. A. K. (1985). Systemic background. In J. D. Benson & W. S. Greaves (Eds.), *Systemic Perspectives on Discourse, Volume 1: Selected Theoretical Papers from the Ninth International Systemic Workshop* (pp. 1–15). Norwood, NJ: Ablex.
Halliday, M. A. K. (2003). *On Language and Linguistics: Volume 3 in the Collected Works of M.A.K. Halliday*. J. J. Webster (Ed.). London: Continuum.
Halliday, M. A. K. (2008). Working with meaning: Towards an appliable linguistics. In J. J. Webster (Ed.), *Meaning in Context: Implementing Intelligent Applications of Language Studies* (pp. 7–23). London: Continuum.

Halliday, M. A. K., & Hasan, R. (1976). *Cohesion in English.* London: Longman.
Halliday, M. A. K., & Hasan, R. (1985). *Language, Context and Text: Aspects of Language in a Social-semiotic Perspective.* Geelong: Deakin University Press.
Halliday, M. A. K., & Matthiessen, C. M. I. M. (2014). *Halliday's Introduction to Functional Grammar.* London: Routledge.
Hasan, R. (1979). On the notion of text. In J. S. Petöfi (Ed.), *Text vs Sentence: Basic Questions of Textlinguistics* (pp. 369–90). Hamburg: Helmet Buske.
Hasan, R. (1985). *Linguistics, Language and Verbal Art.* Geelong: Deakin University Press.
Hasan, R. (2009). *Semantic Variation: Meaning in Society and in Sociolinguistics. The Collected Works of Ruqaiya Hasan, Volume 2.* J. J. Webster & C. Cloran (Eds.). London: Equinox.
Hasan, R. (2011). *Language and Education: Learning and Teaching in Society. The Collected Works of Ruqaiya Hasan, Volume 3.* J. J. Webster and C. Cloran (Eds.). London: Equinox.
Kress, G. (1985). *Linguistic Processes in Sociocultural Practice.* Victoria: Deakin University Press.
Kress, G., & van Leeuwen, T. (1990). *Reading Images.* Geelong: Deakin University Press.
Labov, W., & Waletzky, J. (1967). Narrative analysis. In J. Helm (Ed.), *Essays on the Verbal and Visual Arts* (pp. 12–44). Seattle, WA: University of Washington Press.
Martin, J. R. (1977). *Learning How to Tell: Semantic Systems and Structures in Children's Narrative.* Unpublished PhD dissertation. Department of Languages and Linguistics, University of Essex.
Martin, J. R. (1981). Conjunction and continuity in Tagalog. In M. A. K. Halliday & J. R. Martin (Eds.), *Readings in Systemic Linguistics* (pp. 310–36). London: Batsford.
Martin, J. R. (1983). Participant identification in English, Tagalog and Kâte. *Australian Journal of Linguistics*, 3(1), 45–74.
Martin, J. R. (1990). Interpersonal grammatization: Mood and modality in Tagalog. *Philippine Journal of Linguistics*, 21(1), 2–50.
Martin, J. R. (1992). *English Text: System and Structure.* Amsterdam: John Benjamins.
Martin, J. R. (1995). Logical meaning, interdependency and the linking particle {na/-ng} in Tagalog. *Functions of Language*, 2(2), 189–228.
Martin, J. R. (1996a). Transitivity in Tagalog: A functional interpretation of case. In M. Berry, C. Butler, R. Fawcett, & G. Huang (Eds.), *Meaning and Form: Systemic Functional Interpretations* (pp. 229–96). Norwood, NJ: Ablex.
Martin, J. R. (1996b). Metalinguistic diversity: The case from case. In R. Hasan, C. Cloran, & D. Butt (Eds.), *Functional Description: Theory in Practice* (pp. 325–74). Amsterdam: John Benjamins.
Martin, J. R. (1996c). Types of structure: Deconstructing notions of constituency in clause and text. In E. H. Houvy & D. R. Scott (Eds.), *Computational and Conversational Discourse* (pp. 39–66). Heidelberg: Springer.
Martin, J. R. (1999a). Mentoring semogenesis: 'Genre-based' literacy pedagogy. In F. Christie (Ed.), *Pedagogy and the Shaping of Consciousness: Linguistic and Social Processes* (pp. 123–55). London: Continuum.
Martin, J. R. (1999b). Grace: The logogenesis of freedom. *Discourse Studies*, 1(1), 29–56.
Martin, J. R. (2000). Design and practice: Enacting functional linguistics. *Annual Review of Applied Linguistics*, 20, 116–26.
Martin, J. R. (2002). Blessed are the peacemakers: Reconciliation and evaluation. In C. Candlin (Ed.), *Research and Practice in Professional Discourse* (pp. 187–227). Hong Kong: City University of Hong Kong Press.

Martin, J. R. (2004a). Metafunctional profile of the grammar of Tagalog. In A. Caffarel, J. R. Martin, & C. M. I. M. Matthiessen (Eds.), *Language Typology: A Functional Perspective*. Amsterdam: John Benjamins.

Martin, J. R. (2004b). Positive discourse analysis: Solidarity and change. *Revista Canaria de Estudios Ingleses*, 49, 179–200.

Martin, J. R. (2010). Semantic variation: Modelling realization, instantiation and individuation in social semiosis. In M. Bednarek & J. R. Martin (Eds.), *New Discourse on Language: Functional Perspectives on Multimodality, Identity and Affiliation* (pp. 1–34). London: Continuum.

Martin, J. R. (2015). One of three traditions: Genre, functional linguistics and the 'Sydney School'. In N. Artemeva & A. Freedman (Eds.), *Genre Studies Around the Globe: Beyond the Three Traditions*. Bloomington: Trafford.

Martin, J. R. (2020). Revisiting field: Specialized knowledge in secondary school science and humanities discourse. In J. R. Martin, K. Maton, & Y. J. Doran (Eds.), *Accessing Academic Discourse: Systemic Functional Linguistics and Legitimation Code Theory* (pp. 114–48). London: Routledge.

Martin, J. R., & Cruz, P. (2018). Interpersonal grammar of Tagalog: A Systemic Functional Linguistics perspective. *Functions of Language*, 25(1), 54–96.

Martin, J. R., & Matruglio, E. (2020). Revisiting mode: Context in/dependency in Ancient History classroom discourse. In J. R. Martin, K. Maton, & Y. J. Doran (Eds.), *Accessing Academic Discourse: Systemic Functional Linguistics and Legitimation Code Theory* (pp. 89–113). London: Routledge.

Martin, J. R., & Quiroz, B. (2020). Functional language typology: A discourse semantic perspective. In J. R. Martin, Y. J. Doran, & G. Figueredo (Eds.), *Systemic Functional Language Description: Making Meaning Matter* (pp. 189–237). London: Routledge.

Martin, J. R., & Rose, D. (2007). *Working with Discourse: Meaning Beyond the Clause*. London: Continuum.

Martin, J. R., & Rose, D. (2008). *Genre Relations: Mapping Culture*. London: Equinox.

Martin, J. R., Unsworth, L., & Rose, D. (2020). Condensing meaning: Imagic aggregations in secondary school science. In G. Parodi (Ed.), *Multimodality: From Corpus to Cognition*. Berlin: Peter Lang.

Martin, J. R., & White, P. R. R. (2005). *The Language of Evaluation: Appraisal Systems in English*. Basingstoke: Palgrave Macmillan.

Martin, J. R., & Zappavigna, M. (2019). Embodied meaning: A systemic functional perspective on paralanguage. *Functional Linguistics*, 6(1), 1–33.

Maton, K. (2014). *Knowledge and Knowers: Toward a Realist Sociology of Education*. London: Routledge.

Maton, K., & Doran, Y. J. (2017). Systemic Functional Linguistics and code theory. In T. Bartlett and G. O'Grady (Eds.), *The Routledge Handbook of Systemic Functional Linguistics* (pp. 605–18). London: Routledge.

Mitchell, T. F. (1957). Language of buying and selling in Cyrenaica: A situational statement. *Hespéris*, 26, 1–41.

Ngo, T., Hood, S., Martin, J. R., Painter, C., Smith, B., & Zappavigna, M. (forthcoming). *Modelling Paralanguage Using Systemic Functional Semiotics: Theory and Application*. London: Bloomsbury.

Painter, C., Martin, J. R., & Unsworth, L. (2013). *Reading Visual Narratives: Image Analysis in Children's Picture Books*. London: Equinox.

Plum, G. (1998). *Text and Contextual Conditioning in Spoken English: A Genre-Based Approach*. Nottingham: University of Nottingham.

Poynton, C. (1990). *Address and the Semiotics of Social Relations: A Systemic-Functional Account of Address Forms and Practices in Australian English*. Unpublished PhD Dissertation, Department of Linguistics, The University of Sydney.
Rochester, S., & Martin, J. R. (1979). *Crazy Talk: A Study of the Discourse of Schizophrenic Speakers*. New York: Plenum.
Rose, D., & Martin, J. R. (2012). *Learning to Read, Reading to Learn: Genre, Knowledge and Pedagogy in the Sydney School*. London: Continuum.
Rothery, J. (1996). Making changes: Developing an educational linguistics. In R. Hasan & G. Williams (Eds.), *Literacy in Society* (pp. 86–123). London: Longman.
Ventola, E. M. (1987). *The Structure of Social Interaction: A Systemic Approach to the Semiotics of Service Encounters*. London: Frances Pinter.
Zappavigna, M., & Martin, J. R. (2018). *Discourse and Diversionary Justice: An Analysis of Youth Justice Conferencing*. Basingstoke: Palgrave Macmillan.

Martin's collected works (all authored by Martin, edited by Wang Zhenhua and published in Shanghai by Shanghai Jiao Tong University Press)

(2010a) *Systemic Functional Linguistics Theory*. Volume 1.
(2010b) *Discourse Semantics*. Volume 2.
(2012a) *Genre Studies*. Volume 3.
(2012b) *Register Studies*. Volume 4.
(2012c) *Text Analysis*. Volume 5.
(2012d) *CDA/PDA*. Volume 6.
(2012e) *Language in Education*. Volume 7.
(2012f) *Forensic Linguistics*. Volume 8.

2

Attitudinal alignments in journalistic commentary and social-media argumentation: The construction of values-based group identities in the online comments of newspaper readers

Peter R. R. White
University of New South Wales

Introduction

In June 2019, Australian Federal Police (AFP) officers entered the home of a prominent political journalist, Annika Smethurst, in search of evidence relating to the sources Smethurst had used for a report published the previous year in News Corporation's Sydney *Daily Telegraph*. The story, based on leaked confidential Australian federal government documents, concerned proposals by senior bureaucrats that a key Australian security agency should be given the power to monitor the electronic communications of Australian citizens. This police action was, predictably, very widely covered in both the Australian and international media.

In the immediate aftermath of the 'raid', *The Daily Telegraph* published multiple news articles on the topic, which, in almost all cases, were critical of the police action in terms of a perceived threat to press freedom. These items proved to be very popular with those readers who contribute online comments in response to these stories – the reader/user postings which appear beneath the article, what I will here term the 'comment trail'. These comment trails include reader comments presented by way of direct responses to the article and those comments presented as responses to the prior comments of other readers.

This chapter provides an account of findings arising from an analysis of the attitudinal positioning undertaken in these comments and the opinion piece to which they were a response with a view to reaching conclusions as to how contributors to these trails thereby construe for themselves a particular social identity or persona. While these comment trails have received a good deal of attention from journalism scholars and discourse analysts (see, for example, Manosevitch & Walker, 2009; von Sikorski & Hänelt, 2016; Ziegele et al., 2018), to my knowledge there is currently no other literature which reports on how they might function with respect to attitudinal alignment and the performance of identity. In this, of course, the chapter connects with a longstanding interest in socio-linguistics, applied linguistics and discourse analysis – interest in discursively performed 'group identity' and 'persona' (see, for example, Edwards,1985; Hyland, 2010; Pérez-Milans, 2016). More specifically, such a consideration of these comments trails provides the opportunity for the further development of ideas emerging from the work of J. R. Martin and his collaborators into how speakers 'affiliate/dis-affiliate' through the enactment of relations of solidarity and thereby indicate their membership in communities of shared value. Key earlier work by Martin on 'affiliation' and the performance of identity can be found in Martin (2008, 2009, 2010). Related work on how communality and social identity are based on shared values can be found in Stenglin (2009) and in Tann (2010, 2012). In Knight's work (2008, 2010), a framework was developed for the analyses of the values-based dialogic negotiation of such 'group identities' in face-to-face conversation – specifically casual conversations between friends. Somewhat more recently, Zappavigna (2011, 2012, 2014a, b, 2018, 2019) and Zappavigna and Martin in collaboration (Zappavigna & Martin, 2018) have developed analyses of the performance of social identity via what Zappavigna has termed the practices of 'ambient affiliation' – as afforded by microblogging platforms such as Twitter.

In this context, these sequences of reader comments are of interest in that they very clearly involve what Martin and his colleagues have placed at the centre of the communicative processes by which social identities are discursively enacted and negotiated – assertions by which speakers[1] position addressees to accept and/or infer positive and negative evaluations. Such assessments involve positive or negative evaluations of some 'target' or 'trigger' – persons, human behaviours, objects, artefacts, situations and processes – and for Martin and his colleagues, it is through the sharing or rejecting such assessments of particular targets that speakers indicate or negotiate membership in the social networks which constitute group or communal identities. In this scholarship, this attitudinal targeting is analysed as a mechanism by which an interpersonal meaning (a positive or negative assessment) is 'coupled' with an ideational meaning (the referenced/construed person, object, artefact, situation or process). For these scholars, the sharing of such 'couplings' of attitudinal meanings with experiential references creates 'bonds' between interactants and as Martin proposes: 'It is these bonds which form the building blocks of the individuation hierarchy [a hierarchy of identities], clustering into sub-cultures and master identities to which the community members subscribe' (Martin, 2010, p. 26).

The most cursory viewing of the online reader comments attached to news media articles reveals that one key purpose they serve is the enactment of 'identity', in the sense outlined above – as contributors forthrightly declare their membership in a range of culturally, politically and ultimately ideologically charged communities of shared value. Here 'identity' is both an effect of the commenters' indicated alignments with particular value positions (and the other commenters who share these value positions) and an effect of their indicated dis-alignments with competing value positions (and the other commenters who advance these competing positions). Thus, Knight notes: 'Communal identities are negotiated by participants according to who they are, who they are not, and who they might otherwise be or affiliate with …' (Knight, 2010, p. 49).

Data, methodology and key questions

This chapter reports the findings of an analysis of one article and a selection of the online reader comments 'trail' which were attached to it online. The article is an 'opinion' or 'comment' piece – termed an 'op-ed' – published in News Corp's *The Daily Telegraph*, a Sydney daily newspaper generally characterized as 'tabloid' in its style and intended audience.

In addition to dealing with the 'affiliatory' workings of the op-ed piece itself, I report findings arising from an analysis of just those comments which I classify as 'Openings' – comments where the commenter is responding directly to the article, and not to some other prior commenter. (This is for reasons of space limitations.)

An abbreviated version of the article is provided below.

Annika Smethurst raid was more than an invasion of privacy

Seven federal cops. Seven hours. The rubbish bins. The oven. The underwear drawers.

Tuesday's raid on the home of our national political editor Annika Smethurst was a shocking invasion of privacy – but it was much more sinister than that.

This is an attempt to intimidate journalists, and more importantly their sources, who attempt to reveal information that is in the public interest.

Annika's story, published in April 2018, was absolutely in the public interest: it revealed secret plans at the highest levels of the Canberra bureaucracy to allow the Australian Signals Directorate to cyber-spy on Australian citizens.

That's a chilling prospect: this agency was created to keep Australia safe from external, i.e. foreign, threats. […]

[The police officers] went through every drawer and cupboard from the bedrooms to the living room and, in the kitchen, knelt on the floor rummaging through drawers of whisks and spoons. They looked in the oven. They looked at every page of every cookbook.

Now Annika is left wondering whether she'll be charged with a breach of the Crimes Act relating to official secrets.

News Corp Australia, which publishes this masthead, has been campaigning for many years for politicians to explicitly protect journalists from laws that infringe upon the freedom of the press. They have failed to do so – and today we see that in fact federal agencies are inclined to do absolutely the opposite. This raid was about intimidation, pure and simple.

(*The Daily Telegraph*, 4 June 2019)

The opinion piece was downloaded, along with its comments 'trail' (sixty-eight individual comments), for analysis. There were some twenty-two individual commenters who contributed to the trail – some making just the one contribution and others commenting multiple times as they engage interactively with other commenters. The trail was composed of eighteen different comment chains, where a 'comment chain' (or thread) is made up of an initiating comment (i.e. what, as indicated above, I have termed an Opening) and subsequent interconnected reactions and responses (i.e. termed Follows).

Plainly, Openings present as offering some sort of reaction to the original opinion piece, and, as such, potentially enter into relations of attitudinal alignment ('affiliation') or dis-alignment ('disaffiliation') with the opinion piece's author. As well, of course, as social media texts, they can be viewed as communications offered up to the unknown mass audience of those readers of the article who have chosen to attend to the comments trail. In this sense, there is the potential construal of what Zappavigna has termed 'ambient affiliation', a process by which 'imagined' rather than directly addressed respondents are invited, or called upon, to align attitudinally with the commenter. Issues around such 'imaginary' addressees (otherwise variously termed the 'implied', 'putative' or 'virtual' reader) are taken up below.

There were eighteen of these Opening in the data set, twelve of which were at-odds with the op-ed (dis-affiliatory) and six of which were supportive (affiliatory).

The chapter is thus concerned with the construal of communities of shared value (lines of affiliation/dis-affiliation) in the op-ed piece itself and these Openings. Obviously, the op-ed is 'monologic' in the traditional sense of the term while the Openings are 'dialogic' in that they involve the commenter reacting directly to the article. It might, therefore, be anticipated that different frameworks of affiliation strategies (different possibilities for relations of attitudinal alignment/dis-alignment) would be applied – one for the analysis of the 'monologic' text and another for the 'dialogic' texts. This is certainly an approach which is suggested by recent work by Zappavigna (2018) and Zappavigna and Martin (2018). Here is it indicated that 'dialogic affiliation' (when relations of attitudinal alignments/dis-alignments are being directly and interactively negotiated through turn-taking) should be analysed separately from 'ambient affiliation' (operational, for example, when a Twitter user conveys an attitude in a 'tweet' apparently directed at the 'Twitterverse' in general – rather than by way of a response to a specifically identified tweet or tweeter). Thus, for example, building on prior work by Knight, Zappavigna offers the following taxonomy for the analysis of 'affiliation strategies' in 'dialogic affiliation' (see Figure 2.1 below).

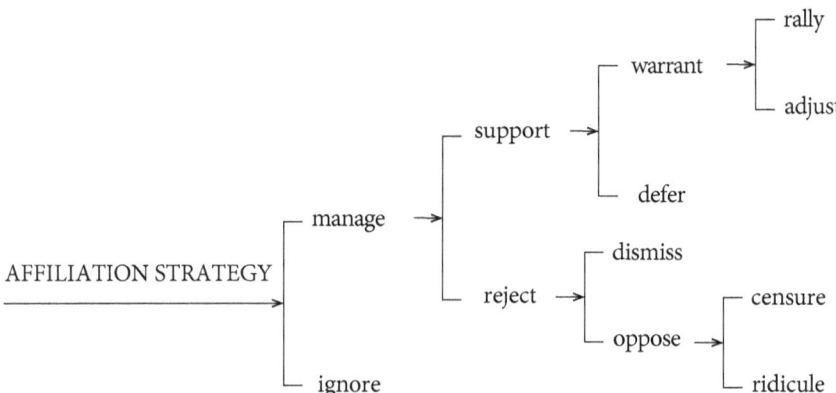

Figure 2.1 Strategies of dialogic affiliation, adapted from Zappavigna (2019, p. 58), and Zappavigna and Martin offer the following framework for the analysis of 'ambient affiliation'. (see Figure 2.2 below).

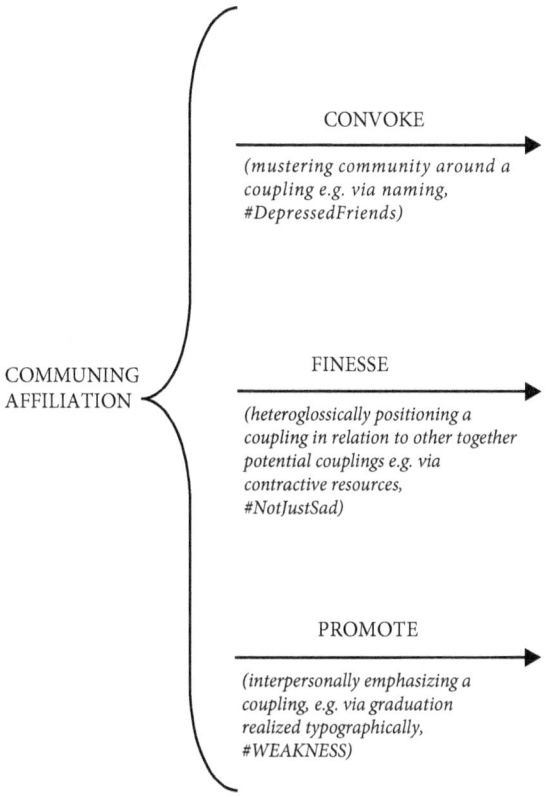

Figure 2.2 System of communing affiliation, adapted from Zappavigna and Martin (2018, p. 8).

This account of mechanisms of 'ambient affiliation' is extremely helpful in terms of the understandings it offers of the specific workings of the highly condensed forms of communicative exchange which operate on the Twitter platform, with specific reference to the particular functionalities of hashtags. However, in what I present below I offer another perspective, by way of a framework for the identification and characterization of discursively performed relations of attitudinal alignment/dis-alignment which can equally be applied to both 'monologic texts' (i.e. the op-ed piece under consideration) and texts which are 'dialogic' in the manner of these news article-attached comments (i.e. the Openings under consideration). The motivation here is both to bring to the fore the fact that even the most 'monologic' texts dialogistically negotiate relations of attitudinal alignment/dis-alignment and, simultaneously, to highlight that, in texts which are overtly dialogic, there is often more at stake in terms of attitudinal alignment/dis-alignment than what is being overtly signalled. In order to develop such a framework, it is necessary to attend not only to construed alignment/dis-alignment relations with any directly addressed interactants (when these are indicated) but also to relations with what, as indicated above, has been termed the 'implied', 'putative' or 'virtual' reader/addressee (see, for example, Thompson & Thetela, 1995; Hasan, 1999, p. 228; Schmid, 2014). A significant part of the following discussion, therefore, is devoted to a consideration of how beliefs, feelings and values may be projected onto this implied/putative/virtual addressee and what may be the (often) covert signals of authorial attitudinal alignment/dis-alignment with this thereby construed addressee.

The framework I have proposed and demonstrated below is as follows. Firstly, the relationship might be what, for ease of reference, I will term 'embracing' (broadly corresponding to Zappavigna's 'dialogic affiliation' strategy of 'support'). Obviously and most straightforwardly, an 'embracing' relationship can be retrospective, involving some concurrence with a prior attitudinal assertion by some external source. For the commenters, this would be a matter of concurring with the value positions advanced in the op-ed, with an earlier commenter (not dealt with in this chapter), or with some other prior external source whose views are referenced (also not dealt with in this chapter). For the op-ed author, this would occur were they to choose to reference the views of some prior speaker on the current subject so as to indicate agreement or approval. (As it turned out, there were no such instances in the opinion piece of the author overtly 'embracing' a prior source.)

Less straightforwardly, 'embracing' can involve a prospective rather than a retrospective relation when the text signals some expectation of how an actual or potential respondent might react, and in so doing signals an assumption of agreement or compliance on the part of this anticipated respondent. Here we are dealing with this notion of the 'implied/putative/virtual' reader/addressee (the reader written into the text). Here 'embracing' is a matter of the speaker deploying formulations which signal an assumption that the addressee will necessarily share the speaker's views – i.e. find a particular value judgement unproblematic. Such prospective addressivity will clearly be deployed not only by the author of the op-ed but also by the commenters, since, addressing as they do the 'ambient audience' of other readers of the article, they can be interpreted as projecting beliefs and values onto both the op-ed author and/or the members of this unknown audience. In this sense, the comments can be seen as 'polylogical'.

Secondly, the relationship might be what, for ease of reference, I will term 'spurning' (broadly corresponding to Zappavigna's 'dialogic affiliation' strategy of 'reject'). This is obviously the converse of 'embracing'. Most straightforwardly, a 'spurning' relationship involves the contradicting or repudiating of some prior attitudinal proposition. For the commenters this is a matter of repudiating value positions advanced by the op-ed's author, or a prior commenter (not dealt with in this chapter), or by some other external source (not dealt with in this chapter). For the author of the opinion piece this would occur were they to explicitly reference the views of some (not necessarily specifically identified) prior speaker on the current subject so as to repudiate these views. In order to prospectively 'spurn' the implied/putative reader, it would be necessary for the speaker to explicitly address the reader so as to indicate an anticipation that they will be intractable in their rejection of the author's own viewpoint – for example, by way of an invented illustration: 'I accept that you, the reader/some readers/some of you, will never find this an acceptable, fair or plausible proposition but ….' (Predictably there were no instances of this in the opinion piece.) Through such 'spurning', the addresser construes the addressee as having membership in some alternative or adversarial community of shared values.

Finally, the relationship might be what, for ease of reference, I will term 'proselytizing'. This is a prospective relationship with the implied/putative addressee by which the speaker presents as 'reaching out' to an undecided, doubtful or even dissenting addressee by supplying his/her attitudinal assertion with motivating argumentative support and justification. By this, the value position is framed as, to some degree, contentious or problematic and the addressee as potentially needing to be won over to the value position at risk. In this sense, the speaker/writer presents as acting to win over or to 'convert' the addressee so as to 'induct' the addressee into the speaker's community of shared value.

These three alignment relations can be summarized thusly:

- 'Embracing': retrospectively concurring with prior speakers or prospectively construing a putative addressee as likeminded (aligning with the addressee in a values-based identity);
- 'Proselytizing': treating other interactants, or construing the putative addressee, as 'persuadable' (construing the addressee as 'inductible' into the speaker's group identity);
- 'Spurning': treating other interactants or the putative addressee as implacably at odds.

The above proposals as to alignment relations rely on an account developed in the appraisal framework literature (Iedema et al., 1994; White, 1998, 2002, 2016; Martin, 2000; Macken-Horarik, 2003; Martin & White, 2005) with respect to the options in English for dialogistic positioning (the stances the speaker/writer can take vis-à-vis prior utterances on the current topic or vis-à-vis potential responses to the current proposition) – options set out as options for 'engagement', as the term is used in this literature (see, for example, White, 2000, 2003, 2010).

By reference to these three possibilities, the first stage of the analysis aimed to reach conclusions as to the nature and manner of formulation of value positions advanced by the author of the opinion piece and thus as to the relations of alignment/dis-alignment thereby entered into. The second stage was concerned with which of the options for alignment relations were taken up by the commenters as they positioned themselves reactively to the value positions (assessments of particular targets) asserted or implied in the article. This discussion involves some comparisons with Zappavigna's proposals for strategies of 'dialogic affiliation' as outlined in Figure 2.1.

With respect to the nature of the value positions at stake, the analysis relied on the APPRAISAL framework's proposals as to the different types and realizations of attitudinal meanings (positive or negative assessments) available in English – what the literature terms the system of ATTITUDE (Martin & White, 2005). Under this account, attitudinal assessments of particular targets (e.g. of human actors, artefacts, objects, happenings and situations) are sub-classified as: (1) Judgement (assessments of human behaviour and character by reference to systems of social norms), (2) Appreciation (assessments of entities, situations and happenings in terms of their aesthetic qualities or their social value) and (3) Affect (indications of positive or negative emotion towards some trigger or target). A key distinction, also relevant to the concerns of this chapter, is between explicit expressions of ATTITUDE (termed 'inscriptions' – e.g. 'the raid was a shocking invasion of privacy') and implied activations of ATTITUDE (termed 'invocations of ATTITUDE', e.g. 'The police officers went through every drawer and cupboard from the bedrooms to the living room and, in the kitchen, knelt on the floor rummaging through drawers of whisks and spoons'). In the case of such 'invocations', even while the writer may provide indicators as to the attitudinal assessment which is at stake, there is no explicitly and stably positive/negative lexis offered, with the reader being relied on to supply some attitudinal assessment through a process of inference. Thus, in the case of invocation just cited, the police actions are not explicitly characterized as exceptional or untoward. Rather, it is left up to the reader to provide an interpretation of the described action as in some way wrong or inappropriate. In this, attitudinal invocation is also implicated in construing addressees (either actual or putative) as 'likeminded', as 'affiliated' with the speaker, at least to the extent that they reveal an assumption that the addressee will be subject to the same attitudinal entailments as the speaker, will reach the same attitudinal conclusions as are elsewhere indicated in the text.

More specifically, the methodology employed tracked all instances of attitudinal assessment (explicit or implicit) in the op-ed and the subsequent Openings, considering at the same time authorial positioning with respect to these assessments (e.g. were they categorially asserted, justified, presented as contingently grounded in the author's own subjectivity, and so on). In this way, it is possible to be specific about exactly what particular attitudinal assessments were being advanced (which assessment of which attitudinal targets), which attitudes were being projected onto the implied/putative reader and around which attitudinal assessments commenters aligned and dis-aligned with the op-ed author.

This is essentially the same methodology applied in the work on affiliation/dis-affiliation mentioned above. However, this group of scholars choose to operate with the metaphor of 'coupling', specifically that attitudinal assessments can be analysed as a 'coupling' (fusion, combining, co-selection) of ideation and attitude – the 'ideation' element being the human actor, artefact, object, process or situation which is positively or negatively assessed by the 'attitude', that is, the particular value of Judgement, Appreciation or Affect. In the discussion below I will use less technical formulations in which attitudinal assessments are analysed and described by reference to the 'value of ATTITUDE being promulgated' and the specific phenomenon which is the 'target' of this value.

ATTITUDE and alignment in the op-ed piece

The findings emerging from the first stage of the APPRAISAL analysis (as described above) enable a case to be made that the author of the opinion piece very largely 'embraces' a putative reader construed as like-minded – i.e. one who, it is assumed, will find unproblematic the value positions being advanced. Thus, this implied addressee is, for the most part, construed as having membership in the same community of shared value as the author, and as subscribing to the same values-based group identity.

This can firstly be seen in the article's headline:[2]

Annika Smethurst raid was more than an invasion of privacy
('inscribed' judgement/impropriety' of the raid as a human behaviour)

Significant here is the fact that one of the article's key attitudinal propositions – that the police action was improper (an 'invasion of privacy') – is treated as a 'given' via the presuppositional grammatical structure of the sentence. That is to say, to assert that the action was 'more than' an invasion of privacy is to treat the proposition that it *was* an invasion as already decided, that is, as universally accepted.

Elsewhere, like-mindedness is projected onto the putative reader when potentially highly contentious attitudinal propositions are presented as if they are unproblematic and not in tension with alternative viewpoints. That is to say, they are barely and hence categorically asserted without any recognition that they are based in the contingent subjectivity of the author – a formulation that the APPRAISAL literature terms 'monoglossic'.[3]

The first instance of this occurs when the headline is restated in the body:

Tuesday's raid on the home of our national political editor Annika Smethurst was a shocking invasion of privacy

Of note here is that the author has 'upped the attitudinal ante'. The police action is categorically characterized not only as 'an invasion of privacy' (inscribed judgement/impropriety of the police action), but also as 'shocking', an assessment by which the action is said to globally trigger a negative reaction (negative appreciation with the 'raid' as its evaluative target). Thus, the author doesn't present as personally being 'shocked' by the action, rather presenting the quality of being 'shocking' as inhering in the act itself. And thus, the proposition that the police action is both improper and emotionally troubling is presented as unproblematic for the reader – as a proposition that need not be tempered, justified or grounded in any specific subjectivity.

The attitudinal invocations similarly anticipate a like-minded reader. Consider, for example, the stand-first at the head of the piece:

Seven federal cops. Seven hours. The rubbish bins. The oven. The underwear drawers.

There are several 'flags' here that these informational details should give rise to negative attitudinal assessments of the police action (i.e. an invoked assessment of judgement/ impropriety on the part of police), for example, the unusual grammatical structure – a series of short noun groups, rather than a clause or complete sentence; similarly, the numbering of the police officers; the fortuitous parallelism of 'seven federal cops' with 'seven hours'; the use of the potentially disparaging term 'cops' and the specific details of 'underwear drawers'. The text thus points the reader in one attitudinal direction, but nevertheless still presents as assuming the reader can be relied on to supply the necessary inference.

There is, however, one exception to this rule – the treatment of the proposition that Smethurst's original 2018 article, which has prompted this police action, was 'in the public interest' (positive appreciation of the story and/or positive judgement of Smethurst's actions in publishing the story). Tellingly, in putting into play this proposition, the author both signals recognition that this is in conflict with an alternative viewpoint (even while this viewpoint is not explicitly sourced) and supplies the proposition with extensive argumentative justification:

> Annika's story, published in April 2018, was absolutely in the public interest: [because] it revealed secret plans at the highest levels of the Canberra bureaucracy to allow the Australian Signals Directorate to cyber-spy on Australian citizens. That's a chilling prospect: this agency was created to keep Australia safe from external, i.e. foreign, threats.

To be noted firstly is the use of 'absolutely' in 'was absolutely in the public interest'. Termed 'pronouncements' in the APPRAISAL framework literature, such expressions involve heightened emphasis on the part of author by way of pushing back against rival propositions. Such pronouncements thus recognize heteroglossic alternatives while simultaneously confronting them. This allows for the possibility that the putative reader may be aware of, or party to, this alterative viewpoint. But then the evaluative proposition at stake is bolstered by a series of justifications – that, for example, the story was revealing plans for 'cyber-spying' on Australian citizens. In moving to offer readers these reasons, the author thereby constructs the putative reader as possibly not wedded to the idea that the story was 'in the public interest', but nevertheless as still 'persuadable', as potentially to be won over and thereby capable of being 'inducted' into the author's community of shared values.

Attitude and alignment in the comments trail Openings

Openings: Embracing

I begin the discussion of the attitudinal alignments/dis-alignments in the comment trail by considering the six Openings which were broadly supportive of the opinion and piece (i.e. 'embracing'). These would broadly fall under Zappavigna's dialogic affiliation category of 'support' (see Figure 2.1). An analysis of these 'embracing' Openings reveals three primary modes of, or orientations to, alignment: bolstering, broadening and barracking. In the cases of some of these Openings, the entirety of the comment can be treated as performing just one of these aligning functions, while in other cases, multiple functions will be observable in the one comment.

Bolstering

In 'bolstering', the commenter goes beyond simply indicating agreement with the op-ed's author or applauding her for the positions she has advanced by offering additional argumentative support or evidence for one or more of the author's value positions.

The commenter thus aligns with the author in a values-based identity through strengthening a value position. The following is an example of such an Opening:

1. Vincent: Grossly disgraceful conduct by those responsible for that home invasion. Whoever authorised it should be sacked immediately. All Annika did was to report the fact that our Government is planning to have Australian spies spying on Australian people. That is hardly breaching National Security. I could understand the concern about National Security if she was having dinners with multi-millionaires from a Communist Country.

Here the commenter essentially reiterates the author's negative assessment of the police action (negative judgement/propriety of 'those responsible for the action'), while interestingly being more direct in his/her attitudinal targeting – assessing the behaviour of 'those responsible' as 'disgraceful conduct'. As well, he/she ups the attitudinal force by characterizing the behaviour as a 'home invasion' – a rather more serious 'crime' than an 'invasion of privacy'. The commenter similarly positions the reader to view positively Smethurst's 2018 story in that it revealed that 'our Government is planning to have Australian spies spying on Australian people'. Beyond this, the commenter develops the argument in drawing a distinction between what Smethurst was doing in revealing confidential government information and what others would be doing if, for example, they revealed such information to foreign agents. The value position is thus bolstered as the commenter recognizes that, yes, in some cases revealing confidential information is 'wrong', but this is certainly not always the case.

Broadening

A number of these aligned Openings 'embrace' by broadening the scope of the attitudinal positioning in play. Consider, for example, the following two instances:

2. Stephen: Have a read of 1984 and see where we are heading, the safer we are the more danger we are in, KGB.
3. John: Another Julian Assange moment, we should be protecting journo's [sic], not jailing them.

In both comments, the issue at hand (the police action in searching Smethurst's home) is, by implication, treated as an instance of a much more widely operating 'issue' of concern. 'Stephen' in comment 2 above draws a very long bow, implying that this action by the police takes us down a path towards the totalitarian extremism of George Orwell's dystopian novel *1984* or the excesses of the Soviet Russian secret service. In comment 3, 'John' connects Smethurst's actions with the groundbreaking actions of WikiLeaks over many years in revealing the innermost workings of the US government, military and security services. In both cases we have instances of what Stenglin has termed 'bonding icons' or 'bondicons' (Stenglin, 2004). By 'bonding icon' Stenglin refers to certain experiential references (e.g. Orwell's *1984*, the KGB, Julian Assange) which, for a particular community of shared value, have become so attitudinally charged that they signify a particular value position – to the extent that, for that community, all it takes to invoke a particular value position is to mention the relevant 'bonding icon'. Crucially, of course, the experiential reference will not work in this way for other communities of shared value. In assuming that 'Assange' can be used as a rallying point in this way, 'John' plainly construes his/her addressees as very much like-minded.

Barracking

One further mechanism of 'embracing' could be observed in the opening comments. This is exemplified in the following two Openings:

4. Peter: Strength to Annika. A great journo, an astute commentator, a brilliant mind. Keep on keeping on.
5. Michael: Annika don't feel threatened buy [sic] this. Just keep on keeping on. Just shows some of the forces involved in silencing the right to speech and the Press. On the anniversary of the Tienanmen Square incident, we do have the right to voice an opinion and not be stifled by government. I have your back.

Obviously, comment 4 doesn't set out to engage with any of the substantive issues raised by the article. Instead, the 'embracing' here is more directly personal as the speaker offers 'moral support' and encouragement, in this case to Smethurst, the individual with whom the op-ed aligns and presents as the injured party. The commenter can therefore be said to be 'barracking' for Smethurst, to be indicating that he/she is 'on the same side as' the op-ed and the person it presents as unfairly dealt with.

Comment 5 operates in the same way, even while, of course, it also involves 'broadening' of the type discussed above. Again the police action is construed as just one instance of a much wider phenomenon – the action of 'forces' to suppress democratic freedoms. Note also the rather interesting use of another 'bonding icon' – the reference to the 'Tienanmen [sic] Square' incident.[4] Interestingly, it is left entirely up to the reader to determine the relevance of the 'Tienanmen [sic] Square incident' to the actions of Australian police in undertaking a search of a journalist's home. The commenter construes the addressee as having membership in a community of shared value (a value-based identity) for whom it is not only uncontentiously 'wrong' for the police to take this action but for whom there is an obvious likeness between this action and the Chinese authorities violently suppressing the pro-democracy movement in Beijing in 1989.

Openings – proselytising and spurning

As indicated above, twelve of the Opening comments in the data set indicated broad dis-alignment with the op-ed and its author. (They would fall within Zappavigna's category of 'reject'.) In two of these Openings the commenter did 'reach out' to the addressee by offering reasoning in support of a counter-view – thereby construing the addressee as 'persuadable', as being 'inductible' into the commenter's values-based group identity. In the remaining cases, one or more of the value positions advanced in the op-ed were rejected, repudiated or basically ignored. They thus construe one or more adversarial communities of shared value, one or more values-based group identities.

Openings – proselytizing

The following exemplifies this 'reaching out' or 'proselytising' alignment function just mentioned:

> 6. Damien: I know journo's [sic] have to support each other but this is ridiculous. By your own acknowledgement the documents were secret. They involved our most secret agencies tasked with protecting us from threats both here and abroad. By all means, if a story is handed to her, let her investigate. But if she, as with Assange, decide [sic] to go public with secret documents then you have to expect investigations to ensue. Regardless of whether it's in the public interest or not these agencies have not only the right but the responsibility to investigate the source of the leaks. Being a journo doesn't make you exempt from the laws which govern the rest of us, and her actions have consequences. What she must decide is if the story is worth the pain that will follow.

While the comment does begin by disparaging the op-ed and its directly addressed author in generalized terms ('… this is ridiculous' – non-specific negative attitude directed at a vague target, presumably the article in general or what the commenter views as its key propositions), the key point here is that the remainder of comment does present as a genuine attempt by the commenter to 'reason' with the op-ed author, to win her over by pointing to gaps or inconsistencies in the article and to make a case for the alternative view that the police action was entirely proper. We note that the commenter doesn't present as operating from a position which is diametrically at odds with that of the op-ed. Rather, he/she presents as pointing to certain aspects of the issue which appear to have been overlooked or given inadequate attention in the op-ed – namely the fact that the police were actually operating according to current Australian laws with regards to 'leaked' confidential documents, laws by which it is 'illegal' for anyone – 'journalists' or otherwise – to be knowingly in receipt of leaked classified documents.

Openings – spurning

In Zappavigna's approach (Figure 2.1), tweets which 'oppose' are divided into those which 'ridicule' and those which 'censure'. As it turned out, none of the Openings in my small data set seemed to 'ridicule'. Rather, all the 'spurning' Openings in the data set could broadly fit within Zappavigna's category of 'censuring' – i.e. they all involve negative critiques or contradictions of positions advanced in the op-ed.

disparagement

It is perhaps not surprising that Openings which 'spurn' often deploy disparagement, as the commenter signals his/her membership of values-based identity which is adversarial to that of the op-ed author. For example (disparagements indicated in italics):

7. Ross: She's *crossed a line.* (negative judgement/propriety of Smethurst) It's *delusional* (negative judgement/capacity of the author of the op-ed and anyone who shares the author's views) to think society has right to know everything that's going on .... *grow up people*
8. Damien: I know journo's [sic] have to support each other but *this is ridiculous.* ...

However, as these examples demonstrate, these disparagements are not typically offered in isolation, but are part of a wider-ranging repudiation of the op-ed's value positions.

Bare antithesis

A repeated method of spurning observed in Openings involved what, for ease of reference, I will term 'bare antithesis'. In these cases, none of the value positions advanced in the op-ed are directly engaged with. Instead, a flatly antithetical position is categorically asserted, without any form of argumentative support:

9. Greg: i am glad the afp (Australian Federal Police) take the broadcasting of confidential leaked documents seriously (positive affectual response by the commenter to the mindset of the police)
10. Ross: She's crossed a line. It's delusional to think society has right to know everything that's going on. There always has to be a level of secrecy across various parts of government, grow up people.
11. SCOTT: National security should ALWAYS take precedence.

Such comments clearly function as acts of group identity demarcation. They are contributed simply to signal the commenter's membership of an adversarial values-based identity.

Axiological substitution

The final 'spurning' mechanism observable in this data set involves what I will term 'axiological substitution'. In this I understand 'axiology' to designate a particular system, 'theory' (formal or informal) or set of related assumptions as to what should be the basis by which phenomena are to be assessed as good/bad, laudable/illaudable, right/wrong, pleasing/displeasing and so on. Thus, speakers/writers may operate with different 'axiologies' – with different bases on which a phenomenon will be evaluated positively or negatively. A number of the commenters 'spurn' by substituting their own axiology for that which operates in the article. For these commenters, the rightness or wrongness of the police action is to be determined on the basis of the moral standing of journalists generally, and not on any consideration of benefits or harm associated with the police action itself:

11. Matt: A journalist the victim of an invasion of privacy? How does it feel now the shoe's on the other foot?

12. Col: So it's okay for a journalist to pry into other people's lives in pusuit [sic] of a story, but it's not okay for the police to pry into the journalist's life to find out how she came into the possession of top secret papers?

Comment 11 obviously operates, via the initial rhetorical question-like minor clause, on the assumption that journalists generally are guilty of 'invasions of privacy' (negative judgement/propriety of journalists as a vocational grouping), thereby shifting the attitudinal focus from the police action and/or Smethurst's own action to generalized attitudes towards journalism as social process. It is this assessment which is then treated as providing the 'axiological' basis for the spurning of the value position advanced in the article – specifically that the article has failed to acknowledge the hypocrisy of any journalist complaining about invasions of privacy. Comment 12 operates along very similar axiological lines.

Interestingly, the community of shared value in which the commenters here announce their membership is one broadly based on one's views of journalists/journalism – those who are positively disposed to journalists (the op-ed) versus those who are negatively disposed (these commenters).

Conclusion

Based, as it is, on an APPRAISAL analysis (an analysis of evaluative workings) of part of the comments trail of just one op-ed piece, the above discussion is necessarily of a preliminary nature. Nevertheless, I am hopeful that it does point forward to further, more comprehensive treatments of how the participants in this one-to-one/one-to-many format conduct themselves interactively and rhetorically and of how it is they construe and demarcate values-based group identities. The chapter has demonstrated how both 'monologic' op-eds of this type and the 'dialogic/polylogic' comments attached to them can be analysed from the perspective of the attitudinal alignments and dis-alignments they enter into, and hence how it is possible to identify the particular values-based group identities enacted by author and commenters. It was proposed that between the extremes of the 'embracing' of and the 'spurning' of some prior or prospective speaker lies the intermediate option of 'proselytizing'. In 'embracing', the speaker aligns with the addressee in a values-based group identity, in 'spurning' signals group-identity disjunction, and through 'proselytising' the speaker construes the addressee as 'inductible' into the speaker's values-based group identity.

The chapter also offered some proposals, arising from this admittedly limited data set, as to what appear to be various options by which 'embracing', 'proselytising' and 'spurning' can be managed communicatively. It was shown, for example, that a number of the commenters 'embraced' by bolstering the value positions advance in the op-ed (by providing additional justifications), while others broadened a value position (by presenting the event being assessed as an instance of a much wider social, political and ethical issue). Similarly, a number of the commenters 'spurned' through a process of 'bare antithesis' (simply asserting a contrary assessment to that advanced by the op-ed), while others engaged in 'axiological substitution' (ignoring the principles operating in the op-ed by which positive/negative assessments are made and deploying entirely different bases for attitudinal conclusions). Plainly, this can only be a preliminary sketch as to various options taken up by participants in these comments trails – an analysis which of necessity could only deal with the commenters' attitudinal positionings vis-à-vis value positions advanced in the op-ed, rather than also dealing with the 'polylogical' arrangements by which the commenters also position themselves vis-à-vis other prospective respondents (via signals as to assumptions of the implied/putative addressee's beliefs and values). More research is needed across a much wider data set to determine how these relationships are typically construed and what might be the wider repertoire of options available.

Notes

1. In this chapter I use 'speaker' as a general term for the source of any verbal communication – i.e. it includes those who communicate through writing.
2. The headline, according to customary newsroom practice, may well not have been composed by the journalist author, being added later by a sub-editor. This, however, is irrelevant for our current concerns, since it is with the article as presented – headline + body – that readers, and hence commenters, engage.
3. For extended discussions of bare assertions as 'monoglossic', see White (2000, 2003, 2010).
4. The violent suppression of pro-democracy protests by the mainland Chinese authorities in Beijing in 1989.

References

Edwards, J. R. (1985). *Language, Society and Identity*. Oxford: Blackwell.

Hasan, R. (1999). Speaking with reference to context. In M. Ghadessy (Ed.), *Text and Context in Functional Linguistics* (pp. 219–328). Amsterdam and Philadelphia: Benjamins.

Hyland, K. (2010). Community and individuality: Performing identity in applied linguistics. *Written Communication*, 27, 159–88.

Iedema, R., Feez, S., & White, P. R. R. (1994). *Media Literacy*. Sydney, Disadvantaged schools programs: NSW, Department of School Education.

Knight, N. K. (2008). 'Still cool ... and American too!': An SFL analysis of deferred bonds in internet messaging humour. *Systemic Functional Linguistics in Use, Odense Working Papers in Language and Communication*, 29, 481–502.

Knight, N. K. (2010). Wrinkling complexity: Concepts of identity and affiliation in humour. In M. Bednarek & J. R. Martin (Eds.), *New Discourse on Language: Functional Perspectives on Multimodality, Identity, and Affiliation* (pp. 35–58). London: Continuum.

Macken-Horarik, M. (2003). Envoi: Intractable issues in appraisal analysis? *Text and Talk (Special edition on Appraisal)*, 23, 313–19.

Manosevitch, E., & Walker, D. (2009). Reader comments to online opinion journalism: A space of public deliberation. *International Symposium on Online Journalism*, 10, 1–30.

Martin, J. R. (2000). Beyond exchange: Appraisal systems in English. In S. Hunston & G. Thompson (Eds.), *Evaluation in Text: Authorial Stance and the Construction of Discourse* (pp. 142–75). London: Oxford University Press.

Martin, J. R. (2008). Tenderness: Realisation and instantiation in a Botswanan town. *Odense Working Papers in Language and Communication*, 29, 30–58.

Martin, J. R. (2009). Realisation, instantiation and individuation: Some thoughts on identity in youth justice conferencing. *DELTA: Documentação de Estudos em Lingüística Teórica e Aplicada*, 25, 549–83.

Martin, J. R. (2010). Semantic variation: Modelling realisation, instantiation and individuation in social semiosis. In M. Bednarek & J. R. Martin (Eds.), *New Discourse on Language: Functional Perspectives on Multimodality, Identity, and Affiliation* (pp. 1–34). London: Continuum.

Martin, J. R., & White, P. R. R. (2005). *The Language of Evaluation: Appraisal in English*. London & New York: Palgrave/Macmillan.

Pérez-Milans, M. (2016). Language and identity in linguistic ethnography. In Siân Preece (Eds.) *The Routledge Handbook of Language and Identity* (pp.109–23). London: Routledge.

Stenglin, M. (2004). *Packaging Curiosities: Towards a Grammar of Three-Dimensional Space*, Unpublished PhD thesis, Department of Linguistics, University of Sydney, Sydney, Australia.

Schmid, W. (2014). Implied reader. In P. Hühn, J. C. Meister, J. Pier et al. (Eds.), *Handbook of Narratology* (pp. 301–9). Berlin: Walter de Gruyter.

Stenglin, M. K. (2009). Space odyssey: Towards a social semiotic model of three-dimensional space. *Visual Communication*, 8, 35–64.

Tann, K. (2010). Imagining communities: A multifunctional approach to identity management in texts. *New Discourse on Language: Functional Perspectives on Multimodality, Identity, and Affiliation* (pp. 163–94). London: Continuum.

Tann, K. (2012). The language of identity discourse: Introducing a systemic functional framework for iconography. *Linguistics & the Human Sciences*, 8, 361–91.

Thompson, G., & Thetela, P. (1995). The sound of one hand clapping: The management of interaction in written discourse. *Text-Interdisciplinary Journal for the Study of Discourse*, 15, 103–28.

von Sikorski, C., & Hänelt, M. (2016). Scandal 2.0: How valenced reader comments affect recipients' perception of scandalized individuals and the journalistic quality of online news. *Journalism & Mass Communication Quarterly*, 93, 551–71.

White, P. R. R. (1998). *Telling Media Tales: The News Story as Rhetoric*. Sydney, NSW: University of Sydney.

White, P. R. R. (2000). Dialogue and inter-subjectivity: Reinterpreting the semantics of modality and hedging. In M. Coulthard, M. Cotterill, & F. Rock (Eds.), *Working with Dialog* (pp. 67–80). Berlin: Tübingen, Max Niemeyer Verlag.

White, P. R. R. (2002). Appraisal: The language of evaluation and stance. In J. Verschueren, J. Ostman, J. Blommaert et al. (Eds.), *The Handbook of Pragmatics* (pp. 1–23). Amesterdam: John Benjamins.

White, P. R. R. (2003). Beyond modality and hedging: A dialogic view of the language of intersubjective stance. *Text-The Hague Then Amsterdam Then Berlin*, 23, 259–84.

White, P. R. R. (2010). Taking Bakhtin seriously: Dialogic effects in written, mass communicative discourse. *Japanese Journal of Pragmatics*, 12, 37–53.

White, P. R. R. (2016). Evaluative contents in verbal communication. In A. Rocci & L. de Saussure (Eds.), *Verbal Communication, Vol 3, Handbooks of Communication Sciences*, Berlin, Boston: De Gruyter Mouton.

Zappavigna, M. (2011). Ambient affiliation: A linguistic perspective on Twitter. *New Media & Society*, 13, 788–806.

Zappavigna, M. (2012). *Discourse of Twitter and Social Media: How We Use Language to Create Affiliation on the Web*. London: Continuum.

Zappavigna, M. (2014a). Ambient affiliation in microblogging: Bonding around the quotidian. *Media International Australia*, 151, 97–103.

Zappavigna, M. (2014b). Enacting identity in microblogging through ambient affiliation. *Discourse & Communication*, 8, 209–28.

Zappavigna, M. (2018). *Searchable Talk: Hashtags and Social Media Metadiscourse*. London: Bloomsbury Publishing.

Zappavigna, M. (2019). Ambient affiliation and Brexit. In V. Koller, S. Kopf, & M. Miglbauer (Eds.), *Discourses of Brexit* (pp. 85–113). London and New York: Routledge.

Zappavigna, M., & Martin, J. R. (2018). # Communing affiliation: Social tagging as a resource for aligning around values in social media. *Discourse, Context & Media*, 22, 4–12.

Ziegele, M., Weber, M., Quiring, O. et al. (2018). The dynamics of online news discussions: Effects of news articles and reader comments on users' involvement, willingness to participate, and the civility of their contributions. *Information, Communication & Society*, 21, 1419–35.

3

The foundational role of discourse semantics beyond language

John A. Bateman
Bremen University

Introduction

The notion that language can be usefully characterized as exhibiting a particular stratum of *discourse semantics* mediating between lexicogrammar and context constitutes one of the major contributions of the variant of systemic functional linguistics articulated at length by Jim Martin for over 40 years (cf. Martin, 1992, 2014, 2019). Analyses performed using Martin's discourse semantics have served an important role in clarifying a range of linguistic phenomena that come into play as texts unfold and have revealed the workings of several kinds of intratextual developments – such as larger-scale thematic progressions, argument structures and developing patterns of appraisal – in a more systematic and inclusive fashion than hitherto. A stratum of discourse semantics is also assigned a decisive role in the approach to analysing multimodal communicative artefacts and performances introduced in Bateman (2011, 2016) and forms the basis for Bateman et al.'s (2017) introductory textbook to multimodality as a research field. In this account, the definition of semiotic mode – arguably the central concept of that field – includes a semiotic stratum of discourse semantics lying 'above' semiotic strata of form and material. Here, material generalizes to include all possible materialities that may be 'shaped' for meaning-making (cf., e.g., Kress, 2010, p. 114), while form covered any regularities that may be imposed on such material in the service of that meaning-making. Discourse semantics then plays a crucial role in characterizing how those regularities in material relate to their contextualized interpretations.

Despite the significant potential offered for multimodality by an extended notion of discourse semantics, the majority of multimodal analyses currently performed – including some which in other respects might be expected to be strongly conformant with the view of the linguistic system that Martin sets out (e.g. Painter et al., 2013) – appear to neglect discourse semantics as soon as the boundaries of the linguistic system are left behind. One reason for this in broadly systemic-functionally oriented work may be that discourse semantics played no role in the key texts initiating systemic-functional multimodality, such as Kress and van Leeuwen's (1996) *Reading Images*. Analyses then often follow in a similar style – sometimes, as in Painter et al. (2013, pp. 3, 6–10), explicitly suggesting that extensions will be made with respect to the original Kress and van Leeuwen framework – rather than engaging more directly with considerations of discourse semantics in their own right.

In this contribution, I seek to redress this oversight and set out why a semiotic stratum of discourse semantics, as proposed by Martin for verbal language, needs to be adopted equally as a fundamental component for addressing *all* semiotic modes – particularly when facing the largely empirical questions of just *which* semiotic modes there are (in general) and, more specifically, which semiotic modes are at work in any given object of analysis. I will argue that without an explicit orientation to discourse semantics along the lines set out by Martin, analysis is seriously compromised.

I proceed towards this conclusion in three stages:

- Firstly, I offer a brief reorientation concerning just what discourse semantics was intended to provide for verbal language and its primary *raison d'être* according to Martin. This will culminate in a diagnosis of a central aspect of a discourse semantics so conceived that has not been delivered on and which, within systemic functional linguistics, still stands largely as a promissory note – that is, the *dynamics* of discourse organization.
- Secondly, I recontextualize the discussion to place the moves made towards dynamics in discourse within systemic functional linguistics against the background of a broader set of concerns that arose in the late 1980s in several linguistic traditions concerning the role of dynamics in accounts of language. These provided the particular extensions of the notion of discourse semantics formulated for multimodal use in Bateman (2011). Since readers outside of systemic functional linguistics are sometimes unsure what the notion of discourse semantics applied within this model of semiotic modes is, this section will be relevant for that broader perspective on multimodal research.
- And thirdly, I show how this view of discourse semantics needs to impact directly on all multimodal analyses, drawing on some straightforward examples from the literature to make the point.

I conclude with some general remarks on the nature of discourse semantics when viewed from a multimodal context, and consider some implications that this may have in return for discourse semantics in verbal language.

Discourse semantics: A recap

Among the original motivations for introducing a notion of discourse semantics was the realization that texts exhibit both regularities and variations in expression that are not captured within lexicogrammatical descriptions. These regularities and variations group together linguistic expressions belonging to very different 'areas' when considered from the perspective of a grammatical description, where they would simply stand as unrelated.

Attempts to move from the lexicogrammar into more textually relevant areas were first undertaken within systemic functional linguistics in Halliday and Hasan's (1976) development of *cohesion*. Cohesion sought to explain certain text-level regularities by drawing *non-structural* connections between lexicogrammatically identified elements. Linking together diverse lexicogrammatical elements in a text then operates beyond the confines of lexicogrammar, but remained classificatory; little predictive power appeared to be gained from such descriptions. Most earlier work on texts from a systemic functional perspective then approached texts from the rather different perspective of context rather than patterns within texts. In such accounts, lexicogrammatical features are seen primarily as being correlated with social-contextual features or configurations and so relate to *register* (cf. Hasan, 1985; Bowcher, 2019). Such register-oriented views see certain kinds of lexicogrammatical features as more or less likely to occur in certain contexts of use than others. Textual phenomena may then be placed on a cline from instantial text, through text-type and register/genre, and on to context (Martin, 2006).

Although this may say much about how the possibilities of grammar may be accorded differing likelihoods of occurrence according to context and use and so may participate in realizational relationships, it only relates indirectly and distantly to the properties that a text exhibits *as it is unfolding*. In essence, the *temporal granularity* of context-based accounts is simply too low: much of what makes texts work as texts is not (yet) visible. As a consequence, around and about Martin's (1985) reemphasis of Hjelmslev's claim that text and process are dual and ever-present aspects of semiosis, developments within systemic functional linguistics took up the task of fine-grained textual description attempting to meet the temporal granularity problem head on. Whereas approaches taking their starting point from Hasan's view of context and register increased temporal granularity by allowing context (and register) to change at scales somewhat 'smaller' than entire texts, others began seeing even micro-scale individual contributions to texts (however defined) as following each other dynamically, each contribution leading to the next. O'Donnell (1999) provides a detailed overview of this course of development within systemic functional linguistics, focusing particularly on the fine-grained changes in context that individual turns or messages can enact and how this might be modelled.

The account of discourse semantics set out in Martin (1992) needs to be seen against this background, drawing on both notions involving cohesion and the need to account for temporal text construction, or *logogenesis*. Divided metafunctionally into several main components, the stratum of discourse semantics consisted of a collection of system networks describing discourse level options for continuing discourses or texts. Applying this mode of description to texts allowed Martin to claim that a text holds together precisely because of the *discourse semantic options* that have been taken up. These options have manifestations in particular discourse structures, which in turn find systematic re-expression in particular patterns of lexical and grammatical material. Four regions of discourse semantics were introduced in depth in Martin (1992) – NEGOTIATION, IDENTIFICATION, CONJUNCTION and IDEATION – later filled out with full-blown regions for APPRAISAL and PERIODICITY as well (Martin & Rose, 2003; Martin, 2019). NEGOTIATION (interpersonal metafunction) concerns those resources of discourse semantics that are responsible for the construction of dialogue and interaction. IDENTIFICATION (textual) captures the semantic resources for referring to and tracking discourse participants. CONJUNCTION (ideational) develops the 'logic' of English text in terms of those resources by which semantic messages are combined into larger complex messages, and through which messages are related to previously expressed messages as a text or dialogue unfolds. IDEATION (ideational) attempts to motivate those systematic selections from groups of 'related' lexical items that bring about a text's 'lexical' cohesion. APPRAISAL (interpersonal) brings together the largely prosodically realized enactments of personal and interpersonal evaluations. Finally, PERIODICITY (textual) systematizes integrated waves of textual prominence that may be created by the deployment of a range of resources, such as higher-level themes. Each of the regions addressed provides a different perspective on 'discourse structure', captured by its own system networks governing their own distinctive units and subunits. Bateman (1998) offers a short but relatively complete overview of the ground covered in the 1992 model.

A recurring problem with this approach, however, is the fact that system networks are simply not a kind of formalism that effectively supports treatment of dynamic phenomena. This is the reason that a range of authors, Martin included, have explored other possibilities, such as 'flowcharts' (e.g. Ventola, 1987; Fawcett, 1989); again, O'Donnell (1999) provides details. Unfortunately, moving to a flowchart-like representation is not an effective strategy because it replaces a highly constrained and well-understood formalism (the system network) with a way of writing what are in effect arbitrarily complex computer programs. This does not lend itself readily to capturing *linguistic* generalizations. Attempts more in line with extended uses of system networks include taking instantial 'snapshots' of paradigmatically selected options which may then be arranged in time as 'instantial' networks (cf. Halliday & Matthiessen, 1999, pp. 382–7) – although these are, again, more suggestive than well-specified models. It is possible to characterize each 'state' in a developing text as a particular instantiation of lexicogrammatical and semantic features and structures, but the *transitions* between states and how those transitions themselves construct meanings remain underdeveloped. Individual turns, messages, utterances in a discourse may then receive detailed descriptions.

Martin draws attention to this necessary property of an account of discourse and of discourse's semantics in the following terms: it must be possible to

> interpret discourse semantic systems as ... connecting phases of discourse of indefinite extent. The last point perhaps needs some elaboration. What we are saying here is that discourse semantic structures involve both 'local' and 'extended' realizations. ... It is perhaps in this respect that discourse semantics can be seen as most strongly complementary to lexicogrammatical and phonological resources. (Martin, 2019, pp. 378–9)

In other words, accounts of discourse need to project (discourse) structures 'in advance' that range over entire sequences of discourse contributions and respond flexibly (i.e. dynamically) to contingencies that arise during the performance of those sequences. Martin's (1992) discourse semantics consequently attempts both to provide paradigmatic and syntagmatic discourse semantic descriptions and to show how these relate, that is, how the semantic potential captured by the paradigmatic options described is actualized in possibly extended unfolding discourse structures. To do this, Martin develops system networks that call for a variety of types of syntagmatic realizations for the paradigmatic discourse options defined, whose scope is genuinely extended, or discoursal, rather than local, that is, restricted to that of contributing clauses or messages. These discoursal syntagmatic structures are intended to describe how discourse structures may grow over the life of a text. Examples are the conjunctive relation reticula modelled on ideas from Gleason (cf. Martin, 2014) or cohesive chain structures – all of which fall under Lemke's (1985) notion of extended (and extendable) 'covariate' structures.

However, these representations are, again, actually static characterizations of entire texts or text fragments. They may be *described* as developing as a text develops, but do not themselves have any dynamic properties. This is analogous to a reading order for a page: a static page of information may be read in a particular order but the information on the page is not in itself dynamic or ordered. Agreeing to read, for example, a collection of conjunctive relations between messages from the beginning of the text to the end does not itself mean that the formalism is dynamic in nature, nor that it has captured dynamic phenomena. For dynamism that is embedded into the framework at a more foundational level, we need to turn to another development in linguistics: that of *formal* discourse semantics.

Dynamics: A broader perspective

By the end of the 1970s, theories drawing on formalizations using logic had developed into a powerful and widely adopted approach to linguistic semantics. Often cited as being heralded by the descriptions of an (extremely) small fragment of English set out by Montague (1973), formal logic approaches see the operations of syntax and of semantics as closely linked. In general, syntactic operations are placed in a one-to-one correspondence with the mechanisms that construct (ideational) semantic descriptions. In several contemporary linguistic theories, this is taken to the limit by making the construction of syntactic descriptions and the construction of semantic descriptions one and the same process.

For all its success at characterizing predictively a range of syntactic and semantic phenomena, linguists developing formal accounts of discourse and connected text quickly established a rather fundamental problem for any straightforward extension of the alignment of syntactic configurations and semantic configurations beyond sentence and clause boundaries using traditional logic. This is already evident in the most simple of examples, as seen in the fact that the two sentences

1. Jane went to the park and played football.
2. Jane played football and went to the park.

might not have the same meaning since, in a narrative text, the temporal relations assumed could well lead to quite different situations being described (cf. Halliday & Matthiessen, 2004, pp. 428–9). While trivial, the formal consequences are profound: quite simply, it means that it is not possible to construct a logical form by relying on a straightforward conjunction. Whereas in a traditional logic 'p and q' is necessarily identical in meaning to 'q and p', this is not the case with these sentences and so another form of modelling is required. The same applies for sequences of sentences, which means similarly that it is not possible to model discourse as simply accumulating semantic configurations in a long conjunction 'p and q and r and …'. Building in a direct temporal relationship, such as 'p and then q', does not help either. In fact, this is equally problematic because the sentences do not always have this temporal interpretation: they could equally be a simple list of things that Jane did at some point: that is, simply an explicit extension rather than an 'implicit successive' in the terms of Martin's conjunctive relations (Martin, 1992, p. 239).

Several formal accounts consequently started proposing a very different approach to logic-based treatments of text and discourse in which logical expressions, broadly corresponding to the ideational semantics of clauses, were no longer combined with logical operators of the traditional kind (e.g. conjunction and disjunction) but rather with a logically more complex operation of 'update' (cf. Kamp, 1981; Heim, 1983). The essential notion here is that when a new piece of semantics is to be added into a growing semantic representation, a function is defined that takes the existing semantic representation as a starting point and extends this with the new semantics. For our example sentences above, this means that the first part of each sentence would define a starting point (i.e. either Jane going to the park or Jane playing football) and the semantics of the second part is then used to enrich the semantics of the first part. How precisely it does this is then the task of formal discourse semantics: some relationship has to be established for 'gluing' the new information into the old, but that relationship may not be immediately or explicitly given by the parts themselves.

The types of logic developed to express this mechanism of discourse growth have the common property that they are *dynamic logics*. In such logics, the order of relating semantic fragments is crucially important since the options available for linking some second part into a first part will naturally be dependent on just what that first part is. It is no longer the case that one can simply swap 'p' and 'q', as in 'p and q' is identical to 'q and p', because the internal details of 'p' (or 'q') may be different. Providing principled access to particular kinds of internal details led to new accounts capable of characterizing a range of discourse-related phenomena (such as extended references to discourse entities) that had previously not been well captured in logic-based accounts.

The most developed account of this kind currently available is Lascarides and Asher's (1993) Segmented Discourse Representation Theory (SDRT), introduced and described at length in Asher and Lascarides (2003). Within SDRT, incoming semantic configurations forming a text are anchored into the existing semantic representation by finding those specific discourse relations whose formal definitions fit with the preceding semantics, the incoming semantics and the 'context', that is, additional knowledge that may be held or presumed concerning any situation being constructed by the discourse. Relations thus look both 'downwards' towards concrete linguistic forms (and their semantics) and 'upwards' towards context. SDRT defines a relatively small set of discourse relations that nevertheless manage to cover a considerable range of naturally occurring discourse phenomena. These relations are all characterized from two perspectives.

The first perspective specifies hard constraints that need to be met from context knowledge for a discourse relation to obtain at all. These are termed *meaning postulates* and are expressed in a logic of a traditional kind, whereby facts are asserted to hold or not to hold and there is no inherent dynamism. If, for example, an interpreter was pursuing the idea that a temporal sequence relation could be the appropriate relation to apply in order to bring the two parts of the first of our sentences above together, then the relevant meaning postulate would be that, indeed, the event of going to the park preceded the event of playing football. If this was known on other grounds not to be the case, then the use of the temporal sequence would be blocked at that point (by virtue of the logical contradiction) and some other discourse relation would need to be found. Conversely, if nothing against this temporal ordering were known, then the meaning postulate would be asserted (or 'accommodated') for the growing discourse context.

The second perspective on discourse relations involves the new, dynamic component of the account and uses *abductive* inference rules, called *default axioms*, that specify which discourse relations may apply given specified properties of the discourse elements being related. Default axioms describe which information the discursive context must provide in order to interpret discourse relations between the segments. The general form of default axioms is to say that if one is attempting to add some new material to the existing discourse structure and certain other specified information is present, then *normally* one can assume that a discourse relation of a particular kind holds. The 'normally' here means that the axiom is not a hard-and-fast logical implication but that an interpreter *may assume* that the given relation holds until further information indicates otherwise. If the hypothesis is never contradicted, then it may stand as a coherent interpretation of the text.

Again, for our example sentence, in the situation where an interpreter is attempting to add the second clause to the first clause, the presence of simple past tense in both clauses and the bare conjunction 'and' might be taken as 'normally' suggesting that a temporal succession relation holds. Given this hypothesis, the interpreter must then also consider the meaning postulates of the discourse relation to check that these are not violated in any way. In the present case, if we assume they are not violated, then this would be sufficient to abduce a discourse relation of temporal succession as a way of joining the clauses. This indirection involving the two perspectives, made up of the meaning postulates and the default axioms, is necessary to allow the 'same' sentence to receive different semantic interpretations in different discourse contexts. In the following 'text', for example,

Jane did two things during the holidays. She went to the park and played football.

the likelihood of a temporal succession relationship for joining the clauses at issue is much reduced. The preceding sentence sets up a discourse context in which a listing (or extending) discourse relation would achieve a higher coherence and so is to be preferred. The meaning postulates for listing contain no commitment to temporal ordering and so can apply freely.

SDRT's formalization of a dynamically growing discourse structure also contributes at this point. The prior discourse context introduces two underspecified events as potential topics (the two things Jane did) and so leaving those events underspecified would score relatively poorly on coherence. The situation changes once again, if the text were to continue thus:

> Jane did two things during the holidays. She went to the park and played football. And she ate a lot of pizza.

Here the temporal succession relation might still apply between going to the park and playing football *within* a single complex event because a further specification of the second thing she did also follows. This produces a coherent overall discourse structure with a macro-theme introducing the thing done filled out by two subtopics, the first of which is itself complex. It is therefore crucial to emphasize here that these kinds of structures are *grown* dynamically precisely as a consequence of the formal discourse relation definitions: abducing a particular discourse relation as holding is at the same time the growth of discourse structural configurations with specific further properties and consequences. One of these consequences involves the automatic creation of intermediate 'topic nodes' within a discourse structure whenever necessary to maintain coherence (cf. Asher & Lascarides, 2003, pp. 164, 219).

The presence of abduction, that is, of only assuming information to hold as the 'best' hypotheses that one can make at a particular point in the interpretation process and which may subsequently need to be altered, is what renders the account a dynamic one. The operation of abduction was first defined in Peirce's account of logic and was used extensively in his semiotics (cf. Peirce, 1931–58: §2.270). In more recent times, abduction is commonly taken as the crucial mechanism that makes discourse and, indeed, interpretation in general, possible at all. Abduction always requires that more be brought to the interpretation process than the information that is simply 'there': there needs to be a jump in interpretation in order to *explain* why the items being brought together combine coherently. The growth of discourse structure in SDRT is then dynamic and abductive in precisely this sense. Such discourse structures can thus be extended arbitrarily as a discourse unfolds and offer a natural candidate for a formalization for the 'extended' realizations for discourse semantics in 'covariate' discourse structures as described above. The use of abduction for discourse relations is also closely related to the notions of *implicit assertions* in Mann and Thompson's (1988) Rhetorical Structure Theory and of 'interpretative gaps' in reader-response theories such as Iser (1978). By adding abduction to its formal modelling, however, SDRT goes beyond these previous approaches to provide a completely explicit account of how discourse interpretation can proceed. Discourse interpretation is thus always seen in SDRT as a process of dynamically selecting discourse relations in order to maximize the coherence of the interpretation achieved thus far.

There is a relatively straightforward connection to be drawn between the kinds of organizations produced dynamically during an SDRT interpretation and the

CONJUNCTION area of Martin's discourse semantics. The discourse relations defined within SDRT already partially overlap with the conjunctive relations given in Martin (1992); a more extensive comparison and contrast of the two frameworks is given in Bateman and Rondhuis (1997). Thus, on the one hand, the actual relations described by Martin may usefully extend the relations available for building interpretations beyond those currently present in SDRT: for example, the rather specific relations that might inform the example texts discussed here, such as particularizing and correcting as subtypes of reformulations (Martin, 1992, pp. 214, 217), are not at present available for SDRT. On the other hand, we can see the formal underpinnings of SDRT as providing a more solid foundation for the rather more sketchy notions of syntagmatic discourse structure provided to date for functional discourse semantics.

Discourse semantics and multimodality

The idea of using facets of Martin's discourse semantics for descriptions of semiotic artefacts utilizing resources other than verbal language has been around at least since van Leeuwen's (1991) application of conjunctive relations to the description of film and TV. It has therefore been logical to explore this approach further, drawing additionally on the formal underpinnings offered by SDRT. This was originally proposed for film in Bateman (2007) and developed considerably further in Wildfeuer (2014). In a similar vein, Tseng (2013) applies the functional discourse region of IDENTIFICATION to film as well. Since then we have been exploring a growing range of media in a similar fashion and the formal side of discourse semantics offers several properties that are useful for guiding this kind of research.

Because the basic mechanism of discourse semantics is taken to be the abductive construction of discourse structures, we know that discourse semantics is at work whenever: (a) particular material regularities can support *differing* interpretations and (b) those interpretations may at any point need to be subject to *revision*. Page layout offers a simple illustration. Two visually distinguished blocks of text placed next to one another on a page indicate on the basis of their form alone only that there is some kind of segmentation into textual units. The functional work that segmentation does for the artefact under analysis can only be abduced on the basis of making further assumptions, or hypotheses, concerning how to impose coherence on the page. For example, the two blocks may be contrasting two opinions, or they might be two successive stages in a developing argument, or they might have no relationship beyond being offered together for consumption. All of these possibilities are commonly found in the medium of newspapers. Thus, one might assume that the medium of newspapers makes use of a semiotic mode (page layout) whose discourse semantics at least provides relations of contrast/comparison, sequence and disjointness. Which of these applies to a particular case needs to be derived on the basis of formal cues in the blocks' realization in form and additional knowledge used to 'explain' the blocks' placement.

Further diverse kinds of discourse relations, and the corresponding discourse structures that support them in the sense of giving evidence in favour of hypothesizing their presence as coherence-building organizations of material, are widespread. Many traditional 'structures' in a variety of media are of this kind. For example, as discussed particularly in Bateman (2009), classical 'point-of-view' shots in film (cf. Branigan, 1986) are precisely such discourse constructions. On the basis of studies of these kinds, we now assume that a semiotic stratum of discourse semantics operates in *all* 'semiotic modes'; indeed, Bateman (2011) argues that the presence of a functioning discourse semantics should be taken as *definitional* for a semiotic mode since, otherwise, there is no formally defined basis for flexibly relating distinctions in technical features to coherence-raising interpretations. In other words, for a semiotic resource to be taken as a semiotic mode, it must of necessity exhibit a semiotic stratum of a discourse semantics, although the internal details, or contents, of that stratum may well differ across distinct semiotic modes as suggested in our contrastive studies of film, comics, newspapers, diagrams and so on. Some semiotic modes may have developed fairly rudimentary discourse semantics, while others may be extensive.

Consequences of the discourse semantics assumption

Given the line of discussion followed in the previous section, it is possible to return to several styles of analyses suggested in the multimodality literature in order to re-assess their theoretical positions and modelling decisions.

One of the clearest to consider is the notion of 'visual grammar' encouraged by Kress and van Leeuwen's (1996) *Reading Images*, although very similar points can be made with respect to O'Toole's (1994) application of a broadly Hallidayan account to artworks as well. In the case of Kress and van Leeuwen, several classification networks are proposed for characterizing the options available in visual materials, primarily static images and printed document pages. These networks are suggestive of a Hallidayan-style grammar, and often direct realizations in material form are given for the alternatives described just as would be required of a grammatical account. So-called 'narrative representations' are, for example, realized by the presence of 'vectors' in the image material; images not exhibiting vectors are seen as realizing 'conceptual representations'. There is no explicit further stratification.

From the perspective set out here, such a position appears unlikely. The interpretation of an explicit vector in an image, such as an arrow, materially expresses (i.e. commits via form) connection and directionality, but the extent to which this may be sensibly generalized to 'narrative', or even 'action', is limited. In the semiotic modes of the media family of diagrams, for example, arrows will often connect verbal labels to visual components or join components in ways that would most naturally be glossed in verbal language by *relational* processes, not material processes of action (cf. Bateman, 2008). A suggestion that diagrams are by virtue of their use of arrows largely narratival would consequently distort analyses rather than inform. Adding a stratum of discourse semantics that is, moreover, dependent on which particular semiotic mode is being deployed provides a stronger hold on the data by allowing a variety of possible interpretations of materially present vectors to be pursued, again always driven by the overarching goal of raising the coherence of such interpretations and guided by empirical research. Similar comments can be made concerning all of the networks proposed by Kress and van Leeuwen. Interpretation depends on many further factors, mostly characterizable in terms of discourse coherence.

One advantage, therefore, of the stratification offered by discourse semantics and the embedding of such a semantics first within semiotic modes, and then further within individual media, would be that this would allow categories such as Kress and van Leeuwen's conceptual/narrative, given-new/ideal-real, powerful/powerless, to be abduced in just those cases where the distinctions might be found (empirically) to operate without enforcing them as necessary interpretations for page composition in general and for all media. Moreover, making explicit the status of any realizations given as applying to discourse system networks would show them best interpreted as cues for potential abduction, that is, as 'default axioms' as introduced above, and not as hard and fast constraints – this is again quite different to realization statements within the grammatical stratum. Maintaining explicit stratification may also improve modelling by forcing re-assessments of proposals concerning how meaning is being made whenever those proposals would violate the logic of the stratification required. As examples of this we can take a further look at some of the treatments offered of some visually based media such as comics, graphic novels, picturebooks and the like. For all treatments, we must explicitly raise the question as to what kind of meaning is being made where. This is important since the formal and material semiotic strata available to the semiotic modes of media of this kind are often very different to those found for verbal language. The consequences of this are easy to underestimate and so to round off the discussion I will pick out just three related sets of consequences as follows.

Firstly, whereas verbal language has few inherent 'meanings' apart from those given to it by the relevant strata of the language system, iconic pictorial semiotic modes support a further path to meaning: one which is provided directly by the perceptual system of recipients. This is often confused with an ideational semantic representation. A semantic description can be constructed with respect to the material perceived but that perception is not the semantic description itself: the semantic (semiotic) description is an *interpretation* of the visually (iconically) presented material. Moreover, that semantics is no 'grammatical' interpretation, that is, it does not occupy a semiotic stratum analogous to lexicogrammar in language, it is instead a *discourse* semantic interpretation. Any attribution of elements, relations and configurations of kinds similar to Processes, Participants, or Circumstances within the visual materials are discourse interpretations, not 'grammar'-like category attributions: just being 'present' in a pictorial image (e.g. some obscure detail in the extreme background in the drawing of a setting in a comic) is not sufficient to posit discourse descriptions. Any such visual elements perceptually available may be *drawn into* a semantic description by the developing discourse (in order to increase coherence) but are not 'automatically' there. Stronger stratification then similarly explains observations such as those of Painter et al. (2013, p. 58) that the interpretations of images in picturebooks offered by adults and by children can be radically different – again this is an indication that we are centrally concerned with discourse semantics and with growth in competence with respect to the discourse semantic strategies that a semiotic mode deploys – such as showing multiple versions of a single character within single frames or panels to construct temporal relations – not with an increase in competence in 'seeing'. This is the generalization of the point made above concerning the classifications set out in Kress and van Leeuwen's *Reading Images*.

Secondly, enforcing a stricter semiotic stratification also has considerable impact on how pictorial materials orchestrated together in media can be related, insisting on a clearer identification of just which strata are involved at any point in the description. For example, Painter (2007), again discussing children's picturebooks, suggests that:

> As the visual semiotic is not inherently time-based in the same way as language is, the essential relation between any two juxtaposed images is not one of addition or sequence but of comparison and contrast. Two successive images invite comparison and any further semantic relations must be inferred by attending to sameness and difference. For this reason comparison/contrast relations are available whenever two images are juxtaposed. … Comparison/contrast relations are thus always present between images at the same time as any of the other relations to be discussed below. (Painter, 2007, p. 49)

The precise nature of this 'being available at the same time' is less clearly expressed than it could, and arguably should, be. The need to 'infer' any further relationships is compatible with the view that such relationships are, indeed, discourse connections of the kind discussed in this contribution, but these are not less 'essential' than descriptions at other semiotic strata.

The relations of comparison and contrast are consequently used here in a manner that still invites ambiguity: they can appear to refer both to *formal* distinctions, which are necessarily present in the material being interpreted, *and* to discourse interpretations that are used to achieve discourse coherence. These two statuses are fundamentally different and this may be the reason why the comparison/contrast options do not then appear in the system network Painter offers. But the quotation muddies these statuses by talking of comparison and contrast and 'further' semantic relations, rather than maintaining a discourse semantic stratum (that may include *semantic* relations of contrast and comparison standing in contrast to other semantic relations such as temporal succession or cause) and a formal stratum (that may include *formal* relations of similarity/difference, but which do *not* stand in contrast to 'other' semantic relations). This may be what was intended, but then also leaves it unclear why corresponding *semantic* relations of contrast and comparison rarely appear in the discourse options offered.

The observations made in the more extended picturebook analyses given in Painter et al. move closer to an explicit consideration of discourse semantics and there is frequent reference to the need to consider the alternatives offered in system networks as requiring inference to resolve whether or not they apply (e.g. Painter et al., 2013, p. 71). However, this remains a comment on how the networks are intended to be read rather than part of the formally specified model. Many system networks given in the discussion still make reference to explicit properties of form but, as suggested above for Kress and van Leeuwen's networks, these cannot be realizations in any sense traditional within systemic functional linguistics. For example, there are networks suggested for focalization, construed more as 'point of view', which specify realizations in terms of direction of gaze. This conflates a description of what is in the image (form) with a discourse semantic interpretation. In other cases, the realization statements do appear to be characterizing form more straightforwardly, as in, for example, classifications of type of frames used around images. Taken together, therefore, this is misleading because complex discourse interpretations may be being given simple form realizations, thus oversimplifying the story and, indeed, making weakened empirical predictions.

Third and finally for current purposes, enforcing stratification also allows a corrective to be made of a position entailed by some of these discussions concerning the relative statuses of the metafunctions. For visual resources, for example, it is sometimes argued that the ideational metafunction must, in some sense, be primary because all other relations must be 'inferred' from that information. This would entail a rather substantial reorganization of the systemic functional understanding of metafunctions as applying equally and in parallel to the materials they are (co-)classifying – indeed, the result would appear far more traditional in that we would have a 'semantics' that only 'afterwards' receives a 'pragmatic' interpretation. This would have the realizational relationship between discourse semantics (including ideational discourse semantics) and form being reconstrued as a precedence relationship between metafunctions.

This leads to several uneasy tensions, or contrasting modelling decisions, made in Painter et al.'s (2013) discussion. For example, they state both that 'all metafunctions are simultaneously in play' (Painter et al., 2013, p. 87) and that 'it is necessary to construe character identity from the ideational representation rather than from a system of deixis: it is through ideation rather than phoricity that we recognise the characters' (Painter et al., 2013, p. 60). This proposal downplays the difference between media constructions, such as films, picturebooks, comics, and natural perception. Whereas it is evident that we need to recognize (perceptually) what we are seeing, the explicit absence or withholding of information in a *medial* construction is generally best considered a discourse strategy, not a natural occurrence. If in such constructions something is made difficult to see, or to know, this is usually motivated on *textual* grounds.

Painter et al. (2013, pp. 64–5) suggest instead that such tracking of characters is ideational in nature, thus contrasting both with Martin's functional discourse region of IDENTIFICATION in verbal language and Tseng's (2013) generalizations of IDENTIFICATION for film and comics:

A visual narrative differs markedly from a verbal one in the lack of anything equivalent to the explicit system of 'REFERENCE' (Halliday & Hasan, 1976) or 'IDENTIFICATION' (Martin, 1992), whereby a presuming pronoun like *she* is used to avoid constantly reintroducing a character by name or description. In a purely visual story, a character is inferred to have the same identity when salient features of his/her appearance are represented in subsequent images. (Painter et al., 2013, p. 59)

Different kinds of visual reappearance or presentation are consequently taken by Painter et al. as parts of their 'ideational' description of images. Note, however, that precisely similar arguments could be made concerning the use of gaze or eye contact, which Painter et al. maintain as interpersonal, even though an interpreter can only reach such classifications via perception of what is seen.

In contrast to this view, competent viewers or readers are well aware of the conventions at play and can interpret offered gaps as discourse 'instructions' to pursue reference resolution – that is, absence of information or the presence of partial information may function phorically. Moreover, even the simple reappearance of some character, object or location in a visual medium is never simply the same thing being shown twice (or more): reappearance is generally *intended* reappearance in the sense that viewers or readers are expected to make the connection with what they have seen before in order to assign coherence. This is, again, a critical property for the functioning of the medium and, as Painter et al. point out, children engaging with picturebooks certainly have to learn that these connections are to be drawn. One can therefore contrast a bare visual analysis of content with what is being done with that content for the *purposes of text construction*. Moreover, part of that text construction is, as Painter et al. (2013, p. 63) also note, to do with changing the status of characters 'towards or away from participant-hood': this supports both the important separation between what is shown and an ideational construal of what is shown and the sharing of work across textual and ideational meaning construction.

It is nevertheless quite crucial that in many visual media the construal of a gap as functioning in this way is itself seen as a *discoursal* construction. In contrast to the explicit phoricity forms of verbal language (pronouns and the like), visual medial forms can indeed only give formal cues that a discourse interpretation of some visual as phoric could be a good candidate for pursuing the construction of discourse coherence. It does this, however, not on the basis of an ideational reading but on the basis of material form that is available, potentially, for parallel ideational, interpersonal and textual interpretations. It can thus readily be the case that recognition of some unidentified element in an image (such as a 'hand' or 'arm' without the rest of the figure) proceeds precisely because of the discourse expectation that particular discourse cohesive chains are being developed, not because of what is shown alone. Freeing up the 'stratal space' between perceptible content and discourse semantics might then allow such character tracking alternatives to migrate back to their former, and arguably more appropriate, position within the textual metafunction.

Conclusions and outlook

In this contribution I have explained why discourse semantics in the sense discussed by Martin (1992) has now become an essential and integral component of our approach to multimodality and is necessarily present in all our analyses of semiotic modes. This view of discourse semantics has also now been complemented by the dynamic discourse structures developed within formal discourse semantic models, resulting in a formal dynamic model of logogenesis. Nevertheless, all of our work reported here concerning multimodality builds on Martin's notion of discourse semantics and would not have been possible without this foundation in place. The importance of *continuing* to consider multimodal phenomena from the perspective of strict stratification of form and discourse semantics must also be emphasized, however. Taken together, the discussion has argued not only that discourse semantics needs always to be present but also that there is now much to do in re-evaluating extant accounts from the perspective of their conformance to this stratificational principle. Making the framework as precise and robust as possible in this regard becomes increasingly urgent as the complexity of the media addressed in analyses grows. Explicit stratification of the kind illustrated above also then makes important contributions to *methodology* by supporting clearer criteria for drawing distinctions (cf. Bateman et al., 2017).

Developing the consequences of this model further remains important for treatments of verbal language as well. The view from multimodality sees discourse semantics as a means of orchestrating embodied experience (cf. Bateman, 2019). It is just as likely that this will be relevant for the treatment of important properties of texts, including issues of aesthetics, intelligibility, persuasion and affect in general. However, any such considerations also demand that the formal underpinnings of treatments of the dynamics of text be strengthened in order to bear this load and to help form more predictive accounts in the future.

References

Asher, N., & Lascarides, A. (2003). *Logics of Conversation*. Cambridge: Cambridge University Press.

Bateman, J. A. (1998). Review article. James R. Martin's *English Text: System and Structure. Functions of Language*, 5(2), 213–47.

Bateman, J. A. (2007). Towards a *grande paradigmatique* of film: Christian Metz reloaded. *Semiotica*, 167(1/4), 13–64.

Bateman, J. A. (2008). *Multimodality and Genre: A Foundation for the Systematic Analysis of Multimodal Documents*. Basingstoke: Palgrave Macmillan.

Bateman, J. A. (2009). Film and representation: Making filmic meaning. In W. Wildgen & B. van Heusden (Eds.), *Metarepresentation, Self-Organization and Art* (pp. 137–62). European Semiotics. Bern: Lang.

Bateman, J. A. (2011). The decomposability of semiotic modes. In K. L. O'Halloran & B. A. Smith (Eds.), *Multimodal Studies: Multiple Approaches and Domains* (pp. 17–38). Routledge Studies in Multimodality. London: Routledge.

Bateman, J. A. (2016). Methodological and theoretical issues for the empirical investigation of multimodality. In N. M. Klug & H. Stöckl (Eds.), *Handbuch Sprache im multimodalen Kontext* (pp. 36–74), number 7 in Handbooks of Linguistics and Communication Science (HSK). Berlin: de Gruyter Mouton.

Bateman, J. A. (2019). Multimodality and materiality: The interplay of textuality and texturality in the aesthetics of film. *Poetics Today*, 40(2), 235–68.

Bateman, J. A., & Rondhuis, K. J. (1997). 'Coherence relations': Towards a general specification. *Discourse Processes*, 24, 3–49.

Bateman, J. A., Wildfeuer, J., & Hiippala, T. (2017). *Multimodality – Foundations, Research and Analysis. A Problem-Oriented Introduction*. Berlin: Mouton de Gruyter.

Bowcher, W. L. (2019). Context and register. In G. Thompson, W. L. Bowcher, L. Fontaine, & D. Schöntal (Eds.), *The Cambridge Handbook of Systemic Functional Linguistics* (pp. 142–70). Cambridge Handbooks in Language and Linguistics. Cambridge: Cambridge University Press.

Branigan, E. (1986). Point of view in the fiction film. *Wide Angle*, 8(3), 4–7.

Fawcett, R. P. (1989). Towards a systemic flowchart model for discourse analysis. In R. P. Fawcett & D. Young (Eds.), *New Developments in Systemic Linguistics: Theory and Application* (pp. 116–43). London: Pinter.
Goodman, N. (1969). *Languages of Art. An Approach to a Theory of Symbols*. London: Oxford University Press.
Halliday, M. A. K., & Hasan, R. (1976). *Cohesion in English*. London: Longman.
Halliday, M. A. K., & Matthiessen, C. M. I. M. (1999). *Construing Experience through Meaning: A Language-Based Approach to Cognition*. London: Cassell.
Halliday, M. A. K., & Matthiessen, C. M. I. M. (2004). *An Introduction to Functional Grammar* (3rd ed.). London: Edward Arnold.
Hasan, R. (1985). Meaning, context and text: Fifty years after Malinowski. In J. D. Benson & W. S. Greaves (Eds.), *Systemic Perspectives on Discourse*, 16–49. Norwood, NJ: Ablex.
Heim, I. (1983). File change semantics and the familiarity theory of definiteness. In C. Schwarzeand, A. von Stechow (Eds.), *Meaning, Use and Interpretation of Language* (pp. 164–78). Berlin: De Gruyter.
Iser, W. (1978). *The Act of Reading: A Theory of Aesthetic Response*. Baltimore: Johns Hopkins University Press.
Kamp, H. (1981). A theory of truth and semantic representation. In J. A. Groenendijk, T. Janssen, & M. B. Stokhof (Eds.), *Formal Methods in the Study of Language. Part 1* (pp. 277–322), number 136 in Mathematical Centre Tracts. Amsterdam: Mathematisch Centrum Amsterdam.
Kress, G. (2010). *Multimodality: A Social Semiotic Approach to Contemporary Communication*. London: Routledge.
Kress, G., & van Leeuwen, T. (2006 [1996]). *Reading Images: The Grammar of Visual Design*. London and New York: Routledge.
Lascarides, A., & Asher, N. (1993). Temporal interpretation, discourse relations, and common sense entailment. *Linguistics and Philosophy*, 16(5), 437–95.
Lemke, J. L. (1985). Ideology, intertextuality, and the notion of register. In J. D. Benson & W. S. Greaves (Eds.), *Systemic Perspectives on Discourse, Volume 1; Selected Theoretical Papers from the Ninth International Systemic Workshop* (pp. 275–94). Norwood, NJ: Ablex.
Mann, W. C., & Thompson, S. A. (1988). Rhetorical structure theory: Toward a functional theory of text organization. *Text*, 8(3), 243–81.
Martin, J. R. (1985). Process and text: Two aspects of human semiosis. In J. D. Benson & W. S. Greave (Eds.), *Systemic Perspectives on Discourse, Volume 1; Selected Theoretical Papers from the Ninth International Systemic Workshop* (pp. 248–74) number 15 in Advances in Discourse processes. Norwood, NJ: Ablex.
Martin, J. R. (1992). *English Text: Systems and Structure*. Amsterdam: Benjamins.
Martin, J. R. (2006). Genre, ideology and intertextuality: A systemic functional perspective. *Linguistics and the Human Sciences*, 2(2), 275–98.
Martin, J. R. (2014). Evolving systemic functional linguistics: Beyond the clause. *Functional Linguistics*, 1(1), 3.
Martin, J. R. (2019). Discourse semantics. In G. Thompson, W. L. Bowcher, L. Fontaine, & D. Schöntal (Eds.), *The Cambridge Handbook of Systemic Functional Linguistics* (pp. 358–81). Cambridge Handbooks in Language and Linguistics. Cambridge: Cambridge University Press.
Martin, J. R., & Rose, D. (2003). *Working with Discourse: Meaning Beyond the Clause*. London and New York: Continuum.

Montague, R. (1973). The proper treatment of quantification in ordinary English. In K. J. J. Hintikka, J. M. E. Moravcsik, & P. Suppes (Eds.), *Approaches to Natural Language: Proceedings of the 1970 Stanford Workshop on Grammar and Semantics* (pp. 221–42). Dordrecht: Springer Netherlands.
O'Donnell, M. J. (1999). Context in dynamic modelling. In M. Ghadessy (Ed.), *Text and Context in Functional Linguistic* (pp. 63–99). (CILT Series IV). Amsterdam: Benjamins.
O'Toole, M. (2011 [1994]). *The Language of Displayed Art*. Abingdon, Oxon: Routledge.
Painter, C. (2007). Children's picture book narratives: Reading sequences of images. In A. McCabe, M. O'Donnell, & R. Whittaker (Eds.), *Advances in Language and Education* (pp. 40–59). London and New York: Continuum.
Painter, C., Martin, J. R., & Unsworth, L. (2013). *Reading Visual Narratives: Image Analysis of Children's Picture Books*. London: Equinox.
Peirce, C. S. (1931–58). *Collected Papers of Charles Sanders Peirce*, Cambridge, MA: Harvard University Press. Vols. 1–6, 1931–35, edited by C. Hartshorne and P. Weiss; Vols. 7–8, 1958, edited by Arthur W. Burks.
Tseng, C. (2013). *Cohesion in Film: Tracking Film Elements*. Basingstoke: Palgrave Macmillan.
van Leeuwen, T. (1991). Conjunctive structure in documentary film and television. *Continuum: Journal of Media and Cultural Studies*, 5(1), 76–114.
Ventola, E. (1987). *The Structure of Social Interaction: A Systemic Approach to the Semiotics of Service Encounters*. London: Frances Pinter.
Wildfeuer, J. (2014). *Film Discourse Interpretation. Towards a New Paradigm for Multimodal Film Analysis*. Routledge Studies in Multimodality. London and New York: Routledge.

4

Construing entities through nominal groups in Chinese

Pin Wang
Shanghai Jiao Tong University

Introduction

This chapter pays tribute to important aspects of J. R. Martin's research interests – grammatical description and functional language typology – and is accomplished under the direct, profound influence of his academic achievements in these areas. Following seminal papers on the grammar of Tagalog before the turn of the century (Martin, 1981, 1988, 1990, 1995, 1996), Martin served a substantial role in fostering the growth of functional language typology as a co-editor of *Language Typology: A Functional Perspective* (Caffarel, Martin, & Matthiessen, 2004) and also as contributor of a systemic functional profile of Tagalog (Martin, 2004). His more prominent position in further promoting language descriptions based on systemic functional linguistics (hereafter SFL) theory emerged after a series of fora and colloquia focusing on SFL language description, which started at Shanghai Jiao Tong University (December 2015), and continued at the Indonesia University of Education (July 2016), the University of Wollongong (July 2017), the Pontificia Universidad Católica de Chile (November 2017), Boston College (July 2018), the University of Sydney (November 2018) and the Pontificia Universidad Católica de Chile again (July 2019).

To be more specific, this chapter aims at modelling the reasoning through which grammatical descriptions of languages are formulated. This reasoning is illustrated for the description of systems and structures in relation to nominal groups in Chinese. The present study is inspired by the SFL-informed grammatical descriptions that Martin and his colleagues have developed in their recent works (e.g. Martin, 2018; Martin et al., 2020; Martin et al., forthcoming a; Martin et al., forthcoming b), where Martin and his colleagues demonstrate important methodologies whereby SFL language description is advanced. The most significant, innovative aspects include:

1. Text-based data collection: Drawing on SFL contextual theory concerning genre and register, language description is based on spontaneous production of natural language, with text as the fundamental unit of meaning and analysis.

2. Approaching grammar 'from above' (Halliday, 1996, p. 16): In SFL, grammatical resources are seen as being responsible for fulfilling discourse semantic tasks, so that grammatical description is approached from discourse semantic systems as point of departure – IDEATION and IDENTIFICATION for this particular study.
3. Axial argumentation: In SFL, grammar is modelled as a system of paradigmatic oppositions, each with syntagmatic implications, that is, system is realized in structure. On the other hand, system is motivated by structure. SFL-informed language description explores the complementarity between system and structure, delving into both systems and their realizations in function structures and class syntagms.

This study approaches the grammatical description of Chinese nominal groups from an ideational perspective first and a textual perspective second. It gives priority to the 'from above' approach, taking as its point of departure the discourse semantic systems of IDEATION and IDENTIFICATION (Martin, 1992; Martin & Rose, 2007). The text on which our grammatical analysis is focused is a story about bringing under control the sea lettuce, a kind of green algae, that once grew fast and wild along the coast in East China's Qingdao city and threatened the sailing competitions of the Beijing Olympics in 2008. The text is published on the website of the Chinese Academy of Sciences.[1]

Nominal groups: A look from above

According to the SFL model of stratification and realization, grammatical systems realize other meaning-making systems at higher levels, that is, discourse semantics, register and genre. Lexicogrammar is designed in the model as being responsible for realizing discourse semantics, which in turn realizes choices in context (register and genre). In the stratified model for context developed by Martin and his colleagues (Martin, 1992; Martin & Rose, 2008), genre is a higher-level contextual abstraction above register, which is composed of the three variables of field, tenor and mode. This model is summarized in Figure 4.1.

The text focused on in this chapter belongs to a story genre in a web-based news article written in a monologic, formal register (mode), enacting a distant, unequal relationship between the writer and readers (tenor), and construing natural phenomena and human experience in a disaster-combatting event (field). Particularly pertinent to this study is the register variable of field, which gives us a sufficient number and variety of nominal groups for analysis.

Field is the ideational contextual variable that construes phenomena as activities oriented to a certain global institutional purpose, or as items involved in activities, along with associated properties (Martin, 1992; Doran & Martin, 2020). The construal of phenomena as activities represents a dynamic perspective of field, whereas the construal of phenomena as items represents a static perspective. Figure 4.2 is an outline of field based on Doran and Martin (2020). Nominal groups construe a static perspective, providing resources for the classification and composition of items and their associated properties.

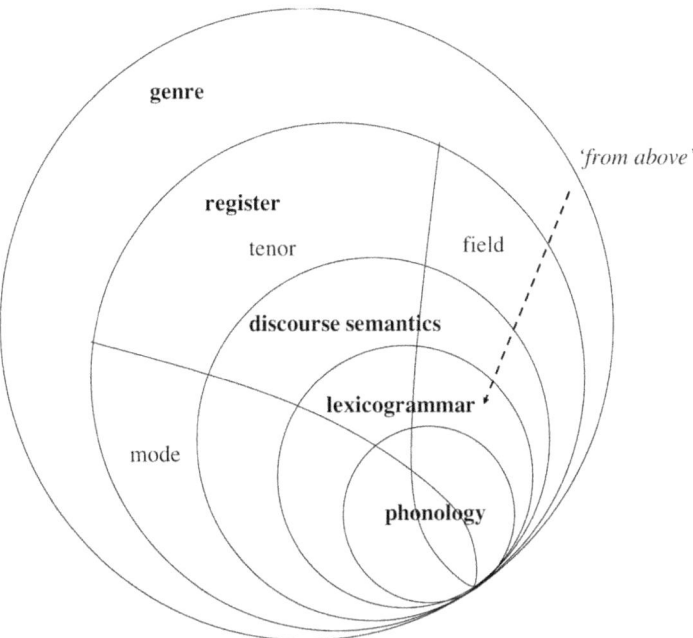

Figure 4.1 SFL model of stratification (with stratified context), based on Martin (2014, pp. 35–7).

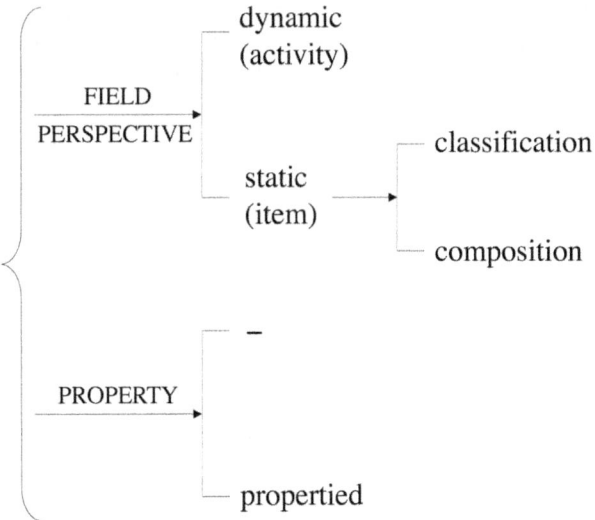

Figure 4.2 Systemic representation of field, based on Doran and Martin (2020).

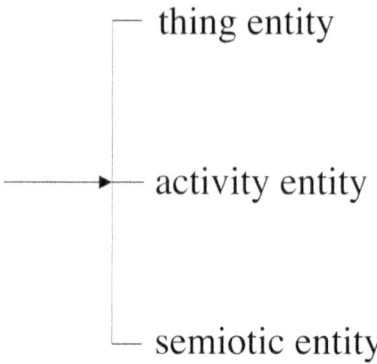

Figure 4.3 Types of entity.

Items in field are realized through entities at the stratum of discourse semantics in terms of the discourse semantic system of IDEATION. Most commonly, these entities are 'thing entities', such as objects, places, institutions and people. However, there are other kinds of entities – 'activity entities', realizing activities in field – and 'semiotic entities', realizing discourse. Figure 4.3 is an entity system based on Hao (2015, 2020). At the stratum of lexicogrammar, the various types of entities are realized through nominal groups. In this chapter, however, we focus mainly on nominal groups that construe 'thing entities', setting aside those realizing activity entities and semiotic entities.

Nominal groups have developed very complex grammatical systems and structures in fulfilling their ideational discourse semantic roles, including classifying, describing and quantifying entities. Their complexity is also attributable to the textual contextual variable of mode. In our news report text featuring a monologic mode, nominal groups play an important role in determining and qualifying entities. In terms of the textual discourse semantic system of IDENTIFICATION, many entities are introduced and tracked throughout the text. The next two sections explore the ideational and textual resources respectively in Chinese nominal groups, drawing on the theoretical foundations reviewed above.

Ideational resources in Chinese nominal groups

In their grammatical structure, all Chinese nominal groups include a nuclear function known as Thing. In this section we focus on Things realized by common nouns, leaving those realized by proper nouns and pronouns for the next section.

In terms of field, from a static perspective, our focus text construes both classification and composition. In the beginning stage of the text, the main taxonomies are concerned with geographical conditions and the offshore sea lettuce. The Things realized by common nouns having to do with these taxonomies are bolded below.

*2008 nian 6 yue, shi juli di 29 jie Beijing Aoyunhui kaimu jinjin liang ge **yue** de **rizi**, ruguo ni zoujin Zhongguo Kexueyuan Haiyang Yanjiusuo, ni jiang bei yanqian kongdi shang liangshai de yi pian lüyouyou de **haizao** suo xiyin, zhexie haizao jiu shi bei chengwei 'turuqilai de haiyang ziran **zaihai**' de **zhujue** – hutai.*

(June 2008 was the **time** only two **months** away from the 29th Beijing Olympic Games. If you walked into the Institute of Oceanology, Chinese Academy of Sciences, you would be attracted to a mass of green **seaweed** being dried on the ground. This seaweed was known as the **protagonist** of the 'unexpected ocean natural **disaster**' – sea lettuce.)

*2008 nian 5 yue 31 ri, da mianji hutai jinru Qingdao jin'an **haiyu**, shi binhai ming cheng Qingdao de lan **hai** chengxian lüse. suizhe **shijian** de tuiyi, yue lai yue duo de hutai sui **chaoshui** yong shang **an**, tamen daoda le Qingdao zhuming de **zhanqiao**, diyi haishui **yuchang** he Qianhai fengjing youlan **qu** yidai de **shatan**, mei ji **tian** bian duiqi le houhou yi ceng, bing xunsu kuosan, zai **taiyang** shai hou geng shi chouqixuntian, chengwei wuran **dai**.*

(On 31 May 2008, expansive sea lettuce invaded Qingdao's offshore **area**, causing the famous coastal city Qingdao's blue **sea** to turn green. As **time** went by, more and more sea lettuce rushed onto the **shore** with the **tidewater**; it reached Qingdao's famous **pier**, the First Seawater **Resort**, and the **beach** near the Qianhai scenic **spot**. Within just a few **days** a thick heap formed and spread fast. Rotting away in the **sun**, it stunk to high heaven and turned into a **belt** of pollution.)

The nominal groups with Thing only, such as *haizao* (seaweed), *hai* (sea) and *shatan* (beach), can be analysed as follows for group class and function, and word class. Each example is provided with word-for-word glossing and a full translation.[2]

(1)	Example	*haizao*
	group class	nominal group
	group function	Thing
	word class	common noun
	gloss	seaweed
	translation	'seaweed'

However, the Thing function alone does not always suffice to delineate the entity that is being construed in the text, such as *haishui yuchang* (seawater resort) above, and *jin hai* (coastal waters) and *dalao jishu* (retrieving technology) elsewhere in the text. In these examples the entities are classified; grammatically, the Thing is subclassified through a Classifier function, which is realized by another common noun, an adjective and a verb, respectively. Detailed analyses are provided in the tabled examples (2)–(4) below.

(2)	Example	*haishui*	*yuchang*
	group class	nominal group	
	group function	Classifier	Thing
	word class	common noun	common noun
	gloss	*seawater*	*resort*
	translation	'seawater resort'	

(3)	Example	*jin*	*hai*
	group class	nominal group	
	group function	Classifier	Thing
	word class	adjective	common noun
	gloss	*near*	*sea*
	translation	'coastal waters'	

(4)	Example	*dalao*	*jishu*
	group class	nominal group	
	group function	Classifier	Thing
	word class	verb	common noun
	gloss	*retrieve*	*technology*
	translation	'retrieving technology'	

The distinction in word class for Classifiers reflects the fact that nouns, adjectives and verbs have different meaning-making potentials. The noun *haishui* (seawater) in *haishui yuchang* (seawater resort) has the potential to realize a Thing, which in turn construes an entity and is subclassified by a Classifier, for example, *bingleng de haishui* (ice-cold seawater). The adjective *jin* (near) in *jin hai* (coastal waters) has the potential to describe another entity, for example, *jin lu* (near road, shortcut), and being graded, for example, *geng jin* (nearer) and *tebie jin* (very near). The adjective *jin*, however, realizes a Classifier here because it demarcates the sea according to the distance from shore, and this construes a taxonomic relationship rather than a property of the sea – we do not use **geng jin de hai* (nearer sea) to grade the sea's nearness to establish contrast with *jin hai* (near sea). The verb *dalao* (retrieve from underwater) has the potential to construe an activity and realizes a Process in a clause, as in *yinni zhengfu jiang dalao heixiazi*[3] (The Indonesian government will retrieve the black box).

To construe the classification of an entity more accurately, a classified entity can take another Classifier, resulting in multiple Classifiers preceding the Thing, as in *haiyang ziran zaihai* and *diyi haishui yuchang* analysed below.

(5)	Example	*haiyang*	*ziran*	*zaihai*
	group class	nominal group		
	group function	Classifier	Classifier	Thing
	word class	common noun	common noun	common noun
	gloss	*ocean*	*nature*	*disaster*
	translation	'ocean natural disaster'		

(6)	Example	*diyi*	*haishui*	*yuchang*
	group class	nominal group		
	group function	Classifier	Classifier	Thing
	word class	numeral	common noun	common noun
	gloss	*first*	*seawater*	*resort*
	translation	'the First Seawater Resort'		

Note that the *diyi* (first) in *diyi haishui yuchang* (the First Seawater Resort) is a numeral in class, but a Classifier rather than a Measurer[4] in function, since it does not quantify the entity; rather, it specifies which seawater resort is in question and distinguishes it from all the other resorts.

The third ideational nominal group function we will consider is Epithet. From the perspective of discourse semantic ideation, this function attributes a quality to an entity; higher above, from the perspective of field, this function assigns a property to an item. There are some examples in the paragraphs quoted above, reproduced below with Epithets highlighted in boldface.

2008 nian 6 yue, shi juli di 29 jie Beijing Aoyunhui kaimu jinjin liang ge yue de rizi, ruguo ni zoujin Zhongguo Kexueyuan Haiyang Yanjiusuo, ni jiang bei yanqian kongdi shang liangshai de yi pian **lüyouyou** *de haizao suo xiyin, zhexie haizao jiu shi bei chengwei '***turuqilai*** de haiyang ziran zaihai' de zhujue – hutai.*

(June 2008 was the time only two months away from the 29th Beijing Olympic Games. If you walked into the Institute of Oceanology, Chinese Academy of Sciences, you would be attracted to a mass of **green** seaweed being dried on the ground. This seaweed was known as the protagonist of the '**unexpected** ocean natural disaster' – sea lettuce.)

2008 nian 5 yue 31 ri, **da mianji** *hutai jinru Qingdao jin'an haiyu, shi binhai* **ming** *cheng Qingdao de* **lan** *hai chengxian lüse. suizhe shijian de tuiyi, yue lai yue duo de hutai sui chaoshui yong shang an, tamen daoda le Qingdao* **zhuming** *de zhanqiao, diyi haishui yuchang he Qianhai fengjing youlan qu yidai de shatan, mei ji tian bian duiqi le* **houhou** *yi ceng, bing xunsu kuosan, zai taiyang shai hou geng shi chouqixuntian, chengwei wuran dai.*

(On 31 May 2008, **expansive** sea lettuce invaded Qingdao's offshore area, causing the **famous** coastal city Qingdao's **blue** sea to turn green. As time went, more and more sea lettuce rushed onto the shore with the tidewater, reaching Qingdao's **famous** pier, the First Seawater Resort, and the beach near the Qianhai scenic spot. Within just a few days a **thick** heap formed and spread fast. Rotting away in the sun, it stunk to high heaven and turned into a belt of pollution.)

An Epithet is used to answer the question 'What like?' and is typically realized through an adjective. Two nominal groups with Epithets from above are analysed below as examples (7) and (8).

(7)	Example	*zhuming*	*de*	*zhanqiao*
	group class	nominal group		
	group function	Epithet		Thing
	word class	adjective	link	common noun
	gloss	*famous*		*pier*
	translation	'famous pier'		

(8)	Example	*turuqilai*	*de*	*haiyang*	*ziran*	*zaihai*
	group class	nominal group				
	group function	Epithet		Classifier	Classifier	Thing
	word class	adjective	link	common noun	common noun	common noun
	gloss	*unexpected*		*ocean*	*nature*	*disaster*
	translation	'unexpected ocean natural disaster'				

The Epithet *turuqilai* derives originally from a clause, but has been lexicalized as an adjective in Modern Chinese and can be graded with adverbs, as in *youdian turuqilai* (a little unexpected) or *tebie turuqilai* (very unexpected).

At this stage we note that there is no one-to-one relationship between function and class; a function can be realized by more than one class (e.g. Classifier realized by noun, adjective, verb or numeral), and a class can realize more than one function (e.g. adjective realizing Classifier or Epithet).

It can be seen from example (8) above that if a nominal group contains both an Epithet and Classifier, both are positioned before the Thing, with the Epithet preceding the Classifier. Other examples from the text are *zhongyao de kexue yiju* (important scientific basis), *shiyong, gaoxiao de dalao jishu* (practical, efficient retrieving technology). The last example contains two Epithets (e.g. *shiyong* (practical) and *gaoxiao* (efficient)), adding qualities at the group rank. If an additive conjunction is inserted between the two adjectives, such as *shiyong bing gaoxiao* or *shiyong qie gaoxiao* (practical and efficient), we analyse it as a paratactic adjective complex realizing a single Epithet, adding qualities at the word rank. This can be seen in examples (9) and (10):

(9)	Example	*shiyong*	*gaoxiao*	*de*	*dalao*	*jishu*
	group class	nominal group				
	group function	Epithet	Epithet		Classifier	Thing
	word class	adjective	adjective	link	verb	common noun
	gloss	*practical*	*efficient*		*retrieve*	*technology*
	translation	'practical, efficient retrieving technology'				

(10)	Example	*shiyong*	*qie*	*gaoxiao*	*de*	*dalao*	*jishu*
	group class	nominal group					
	group function	Epithet				Classifier	Thing
		adjective complex					
		1	+2				
	word class	adjective	conjunction	adjective	link	verb	common noun
	gloss	*practical*	*and*	*efficient*		*retrieve*	*technology*
	translation	'practical and efficient retrieving technology'					

Apart from adjective complexes, an Epithet can also be realized by other types of word complexes describing the Thing. In our text, *da mianji hutai* (expansive sea lettuce) is an example of this kind. Analysis of both function and class is presented in example (11). In this nominal group, *da mianji*, literally 'large area', as an Epithet, describes the quality of the sea lettuce; the Epithet itself is composed of an adjective *da* (large) and a noun *mianji* (area). In discourse semantics, the noun realizes dimension, which is deployed to specify to what facet of the entity the preceding adjective is used to assign the quality, typically size, colour, weight, etc.

(11)	Example	*da*	*mianji*	*hutai*
	group class	nominal group		
	group function	Epithet		Thing
		word complex		
		α	β	
	word class	adjective	noun	common noun
	gloss	*large*	*area*	*sea lettuce*
	translation	'expansive sea lettuce'		

It is obvious from the above examples containing an Epithet that there is sometimes a lexical item *de* after the Epithet. This lexical item is obligatory in some structures, and can be dispensed with in others, as can be seen in the following examples:

zhuming de zhanqiao (famous pier)
zhuming zhanqiao

da mianji de hutai (expansive sea lettuce)
da mianji hutai

lüyouyou de haizao (green seaweed)
*lüyouyou haizao

turuqilai de haiyang ziran zaihai (unexpected ocean natural disaster)
*turuqilai haiyang ziran zaihai

Here we do not pursue further the conditions of the use of *de*; however, considering the fact that *de* is optionally used in certain nominal groups, we do not analyse *de* as a component within the Epithet structure; in terms of class, we do not treat *de* as part of an adjective or a word complex. This lexical item does not realize any function at the group rank, but only serves as a linking element between Epithet and Thing at the word rank, hence only its word-class label 'link'.

As a final step of accounting for the ideational nominal group resources in Chinese, the patterns of quantifying an entity in a nominal group are discussed. This quantification is realized in nominal groups through the function of what we will call Measurer. We do not use the functional label Numerative as in the description of quantification in English nominal groups (Halliday & Matthiessen, 2014) because the two functions give rise to different structures. Nominal groups containing the function Measurer are highlighted in bold in the following excerpts of text:

laizi Zhongguo Haiyang Daxue ... **6 ge keyan danwei** *de* **25 ming keyan renyuan** *canjia le ci ci hangxing. ben ci hangxing lishi* **16 tian**, *gong wancheng le Huangdonghai dianxing haiyu de* **8 ge duanmian, 67 ge zhanwei** *de guance diaocha, qude le* **yi da pi jichu shuju he ziliao**, *wei hutai zaihai de zhili tigong le zhongyao de kexue yiju.*

(**25 researchers** from **6 research institutes** including Ocean University of China ... participated in this exploration on the sea. This voyage took **16 days**, accomplishing observation on **8 sections, 67 stations** in key areas on the Yellow Sea and East China Sea and obtaining **a big batch of basic statistics and data**, which provides important scientific basis for the control of sea lettuce disaster.)

In terms of structure, the Measurer in a Chinese nominal group is not only realized by a numeral, but it also needs to take a word whose class is known as measure, in order to quantify an entity, for example, *6 ge keyan danwei* (6 research institutes), *25 ming keyan renyuan* (25 researchers) in the above excerpt. The most commonly used measure is *ge* in Chinese; other measures specify the shape or nature

(12)	Example	8		ge	duanmian
	group class	nominal group			
	group function	Measurer			Thing
		word complex			
		α		β	
	word class	numeral		measure	common noun
	gloss	8			section
	translation	'8 sections'			

of the quantified entity, for example, *zhang* is used as a measure for thin objects, *liang* is used for land vehicles.

Function and class analysis of the nominal group *8 ge duanmian* (8 sections) is presented above in example (12). Here we analyse the function Measurer as realized by a word complex, with a numeral, and a measure depending on that numeral, forming a hypotactic relationship.

Note that in the above excerpt of text there is a nominal group *16 tian* (16 days), appearing as if there is not any measure between the numeral *16* and noun *tian* (day). According to Zhu (1982, p. 50), this nominal group should be regarded as a Thing-less one, where *tian* (day) is treated as measure rather than noun, since the nominal group can be expanded to its full form *16 tian shijian* (16 days' time).

It has been argued in example (6) *diyi haishui yuchang* (the First Seawater Resort) that a numeral can, on some occasions, realize the function of Classifier. This is attested to by the criterion, mentioned directly above, that a measure word needs to be used immediately after the numeral in the realization of a Measurer function. The numeral *diyi* (first) does not realize Measurer since there is no measure following it.

The fact that this numeral *diyi* (first) does not realize a Measurer is also reflected in the tone value in relation to the number one in Chinese. The numeral *yi* (one) takes the level tone *yī* when it realizes a Classifier, for example, *yī céng* (the first floor), *yī duàn* (level one, the first level), no matter what tone the following syllable takes; whereas it displays the tone sandhi when realizing a Measurer, for example, *yì céng lóu* (one storey), *yí duàn huà* (one passage of text, one paragraph), where *yi* takes the falling tone before a syllable in the rising tone and takes the rising tone before a syllable in the falling tone.[5]

The Measurer function can also be realized by a word complex involving an inexact number, for example, *30 duo ge guojia* (more than 30 countries) in our text. *30 duo* (more than 30) and the measure *ge* form a hypotactic relationship (α and β, respectively); within the α, another layer of hypotaxis is added, with the quantifier *duo* (more), dependent upon the numeral *30*, labelled αβ and αα, respectively.

One Chinese nominal group only allows for one Measurer, which tends to precede the Epithet in structure, for example, **yi pian** *lüyouyou de haizao* (a mass of green seaweed) and **yi chang** *turuqilai de haiyang ziran zaihai* (an unexpected ocean natural disaster),[6] the latter example is analysed below.

(13)

	Example	30		duo	ge		guojia
	group class	nominal group					
	group function	Measurer					Thing
		word complex					
		αα		αβ	β		
	word class	numeral		quantifier	measure		common noun
	gloss	30		more			country
	translation	'more than 30 countries'					

(14)

	Example	yi	chang	turuqilai	de	haiyang	ziran	zaihai
	group class	nominal group						
	group function	Measurer		Epithet		Classifier	Classifier	Thing
		word complex						
		α	β					
	word class	numeral	measure	adjective	link	noun	noun	noun
	gloss	one		unexpected		ocean	nature	disaster
	translation	'an unexpected ocean natural disaster'						

(15)

	Example	yi	da	pi	jichu	shuju	he	ziliao
	group class	nominal group						
	group function	Measurer			Classifier	Thing		
		word complex				noun complex		
		α	ββ	βα		1		+2
	word class	numeral	adjective	measure	noun	noun	conj.	noun
	gloss	one	big	batch	basis	statistics	and	data
	translation	'a big batch of basic statistics and data'						

Before we finish this section, let's consider another kind of complex structure involving the Measurer. The measure in the function Measurer may sometimes be preceded by an adjective, for example, *yi **da** pi jichu shuju he ziliao* (a **big** batch of basic statistics and data) (analysed fully above as example (15)); this demonstrates a similarity between a measure and a noun in that they both can be described by an adjective. Other examples of the numeral–adjective–measure syntagm include *yi chang chuan* (one long string), *liang xiao kuai* (two small chunks), *san man wan* (three full bowls). However, the occurrence of an adjective before a measure is highly restricted: only a small number of monosyllabic adjectives can be thus used, and such an adjective cannot be graded, for example, *yi **geng** chang chuan (one longer string) and *liang **hen** xiao kuai (two very small chunks).

Again, the Measurer is analysed as realized by a double-layered word complex. In the first layer, yi (one) and da pi (big batch) enter into a hypotactic relationship (α and β, respectively), and within β, there is another layer of hypotaxis, with the adjective da (big) depending on the measure pi (batch) (thus ββ and βα, respectively).

If we compare this example with da mianji hutai (expansive sea lettuce) in example (11) above, where da mianji (large area) is also a word complex, we see that the difference lies in the direction of dependency. In da pi (big batch), da (big) is dependent on pi (batch) and thus can be omitted, rendering yi pi jichu shuju he ziliao (a batch of basic statistics and data); in contrast, the adjective da (large) in da mianji (large area) is the host on which mianji (area) is dependent and thus cannot be omitted, for example, *mianji hutai. In terms of word class, da pi (big batch) represents the adjective–measure syntagm, whereas da mianji (large area) represents the adjective–noun syntagm.

Example (15) also illustrates the realization of Thing as a noun complex (i.e. shuju he ziliao (statistics and data)), realizing two entities in the discourse semantics stratum. Also, note that the link de in Chinese is not used after a Measurer or Classifier, but can only occur after an Epithet in the discussion thus far.

Textual resources in Chinese nominal groups

The text used for analysing Chinese nominal groups is an instance of a narrative genre (Martin & Rose, 2008), reconstruing a disastrous event that is evaluated and resolved. As far as the entities involved are concerned, the text has to 'self-contextualize' (Martin et al., forthcoming b); that is, the text has to allow for the entities to be identifiable through introducing them and keeping track of them. The key discourse semantic system responsible for introducing and keeping track of any entity in a text is IDENTIFICATION; at the lowest level of delicacy, there are two choices: presenting an entity whose identity is unknown and presuming an entity if its identity is recoverable (Figure 4.4).

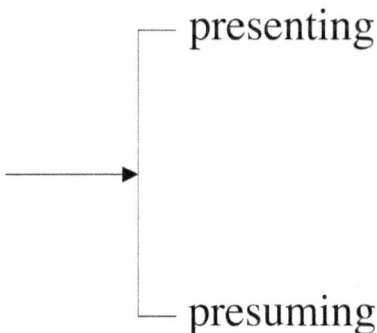

Figure 4.4 Basic IDENTIFICATION system.

A nominal group comprising Thing function only, which is realized by a proper noun or a pronoun, presumes that the identity of an entity can be recovered by the reader. This kind of nominal group has the minimal simplest structure. There are a good number of these Thing-only presuming nominal groups in our focus text, as exemplified below, and two of them are analysed in tables in terms of function and class, as per examples (16) and (17).

*2008 nian 6 yue, shi juli **di 29 jie Beijing Aoyunhui** kaimu jinjin liang ge yue de rizi*
(June 2008 was the time only two months away from the **29th Beijing Olympic Games**)

*2008 nian 5 yue 31 ri, da mianji hutai jinru **Qingdao** jin'an haiyu*
(On 31 May 2008, expansive sea lettuce invaded **Qingdao**'s offshore area)

*yue lai yue duo de hutai sui chaoshui yong shang an, **tamen** daoda le Qingdao zhuming de zhanqiao*
(more and more sea lettuce rushed onto the shore with the tidewater; **they** reached Qingdao's famous pier)

*lianxu de gongzuo yu meiwan chixu dao hou banye de huiyi, rang **Sun Song Suozhang** tili jida de touzhi. you yi ci, **ta** yi tian lianxu gongzuo 20 ge xiaoshi*
(unceasing work and nightly meetings made **Director Sun Song** burn the candle at both ends. Once **he** even worked 20 hours non-stop)

(16)	Example	*Qingdao*
	group class	nominal group
	group function	Thing
	word class	proper noun
	gloss	*Qingdao*
	translation	'Qingdao'

(17)	Example	*tamen*
	group class	nominal group
	group function	Thing
	word class	pronoun
	gloss	*they*
	translation	'they'

Note that proper names for people, places, institutions, dates, etc., are simply treated as realizing the Thing function only, and their internal structure is set aside in the present study, no matter how many words make up a proper name, for example, *di 29 jie Beijing Aoyunhui* (29th Beijing Olympic Games), *Sun Song Suozhang* (Director Sun Song) above, and *Zhongkeyuan Haiyangsuo* (Institute of Oceanology, Chinese

Academy of Sciences), *Shandong Shengwei Shengzhengfu* (CPC Provincial Committee and Provincial Government of Shandong Province), etc., in the text.

It is also worth noting that the clause *meili de Qingdao Aofan Zhongxin zuizhong yinglai le **chenggong de di 29 jie Aofansai*** (the beautiful Qingdao Olympic Sailing Centre finally greeted **successful 29th Olympic Sailing Games**) from our text contains a nominal group *chenggong de di 29 jie Aofansai* (successful 29th Olympic Sailing Games). In this nominal group *chenggong* (successful), as an attitude-conveying Epithet, is positioned before *di 29 jie Aofansai* (29th Olympic Sailing Games) via the link *de*; this gives us reason to treat *di 29 jie Aofansai* (29th Olympic Sailing Games) as a single Thing and regard *di 29 jie* (29th) not as a Measurer quantifying *Aofansai* (Olympic Sailing Games).

(18)	Example	*chenggong*	*de*	*di 29 jie Aofansai*
	group class	nominal group		
	group function	Epithet		Thing
	word class	adjective	link	proper noun
	gloss	*successful*		*29th Olympic Sailing Games*
	translation	'successful 29th Olympic Sailing Games'		

When the identity of an entity cannot be readily recovered by the reader, that is, not presumed, it needs to be presented in the text with an expanded nominal group. The sea lettuce is introduced for the first time in the text through the nominal group ***yi pian** lüyouyou de haizao* (a mass of green seaweed). In terms of word class, unlike English, Chinese does not have articles, but the presenting function is served by a Measurer realized by the numeral *yi* (one) with an ensuing measure.

Once this entity is presented, it is presumed afterwards in the text as *zhexie haizao* (these seaweeds). In the structure of this nominal group (analysed below as example (19)), the presuming function is fulfilled by a Deictic, which is typically realized in Chinese by a demonstrative determiner.

(19)	Example	*zhexie*	*haizao*
	group class	nominal group	
	group function	Deictic	Thing
	word class	demonstrative determiner	common noun
	gloss	*these*	*seaweed*
	translation	'these seaweeds'	

For the realization of the Deictic function in a Chinese nominal group, the demonstrative determiner can be followed by a measure as well, for example, ***ben ci** lüchao* (this green tide), so that the Deictic, like Measurer, is realized by a word complex (analysed below as example (20)).[7] In a Chinese nominal group syntagm, the measure does not occur alone; it is always part of a word complex (realizing β), following either a numeral or a demonstrative determiner.

(20)	Example	*ben*		*ci*	*lüchao*
	group class	nominal group			
	group function	Deictic			Thing
		word complex			
		α		β	
	word class	demonstrative determiner		measure	common noun
	gloss	this			green tide
	translation	'this green tide'			

In addition to demonstrative pronouns, possessives are also deployed to realize Deictics. Possessives include possessive pronouns (e.g. *wo de* (my), *tamen de* (their)) and embedded nominal groups (e.g. **Qingdao** *zhuming de zhanqiao* (Qingdao's famous pier), **Zhongguo Kexueyuan** *de zhuanjia* (experts from Chinese Academy of Sciences), **duo jia she hai danwei** *de zhuanjia* (experts from many ocean-related institutes)). Two representative examples are analysed below as (21) and (22).

(21)	Example	*Qingdao*	*zhuming*	*de*	*zhanqiao*
	group class	nominal group			
	group function	Deictic	Epithet		Thing
		[nominal group]			
		Thing			
	word class	proper noun	adjective	link	common noun
	Gloss	Qingdao	famous		pier
	Translation	'Qingdao's famous pier'			

Here *Qingdao* is analysed as a Deictic because it answers the probe question 'Which pier?'; it is realized by an embedded nominal group rather than directly by a proper noun because it has the potential of being expanded, for example, [*meili de Qingdao*] *zhuming de zhanqiao* (beautiful Qingdao's famous pier).

(22)	Example	*duo*	*jia*	*she hai*	*danwei*	*de*	*zhuanjia*
	group class	nominal group					
	group function	Deictic					Thing
		[nominal group]					
		Measurer		Qualifier	Thing		
		word complex					
		α	β				
	word class	quantifier	measure	[[clause]]	noun	link	noun
	gloss	many		involve ocean	institute		expert
	translation	'experts from many ocean-related institutes'					

In this example, *duo jia she hai danwei* (many ocean-related institutes) realizes a Deictic to determine which specific experts are being identified in the nominal group, and it in itself is an embedded nominal group with a fairly complex structure, involving Measurer (realized by a hypotactic word complex), Qualifier (realized by an embedded clause)[8] and Thing (realized by a common noun) functions.

Since sequentially the Measurer comes before the Thing in the nominal group structure, to discern whether the numeral or quantifier in the Measurer (e.g. *duo* (many) in the above example) is quantifying the Thing in the embedded nominal group (e.g. *danwei* (institute)) or the Thing in the entire nominal group (e.g. *zhuanjia* (expert)) depends on the measure realizing β in the Measurer. Compare the following two nominal groups:

[*duo **jia** she hai danwei*] *de zhuanjia*
(experts from many ocean-related institutes)

*duo **wei** [she hai danwei] de zhuanjia*
(many experts from ocean-related institutes)

The first nominal group has a measure *jia*, which is used for institutions; whereas in the second one, the measure word is *wei*, used to refer to people in a respectful manner. Through the use of different measures, we know that *duo* (many) in the first nominal group is quantifying *danwei* (institutes), while the same lexical item is quantifying *zhuanjia* (expert) in the second nominal group.

To exclusively identify an entity, a nominal group may need a Qualifier function to make explicit which entity is being referred to in the text. In terms of class, a Qualifier can be realized either by an embedded coverbal phrase[9] or by an embedded clause. The following nominal groups from our focus text each contain a Qualifier function:

kongdi shang liangshai de yi pian lüyouyou de haizao
(a mass of green seaweed being dried on the ground)

laizi Zhongguo Kexueyuan Haiyangsuo ... de 14 wei zhuanjia
(14 experts from the Institute of Oceanology, Chinese Academy of Sciences ...)

dalao hutai de xiaolü
(the efficiency of getting sea lettuce out of water)

guanyu hutai de gezhong kexue shuju
(various scientific statistics about the sea lettuce)

zhengzai nan Huanghai zhixing renwu de 'Kexue 3' kekaochuan
('Science 3' scientific research ship that is undertaking a task at south Yellow Sea)

Unlike the case in the English nominal group structure where the Qualifier follows the Thing, in the Chinese nominal group structure, the Qualifier precedes the Thing. What is common in structure for all Qualifiers is that the link *de* is required to immediately follow the embedded coverbal phrase or clause realizing the Qualifier.

Function and class analyses of three examples are provided below. According to SFL convention, the embedded coverbal phrase is enclosed in single square brackets (as has been exemplified in examples (21) and (22) above) to indicate that it is realizing a function in a structure of the same rank (here group/phrase in group/phrase), and the embedded clause is enclosed in double square brackets (as has been used in example (22) above) to indicate that it is realizing a function in a structure of a lower rank (here clause in group/phrase).

(23)	Example	*guanyu hutai*	*de*	*ge*	*zhong*	*kexue*	*shuju*
	group class	nominal group					
	group function	Qualifier		Deictic		Classifier	Thing
				word complex			
				α	β		
	word class	[coverbal phrase]	link	demonstrative	measure	noun	noun
	gloss	about sea lettuce		each	kind	science	statistics
	translation	'various scientific statistics about the sea lettuce'					

(24)	Example	*laizi Zhongguo Kexueyuan Haiyangsuo …*	*de*	*14*	*wei*	*zhuanjia*
	group class	nominal group				
	group function	Qualifier		Measurer		Thing
				word complex		
				α	β	
	word class	[[clause]]	link	numeral	measure	noun
	gloss	come from the Institute of Oceanology, Chinese Academy of Sciences …		14		expert
	translation	'14 experts coming from the Institute of Oceanology, Chinese Academy of Sciences …'				

(25)	Example	*kongdi shang liangshai*	*de*	*yi*	*pian*	*lüyouyou*	*de*	*haizao*
	group class	nominal group						
	group function	Qualifier		Measurer		Epithet		Thing
				word complex				
				α	β			
	word class	[[clause]]	link	numeral	measure	adjective	link	noun
	gloss	dry on the ground		one	expanse	green		seaweed
	translation	'a mass of green seaweed that is being dried on the ground'						

As mentioned above, the Qualifier is positioned before the Thing in the Chinese nominal group, but it does not necessarily come in the initial position of the nominal group (though all examples above might have implied so). Both a Deictic and a Measurer can precede the Qualifier. For example, the following pairs of nominal groups (reproduced and adapted from examples (23) and (24) above) are all grammatical, but these have different structural sequences for textual reasons:

guanyu hutai de gezhong kexue shuju (Qualifier ^ Deictic)
gezhong guanyu hutai de kexue shuju (Deictic ^ Qualifier)
(various scientific statistics about the sea lettuce)

laizi Zhongguo Kexueyuan Haiyangsuo ... de 14 wei zhuanjia (Qualifier ^ Measurer)
14 wei laizi Zhongguo Kexueyuan Haiyangsuo ... de zhuanjia (Measurer ^ Qualifier)
(14 experts from the Institute of Oceanology, Chinese Academy of Sciences ...)

Chinese nominal group systems

The above two sections introduced ideational and textual resources of Chinese nominal groups, approached 'from above' in terms of the ideational and textual discourse semantics, and then reasoned 'from around and below' to analyse nominal group structures and their realizations. In this section we will make explicit Chinese nominal group systems using system networks. Conventions for drawing system networks can be found in Martin et al. (2013).

As an initial step we set aside elliptical nominal groups, that is, Thing-less nominal groups, for example, *houhou yi ceng* ⊘ (a thick layer (of ⊘)), from non-elliptical ones. For the next step we distinguish between Thing-only nominal groups designating presumed entities and nominal groups specifying entities. Then we distinguish designating nominal groups that name entities with proper nouns from those that proname[10] entities with pronouns. These systems and how they relate to each other are represented in Figure 4.5.

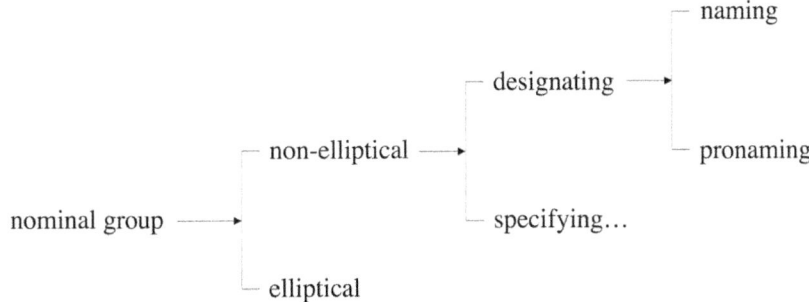

Figure 4.5 General Chinese nominal group systems.

The realization statements for features in the above systems are listed in Table 4.1. In the realization statement column, '+' signifies insertion of a function and ':' signifies realization of a function through a class. For detailed notation conventions of realization statements also see Martin et al. (2013).

The feature [specifying] further opens up five simultaneous systems, making it possible for an entity to be optionally classified, described, quantified, determined and/or qualified.

For [classifying], it offers four more delicate choices, that is, nominal, adjectival, verbal and numeral, depending on what class is realizing the Classifier function. Examples for the four choices are provided above in the analyses as examples (2), (3), (4) and (6). Since more than one Classifier can be selected in a nominal group structure, the system CLASSIFICATION is represented as a recursive one, allowing for more than one option in the system. The system network is outlined in Figure 4.6. The Classifier, if selected, is positioned immediately before the Thing in the structure.

For [describing], the Epithet function needs to be introduced to the nominal group structure, and the realization of the Epithet obligatorily involves an adjective. The adjective can be optionally followed by a noun realizing dimension, on the one hand, and optionally followed by the link *de*, on the other. Therefore, the selections between [dimensioned] or not and between [linked] or not are presented as simultaneous

Table 4.1 Realization statements for general Chinese nominal group features.

Feature	Realization statement
non-elliptical	+Thing
naming	Thing: proper noun
pronaming	Thing: pronoun

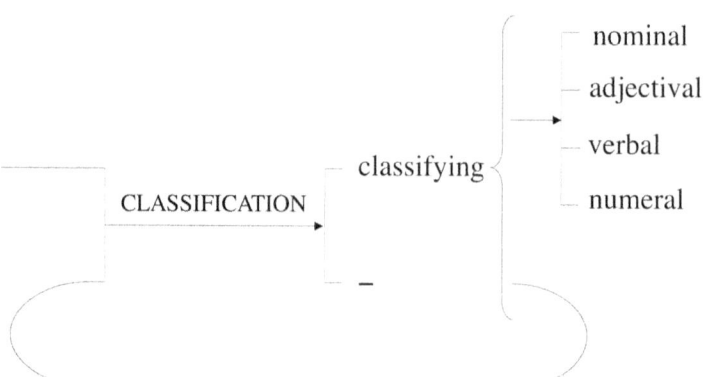

Figure 4.6 The CLASSIFICATION system of Chinese nominal group.

systems, along with an option of further classifying the entity after it is classified once. The recursive system of description for Chinese nominal groups is outlined in Figure 4.7. The Epithet is positioned before Thing; it also comes before the Classifier where there is one in the nominal group structure.

The [quantifying] option requires the insertion of a Measurer function into the nominal group structure, which is realized by a word complex featuring a measure word relating hypotactically to a numeral or a quantifier. The distinction between numeral and quantifier realizes the distinction between features of [exact] and [inexact], which distinguishes digital quantification of an entity from approximate quantification. Simultaneous to the selection between [exact] and [inexact], a system of gradability allows the quantification of an entity to be optionally gradable, realized by an adjective showing degree lodged between the numeral/quantifier and the measure. The system network of QUANTIFICATION is shown in Figure 4.8. In terms of sequence, the Measurer precedes the Classifier, and typically also precedes the Epithet, though for textual reasons some Epithets may come before the Measurer (see example (14) above and note 6).

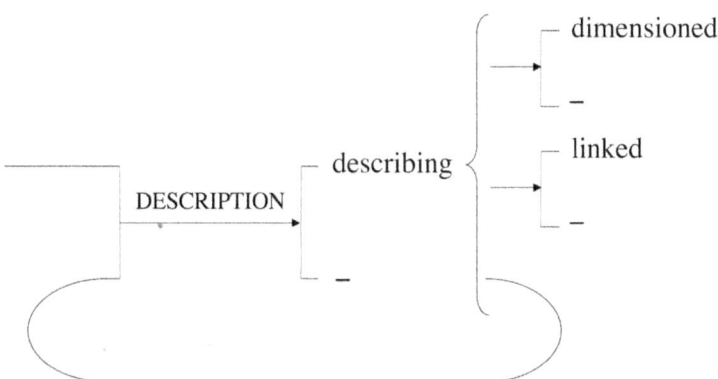

Figure 4.7 The DESCRIPTION system of Chinese nominal group.

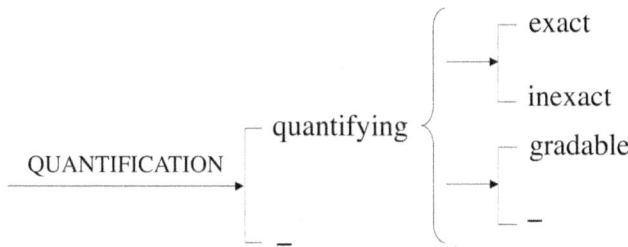

Figure 4.8 The QUANTIFICATION system of Chinese nominal group.

The [determining] feature first provides two options of [demonstrative] and [possessive]. The demonstrative type requires the use of a demonstrative determiner, without being linked by *de*, but which can be subclassified into [measured] or not, depending on whether there is a measure after the demonstrative determiner (as in examples (19) and (20) above). The possessive type is further classified into two subtypes: [pronominal] and [nominal group embedding], featuring a Deictic realized by a pronoun and an embedded nominal group, respectively. Both subtypes can optionally use the link *de* after the possessive determiner (pronoun or embedded nominal group). When there is an Epithet followed by a link *de* in the nominal group structure, the Deictic preceding it tends not to use another link *de*, for example, **Qingdao** *zhuming de zhanqiao* (Qingdao's famous pier) Deictic ^ Epithet ^ Thing, as shown in example (21). For [possessive: pronominal & linked] and [possessive pronominal & not linked], we provide two examples, (26) and (27), which are not from our focus text, to illustrate this structure. The system network of DETERMINATION is outlined in Figure 4.9. In terms of structural sequence, the Deictic is positioned before Epithet or Measurer in the nominal group.

(26)	Example	*wo*	*de*	*pengyou*
	group class	nominal group		
	group function	Deictic		Thing
	word class	pronoun	link	proper noun
	gloss	I		friend
	translation	'my friend'		

(27)	Example	*wo*		*baba*
	group class	nominal group		
	group function	Deictic		Thing
	word class	pronoun		proper noun
	gloss	I		dad
	translation	'my dad'		

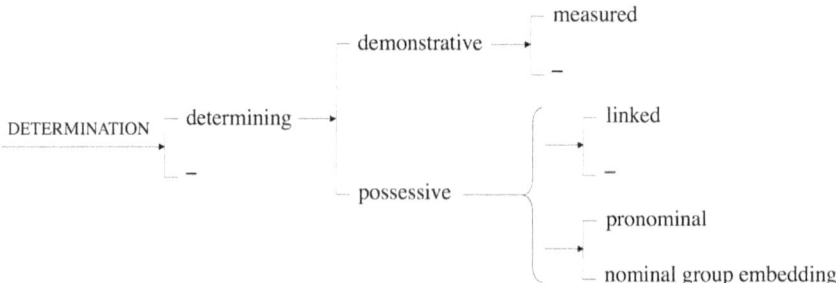

Figure 4.9 The DETERMINATION system of Chinese nominal group.

The feature [qualifying] is subclassified into [phrasal] and [clausal], reflecting the realization features of the Qualifier in the nominal group. The system network of QUALIFICATION is represented in Figure 4.10. Both phrasal and clausal types require the link *de* to connect the Qualifier with the rest of the nominal group. In terms of sequence, the Qualifier precedes the Epithet; however, it is only relative sequencing, when the nominal group also contains a Measurer or Deictic, they can either precede the Qualifier ^ Epithet sequence or appear between the Qualifier ^ Epithet (as discussed and exemplified in the previous section).

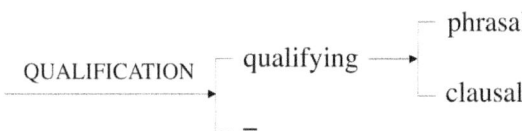

Figure 4.10 The QUALIFICATION system of Chinese nominal group.

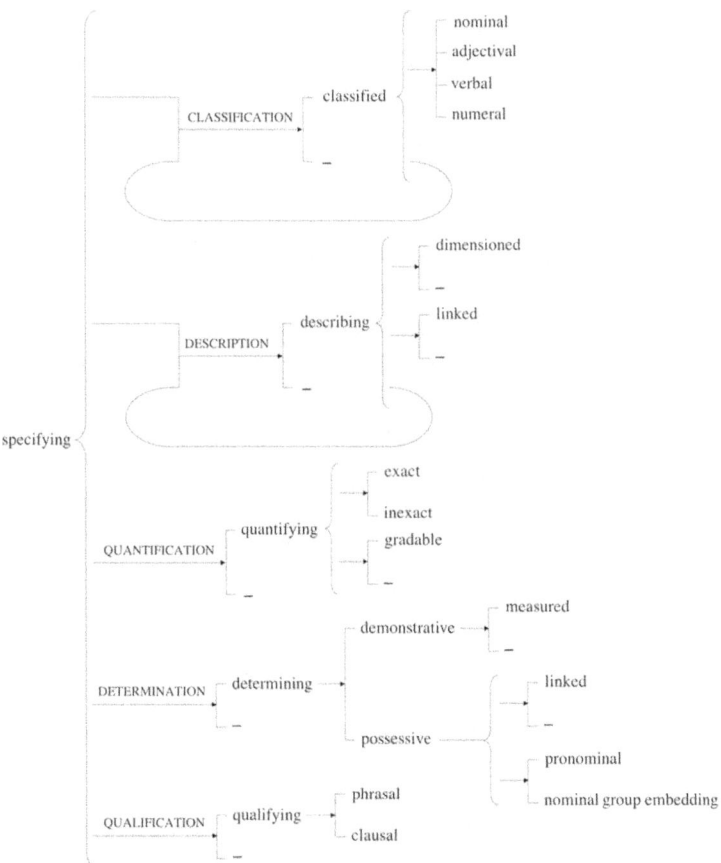

Figure 4.11 Delicate specifying nominal groups in Chinese.

Table 4.2 Realization statements for specifying Chinese nominal group features.

Feature	Realization statements
classifying	+Classifier; Classifier ∧ Thing
nominal	Classifier: noun
adjectival	Classifier: adjective
verbal	Classifier: verb
numeral	Classifier: numeral
describing	+Epithet; Epithet: adjective; Epithet ⤳ Classifier
dimensioned	Epithet: adjective ∧ noun
linked	Epithet ∧ *de*
quantifying	+Measurer; Measurer ⤳ Classifier; Measure: word complex
exact	Measurer: numeral ∧ measure
inexact	Measurer: quantifier ∧ measure
gradable	Measurer: numeral ∧ adjective ∧ measure
determining	+Deictic; Deictic ⤳ Classifier
demonstrative	Deictic: demonstrative determiner
measured	Deictic: demonstrative determiner ∧ measure
possessive	Deictic: possessive determiner
linked	Deictic ∧ *de*
pronominal	Deictic: [nominal group]
nominal group embedding	Deictic: pronoun
qualifying	+Qualifier; Qualifier ⤳ Epithet; Qualifier ∧ *de*
phrasal	Qualifier: [coverbal phrase]
clausal	Qualifier: [[clause]]

As mentioned earlier, the above five nominal group systems are opened up by the feature [specifying] in Figure 4.5. They are consolidated in Figure 4.11, and the realization statements for these system features are summarized in Table 4.2. In the realization statements column, apart from the '+' and ':' signs that have been introduced above, '∧' signifies immediate sequence of functions, classes and lexical items[11]; '⤳' signifies relative sequence of functions.

A homage to J. R. Martin

This chapter has presented a text-based study of the construal of entities through nominal groups in Chinese, which is work inspired by J. R. Martin's active engagement in the development of functional language typology and grammatical description of both English and languages other than English (Martin et al., forthcoming b). The chapter also aimed to demonstrate the methodology of grammatical description informed by Systemic Functional linguistic theory, designed by M. A. K. Halliday and his colleagues. Specifically, this chapter has illustrated three aspects in relation to methodology: text-based data compilation, approaching grammar 'from above' and axial reasoning, all of which are key principles in grammatical description that Martin and his colleagues are endeavouring to pursue and develop in their recent works, as mentioned in the opening section of this chapter.

This chapter serves as a homage to Jim also for the fact that it follows the illustrative and instructive example set by him in his description of English nominal group systems and structures in Martin et al. (forthcoming b). During my work on translating his description of English nominal groups (and also Beatriz Quiroz's description of Chilean Spanish nominal groups) and describing Chinese nominal groups as a visiting fellow at the University of Sydney, I met with Jim in his office regularly and received immense, illuminating advice on this project. Without his professional instruction and generous help this study would never have appeared in its present shape. I feel myself highly privileged to have Jim as a great mentor, and to dedicate this chapter to him in a special Festschrift. As a role model, Jim will continue to inspire us to push forward language description and functional language typology.

Notes

1. URL: http://www.cas.cn/xw/yxdt/200809/t20080905_986639.shtml (retrieved on 15 April 2019).
2. All numbered examples in this chapter follow the interlinear glossing rules developed by the Systemic Language Modelling (SLaM) Network. The glossing conventions can be found at: https://systemiclanguagemodelling.com/glossing/. Last accessed 15 April 2020.
3. This example is taken from a news report at Xinhuanet (URL: http://www.xinhuanet.com/world/2019-01/05/c_1210030343.htm; retrieved on 31 July 2019).
4. This nominal group function will be introduced shortly afterwards in this section.
5. Besides quantifying, a Measurer comprising the numeral *yi* (one) also functions as presenting the identity of an entity. This textual functional of Measurer is to be accounted for in the next section.
6. For textual reasons, an Epithet can precede a Measurer sometimes in nominal group structure, for example *lüyouyou de yi pian haizao* (a mass of green seaweed), *turuqilai de yi chang haiyang ziran zaihai* (an unexpected ocean natural disaster). However, this alternative positioning does not apply to all instances, for example, the Measurer *yi ge* (one) and the Epithet *huai* (bad) in the nominal group *yi ge huai xiaoxi* (a piece of bad news) cannot swap positions to produce **huai (de) yi ge xiaoxi*, with or without the link *de*.
7. Other examples in the text featuring the same structure include **ben ci** *hangxing* (this voyage), **zhe chang** *hutai dazhan* (this fierce battle with sea lettuce). However, the Thing function of these nominal groups realizes activity entities rather than thing entities, thus not the focus of our discussion in this chapter.
8. The Qualifier function and its realizations will be described later in this section.
9. A coverbal phrase is seen as the 'Chinese equivalent of a prepositional phrase' (Li, 2017, p. 349), formed by the combination of a nominal group following a coverb, a class of verb and functioning as minor Process. Almost all coverbs can function also as major Process in the clause (Halliday & McDonald, 2004, p. 317). The coverb is also termed as 'prepositive verb' in Halliday (1956).

10 The term 'proname' is adopted from Martin et al. (forthcoming b), meaning to designate a presumed entity with a pronoun.
11 The sign '^' originally indicates sequence of functions (Martin et al., 2013); in this chapter, its use is expanded to indicate also the sequence of classes, and a lexical item *de*.

References

Caffarel, A., Martin, J. R., & Matthiessen, C. M. I. M. (Eds.) (2004). *Language Typology: A Functional Perspective*. Amsterdam: John Benjamins.

Doran, Y. J., & Martin, J. R. (2020). Field relations: Understanding scientific explanations. In K. Maton, J. R. Martin, & Y. J. Doran (Eds.), *Studying Science: Language, Knowledge and Pedagogy*. London: Routledge.

Halliday, M. A. K. (1956). Grammatical categories in modern Chinese. *Transactions of the Philological Society*, 55(1), pp. 178–224.

Halliday, M. A. K. (1996). On grammar and grammatics. In R. Hasan, C. Cloran, & D. G. Butt (Eds.), *Functional Descriptions: Theory in Practice* (pp. 1–38). Amsterdam: John Benjamins.

Halliday, M. A. K., & Matthiessen, C. M. I. M. (2014). *Hallidays Introduction to Functional Grammar* (4th ed.). London/New York: Routledge.

Halliday, M. A. K., & McDonald, E. (2004). Metafunctional profile of the grammar of Chinese. In A. Caffarel, J. R. Martin, & C. M. I. M. Matthiessen (Eds.), *Language Typology: A Functional Perspective* (pp. 305–96). Amsterdam: John Benjamins.

Hao, J. (2015). *Construing Biology: An Ideational Perspective*. PhD thesis, University of Sydney.

Hao, J. (2020). *Analyzing Scientific Discourse from a Systemic Functional Linguistic Perspective: A Framework for Exploring Knowledge Building in Biology*. New York and London: Routledge.

Li, E. S. (2017). The nominal group in Chinese. In T. Bartlett & G. O'Grady (Eds.), *The Routledge Handbook of Systemic Functional Linguistics* (pp. 338–53). London/New York: Routledge.

Martin, J. R. (1981). CONJUNCTION and CONTINUITY in Tagalog. In M. A. K. Halliday & J. R. Martin (Eds.), *Readings in Systemic Linguistics* (pp. 310–36). London: Batsford.

Martin, J. R. (1988). Grammatical conspiracies in Tagalog: Family, face and fate – with reference to Benjamin Lee Whorf. In J. D. Benson, M. J. Cummings, & W. S. Greaves (Eds.), *Linguistics in a Systemic Perspective* (pp. 243–300). Amsterdam: Benjamins.

Martin, J. R. (1990). Interpersonal grammatization: Mood and modality in Tagalog. *Philippine Journal of Linguistics*, 21(1) (Special Issue on the Silver Anniversary of the Language Study Centre of Philippine Normal College 1964–1989 – Part 2), 2–51.

Martin, J. R. (1992). *English Text: System and Structure*. Amsterdam: John Benjamins.

Martin, J. R. (1995). Logical meaning, interdependency and the linking particle {-ng/na} in Tagalog. *Functions of Language*, 2(2), 189–228.

Martin, J. R. (1996). Transitivity in Tagalog: A functional interpretation of case. In M. Berry, C. Butler, R. Fawcett, & G. Huang (Eds.), *Meaning and Form: Systemic Functional Interpretations* (pp. 229–96). Norwood, NJ: Ablex.

Martin, J. R. (2004). Metafunctional profile: Tagalog. In A. Caffarel, J. R. Martin, & C. M. I. M. Matthiessen (Eds.), *Language Typology: A Functional Perspective* (pp. 255–304). Amsterdam: Benjamins.

Martin, J. R. (2014). Evolving systemic functional linguistics: Beyond the clause. *Functional Linguistics*, 1, 24–47.

Martin, J. R. (2018). Interpersonal meaning: Systemic functional linguistics perspective. *Functions of Language*, 25(1), 2–19.

Martin, J. R., & Rose, D. (2007). *Working with Discourse: Meaning beyond the Clause* (2nd ed.). London: Continuum.

Martin, J. R., & Rose, D. (2008). *Genre Relations: Mapping Culture*. London: Equinox.

Martin, J. R., Wang, P., & Zhu, Y. (2013). *Systemic Functional Grammar: A Next Step into the Theory – Axial Relations*. Beijing: Higher Education Press.

Martin, J. R., Doran, Y., & Figueredo, G. (Eds.) (2020). *Systemic Functional Language Description: Making Meaning Matter*. London: Routledge.

Martin, J. R., Quiroz, B., & Figueredo, G. (Eds.) (forthcoming a). *Interpersonal Grammar: Systemic Functional Linguistic Theory and Description*. Cambridge: Cambridge University Press.

Martin, J. R., Quiroz, B., Wang, P., & Zhu, Y. (forthcoming b). *Systemic Functional Grammar: Another Step into the Theory – Grammatical Description*. Beijing: Higher Education Press.

Zhu, D. (1982). *Yufa jiangyi* (Lecture notes on grammar). Beijing: Commercial Press.

5

Launching research: A Martinian perspective on science pedagogy

Sally Humphrey, Jing Hao and David Rose
Australian Catholic University; Pontificia Universidad Católica de Chile; University of Sydney

Introduction

Perhaps the best known of Jim Martin's work is his contribution to literacy education, which is known as the genre-based pedagogy of the 'Sydney School' (Hyons, 1996; Martin, 2000). Although its origins in Jim's research are often unacknowledged, it is his model of both a stratified content plane in language and a stratified context plane that is the foundation of this genre pedagogy. It is now forty years since this research began, in collaboration with teacher educators. In this time, the emerging model of discourse semantics has been applied to corpora of texts written in schools, to reveal consistent syndromes of features associated with varieties of narrative, informative and argument genres which were previously undescribed but have since entered the repertoires of teachers around the world. These applications have brought many educators to Jim's work, including Sally Humphrey (Humphrey, 1996, 2016) and David Rose (Rose & Martin, 2012), among many others.

Through the 1980s, as Jim was working out the details of discourse semantics, together with his semiotic model of context as register and genre systems, which culminated in *English Text* (1992), teachers were being trained in genre pedagogy alongside extracts from Halliday's functional grammar (Martin, 2000). Ironically, while discourse semantics and register were the bases of genre descriptions, they have rarely been included in teacher training programs, despite the focus on curriculum registers in literacy research projects in the secondary school and workplaces (Christie & Martin, 1997; Martin & Veel, 1998) as well as in tertiary education (Dreyfus et al., 2016), all of which were led by Jim. Work on detailing register descriptions was backgrounded through the 2000s, in favour of sociological takes on knowledge structures and legitimation codes (Christie & Martin, 2007), together with studies in multimodality (Painter et al., 2013), appraisal (Martin & White, 2005), individuation and identity (Zappavignia & Martin, 2018).

> The authors would like to acknowledge the contributions of industry partner participants to this study: Brunswick Secondary College, Caroline Chisholm Catholic College, Penola Catholic College and Roxburgh Secondary College.

Martinian research on discourse semantic and register systems is now entering a new phase with Jing Hao's (2015) description of ideation systems in *Construing Biology*, and Doran and Martin's (forthcoming) description of field systems. In this chapter we bring this new work together with current research in genre pedagogy to describe the semiotic resources that secondary students must bring to the tasks of studying science theory and reporting its practices, in order to succeed in communicating scientific investigations for 'high stakes' assessment.

Theory and research

In this section we outline the educational research project in which our findings have emerged, and the theoretical model of genre and register that we work with.

The research context

The research reported on in this chapter is one aspect of a design-based project exploring multiliteracies in the senior secondary science curriculum (Unsworth et al., 2016). The specific research focus in this chapter is on the discourse semantic resources that students need to report their practical investigations in senior biology for school-based assessment. The discourse semantic metalanguage that emerges from this research also opens the space for analysis of visual dimensions of scientific investigation reports, although such a visual analysis is beyond the scope of this chapter.

In the senior years, school-based science assessment tasks often take the form of practical investigations. For example, in the schools participating in this research, students in their final two years of study are required to report their scientific investigation through designing and making a scientific poster. As posters represent recognized disciplinary practice of scientists and are also highly valued in tertiary science studies, they provide a valuable context for exploring the discourse moves involved in extended scientific writing. Composition of the investigation report in the poster typically concludes a curriculum unit of five to ten weeks duration, in which the class studies a scientific field, through teacher presentations and reading, followed by the practical investigation.

Initial analysis of advice provided by the science curriculum authority to teachers revealed little support for composing the posters, apart from specifications of mandated sections (i.e. Introduction, Methodology, Result, Discussion, Conclusion) and features of poster layout. Instructions on language use relate to the use of voice, that is, 'using first person (rather than third person) and active (rather than passive) voice is acceptable in scientific reports' and to past and present tense, as is shown in the following excerpt:

> When describing something that has already happened (for example, the investigation procedure) then past tense is used …; when describing something that still exists (for example, the report, theory and permanent equipment) then the present tense is used. (VCAA, 2017)

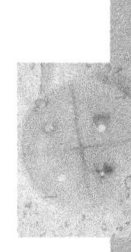

Figure 5.1 Year 12 Biology Poster. Alden.

In this excerpt, tense is related to two different realms of meaning, or fields (i.e. describing something that has already happened and describing something that still exists). However, what is not clarified is how these two realms of meaning are brought together across and within sections of the text, for example, when linking observations of experiments which have already happened to principles which 'still exist'. Such moves cannot be revealed by focusing on tense alone and require attention to interactions amongst the fields therein.

The syllabus advice also touches on the importance of appropriately conveying scientific values in students' writing, particularly in terms of the 'validity' and 'certainty' of hypotheses and findings. This resonates with research on scientific discourse at the tertiary level (Hood, 2010; Hao & Humphrey, 2012a, 2012b). The advice, however, was limited to lists of 'terms' to be avoided or preferred, for example:

> The terms 'proved', 'disproved', 'correct' or 'incorrect' in relation to the hypothesis should be avoided since this level of certainty may be unlikely in a single investigation; terms such as 'supported', 'indicated' and 'suggested' are more appropriate to evaluate the hypothesis. (VCAA, 2017)

A primary objective of participating teachers was to support students' writing of the Discussion section of investigation report posters. Particular concerns were the challenges of generalizing findings from data, developing logical arguments for supporting a hypothesis and evaluating the experimental design. Despite the attention given to Introductory sections of research reports by researchers from the tradition of English for Specific Purposes (e.g. Swales, 1990), teachers considered that the Discussion presented more significant challenges for students at secondary level.

Seventy graded texts from across Years 11 and 12 biology, chemistry and physics classes in the four schools were collected, of which one high-graded biology investigation report poster was analyzed for its discourse patterns. The poster, composed by a student identified as Alden, is shown as Figure 5.1. It reports on an investigation of the effect of herbs and spices on the growth of *Escherichia coli* bacteria. In the experiment, agar plates were smeared with a bacterial lawn of *E. coli*, and discs containing garlic, cloves, cinnamon and turmeric were placed on the plates, together with discs containing an antibiotic and no substance as controls. Antibacterial effects of each type were measured by the size of their zone of inhibition (ZoI) of bacterial growth.

Genre and register

The Martinian theory applied here models social contexts as two levels of semiotic systems, in which systems of genres configure recurrent variations in social activities, social relations and modalities of meaning-making, or field, tenor and mode systems, which are collectively known as register. These register variables tend to be realized by ideational, interpersonal and textual metafunctions of language and other modalities. Within each metafunction, systems in the stratum of discourse semantics realize features of register and are realized in turn by lexicogrammatical systems.

For educational purposes, we will distinguish two broad families of genres. Following Christie (2002), the term *curriculum genres* is used for pedagogic practices through which knowledge and values are negotiated (Rose, 2018). In contrast, the term *knowledge genres* has been applied to the texts that are written and read by learners in schools (Rose & Martin, 2013). Within each of these families, genres are distinguished by their staging. The stages of knowledge genres are realized by register structures termed phases, often expressed as paragraphs in writing (Martin & Rose, 2008). Curriculum genres configure two registers together: a *curriculum register* of knowledge and values is exchanged through a *pedagogic register* of teaching/learning activities, involving various modalities and teacher/learner relations.

From this perspective, the poster assessment is a knowledge genre, termed *experiment* or *investigation report*, with the stages Introduction, Methodology, Results, Discussion, Conclusion. As flagged above, this genre and its staging are explicitly taught by science teachers. Within each stage is a series of more variable phases that may also be taught by science teachers, but may or may not be given explicit labels. Although the teachers were concerned primarily with supporting students to write 'logical' and 'persuasive' Discussions, previous studies and our analysis of the students' posters reveal that such characteristics of language are also salient in the Introduction stage (Hood, 2010; Humphrey & Hao, 2012b). In order to account for the recurrent language patterns throughout the text, in this chapter, we focus on both Introduction and Discussion stages of the report from Figure 5.1. In Table 5.1, we identify three broad phases in the Introduction, and two in the Discussion, labelled in bold, and a series of more delicate phases labelled in italics.

Table 5.1 Extract from investigation report (Figure 5.1).

Introduction	
Classification	E. coli is a bacteria that commonly live in the environment, foods and in the intestines of people.
Issue	Although mostly harmless, there are strains that are lethal to humans according to one fact sheet (WHO, 2016). One strain called STEC releases toxins which can kill humans. Outbreaks are common in meat and can be cured through the use of antibiotics.
Confirming prior research	One report (Chopra, Dale and Blackwood, 1963) investigated the effects of ampicillin on *E. coli* growth. It was found that the ampicillin was effective at inhibiting growth of *E. coli*.
Unconfirmed	It is also believed however that various herbs and spices have similar antibacterial properties. One study conducted (Billing and Sherman, 1998) found that various herbs/spices had antibacterial properties that could inhibit the growth of *E. coli*.
Application	If this is true then millions of people could avoid food poisoning by using herbs and spices in their meat dishes. According to one investigation (WHO, 2015) around 430,000 people worldwide die due to eating contaminated food.
Justification	The results from this experiment could tell us which spices and herbs effectively inhibit *E. coli* growth.

Table 5.1 Extract from investigation report (Figure 5.1). *(continued)*

Introduction	
Steps	The results will be gathered by putting spices and control substances like ampicillin onto discs and placing them inside a bacterial lawn of *E. coli* and observations of growth measured the next day to determine if those spices have antibacterial properties.
Application	These spices can then be used in meat dishes to prevent STEC growth in meat after it has been cooked; this would result in less cases of food poisoning across the world and therefore less fatalities.
Aim	The aim of this experiment is to investigate how different type of spices affect the growth of *E. coli*.
Hypothesis	It is hypothesized that if garlic is effective at inhibiting the growth of *E. coli*, then it should have a larger zone of inhibition surrounding it compared to the disc with no substance on it.
Results	...
Discussion	
Findings	
Findings: Confirmation of hypothesis	From the results gathered it is seen that the hypothesis that garlic is effective at inhibiting *E. coli* is supported because its zone of inhibition (ZoI) had a radius of 5.714 mm (Graph.2) whilst the blank disc had a ZoI of 0 mm (Graph.1). It is seen in the results (Graph.2) that garlic was the most effective (ZoI 5.714 mm), cloves and cinnamon were second most effective (ZoI 2.25mm) and turmeric was the least effective (ZoI 0.25 mm).
Conclusion	
Confirmation of prior research	From these results it can be inferred that certain spices and herbs do have an effect on the inhibition of *E. coli* as each had a ZoI whilst the negative control (blank disc) had no ZoI (Graph.1); therefore, the spices and herbs used were effective at inhibiting bacterial growth. Garlic was effective at this concentration, cinnamon and cloves were slightly effective at this concentration and turmeric had little/no effect at this concentration.
Validation of method	The positive control (ampicillin disc) had an expected result as its ZoI was 12 mm (Graph.1) and was completely clear. This meant that the positive control set up an example of an extremely effective inhibitor of bacterial growth.

A discourse semantic perspective on research writing in science: Knowledge genre

Despite the explicit account of meaning enabled by this delicate metalanguage at the level of register, the focus of language description in genre-based literacy programs in schools has tended to be on lexicogrammatical features of genres, with some attention to variability across stages. Limited attention has been given to the realizations of register across stretches of discourse and across genres. To remedy this and to more directly address the issues raised by teachers in the project, the approach we take here focuses on patterns in discourse semantics. This discourse semantic perspective builds on research on undergraduate writing (Hood, 2010), including Jing Hao's and Sally Humphrey's research in biology in the *SLATE* project (Dreyfus et al., 2016; Hao & Humphrey, 2012a, 2012b; Humphrey & Hao, 2013).

Our examination of students' posters reveals that a significant feature in Introduction and Discussion stages is the appropriate use of 'showing' verbs, such as *suggest, indicate, demonstrate, prove*. From a grammatical perspective, Christie and Cléirigh (2008) found that use of 'showing' verbs in verbal and relational clauses is a significant experiential language development in secondary school student texts. From a discourse semantic perspective, however, such verbs play a critical role in making meanings in all metafunctions (Hao, 2017, 2020). Interpersonally, they enact the evaluations mentioned above by the syllabus and by teachers; experientially, they serve to relate specific data to generalized findings; logically, they contribute to reasoning from results to principles; and textually, they are used to 'launch' fields of scientific phenomena (Hood, 2010). Here we discuss each of these discourse functions in turn, drawing on examples from Alden's text.

Interpersonal perspective

From an interpersonal perspective, 'showing' verbs offer a rich set of choices in the discourse semantic system of ENGAGEMENT (Martin & White, 2005, Martin & Rose, 2007). Choices in ENGAGEMENT negotiate texts as a dialogic space, either expanding negotiability by engaging with alternative voices to agree or disagree with the proposition, or contracting negotiability by presenting a proposition as valid and less contestable. Managing this interpersonal resource allows students to engage with prior scientific studies and argue for their own findings from the investigation.

When engaging with prior research, Alden uses both contracting and expanding strategies. Contracting is exemplified in (1), using *it was found* to convey that the results are not in doubt. In contrast, expanding is exemplified in (2), where *it is also believed* suggests that the 'belief' is open to be contested.

(1) One report (Chopra, Dale and Blackwood, 1963) investigated the effects of ampicillin on E. coli. It was **found** [contract] that the ampicillin was effective at inhibiting growth of E. coli.
(2) It is also **believed** [expand] that various herbs and spices have similar antibacterial properties.

Both examples (1) and (2) are used in the Introduction of the text. They function to relate the prior research to the background on the one hand, and the proposed experiment on the other. The contracting resource *it was found* construes the ampicillin research as confirming the preceding statement, *Outbreaks ... can be cured through the use of antibiotics*. This research will be replicated in the experiment as a control to validate the method. The expanding resource *It is also believed* construes the herbs and spices research as unconfirmed, which opens space for the experiment to confirm it.

After the prior research is set up, Alden introduces his own experiment by offering a hypothesis (3), which keeps the dialogic space open for the experiment to confirm or not.

(3) It is **hypothesized** [expand] that if garlic is effective at inhibiting the growth of E. coli, then it should have a larger zone of inhibition surrounding it compared to the disc with no substance on it.

In the Results stage, Alden interprets the results with *appeared* and *suggesting* which also expand the dialogic space (4).

(4) Cinnamon and the disc with nothing however had a radius of 0mm. The blank disc however **appeared** [expand] to have extra bacteria growth surrounding it, **suggesting** [expand] that it actually amplified the growth of bacteria.

However, as the text unfolds to the Discussion stage, Alden contracts the dialogic space to emphasize the validity of his findings. In (5) the hypothesis *is supported* by the results.

(5) In conclusion the hypothesis that garlic is effective at inhibiting bacterial growth is **supported** [contract] because during the experiment it was gathered that garlic had a 5.714mm ZoI (Graph.2) with 50% E. coli growth.

In addition to functioning as ENGAGEMENT resources, these instances also demonstrate interesting prosodic interactions with choices of ATTITUDE (Martin & White, 2005; Martin & Rose, 2007), particularly in terms of evaluating the effectiveness of herbs and spices. In examples (1) and (5), *ampicillin* and *garlic* are explicitly evaluated as *effective*. Both evaluations are coupled with the contraction of dialogic space. Since the experiment requires students to provide an assessment of different herbs and spices, their scientific values are enacted both by expressing explicit attitude (e.g. *effective*) and by validating the attitudinal proposition through engagement.

Experiential perspective

Alongside their interpersonal role, verbs of 'showing' play an important role in connecting multiple fields in the discipline of science (Hao, 2017, 2020). Two general field types found in investigation reports are research activities and the researched phenomena (cf. Hood, 2010). Researched phenomena may be general principles, such as *E.coli is a bacteria*, or specific depictions, such as *The blank disc appeared to have extra bacteria growth surrounding it*. In terms of the discourse semantic resources construing these fields, we will consider two general experiential choices – a type of element known as *entity* and a configuration of elements known as *figure* (Martin, 1992; Hao, 2020).[1] Entities construe people, things, places and activities in a given field, and are organized into taxonomies, and a figure can realize either an activity or expansion of an entity (Hao, 2020).

An entity can be presented as a 'source' for a figure, by means of a showing verb. The source entities construe taxonomies in the field of research, including people (e.g. *we, I, scientists*), publications (e.g. *Billing and Sherman, 1998; WHO, 2015*), semiotic entities (e.g. *results*) and activity entities (e.g. *method*). The source entity, in combination with the interpersonal engagement enacted by the 'showing' verb, positions the figure in the heteroglossic discourse. Hence, such a figure is known as a *positioned figure*, and the entity plus the engagement is referred to as a *position* (Hao, 2020). This experiential perspective allows us to consider not only the expanding and contracting of heteroglossic space, but also 'who' is positioned to do so.

In Alden's report, the figures construe a phenomenon associated with either a generalized scientific principle (6), a specific depiction in a particular study (7) or a generalized social/economic phenomenon (8). These phenomena are in bold while positions are underlined.

(6) E. coli is **a bacteria** that commonly live in the environment, foods and in the intestines of people.

(7) <u>We saw from the results</u> **its Zone of Inhibition (ZoI) had a radius of 5.714mm** (Graph.2) whilst **the blank disc had a ZoI of 0mm** (Graph.1).

(8) <u>According to one investigation (WHO, 2015)</u> **around 430,000 people worldwide die due to eating contaminated food**.

Generalized phenomena and specific depictions interact with different choices of tense and deixis, as noted in the syllabus advice above. We can see in the examples here that generalized phenomena tend to have entities with generic reference (Martin, 1992; Martin & Rose, 2007), such as indefinite articles (*a bacteria*) or no deixis (*E. coli*; *contaminated food*), and simple present tense (e.g. *is*; *live*). Specific depictions tend to use specific reference (e.g. *its zone of inhibition; the blank disc*) and past tense (e.g. *saw; had*).

Source entities in a position are not always explicit. In (6), the source of the scientific principle is implicitly presumed. In (7), the source is explicitly *we*, and in (8), it is *one investigation (WHO, 2015)*. Returning to example (1) above, we know from the co-text that it is *Chopra, Dale and Blackwood (1963)* who found the effectiveness of ampicillin. This example is reproduced in (9) to make the source entity explicit.

(9) <u>It was found (by Chopra, Dale and Blackwood)</u> that the ampicillin was effective at inhibiting growth of E. coli growth.

In Alden's text, positions include not only the 'showing' verbs but also 'seeing' verbs. In (10), the position construes a semiotic entity, *the results*, as the source.

(10) <u>It is seen in the results (Graph.2)</u> that garlic was the most effective (ZoI 5.714mm), cloves and cinnamon were second most effective (ZoI 2.25mm) and turmeric was the least effective (ZoI 0.25mm).

In Alden's text, positioned figures are salient in both the Introduction and Discussion stages. This is because in these two stages, the positions themselves construe an activity in the research field that bring together multiple fields. This pattern can be better explained when we take a logical perspective, considering how figures are logically connected into a sequence.

Logical perspective

From a logical perspective, 'showing' verbs can be used to encapsulate a complex set of meanings that connects figures into a sequence. This provides an important resource for developing logical arguments in an investigation report. When figures are connected in a sequence, the logical connexions[2] between them may be realized through a conjunction (*so, and, then*) and the sequence is realized through an expanding clause complex (*we saw it was raining heavily outside,* <u>so</u> *we knew we must take an umbrella*). However, it is also possible to realize sequences in a grammatically metaphorical way (Halliday, 1998; Martin, 2008). In doing so, the logical connexions and positions can be realized together through a verbal group, often employing 'showing' verbs.

In example (4) above, the verb *suggesting* metaphorically connects two figures into a sequence: a result figure *suggesting* a finding figure. This construes the result as a source, combining logical connexion and position. We can unpack this metaphorical realization by remapping the connexion congruently as a conjunction *so*, with the expansion of *suggesting* remapped congruently as *we suppose* (12).

(12) Cinnamon and the disc with nothing however had a radius of 0mm. The blank disc however appeared to have extra bacteria growth surrounding it. **So we suppose** that it actually amplified the growth of bacteria.

Through positioning figures and logically connecting them, Alden is able to construe an activity of reasoning in the scientific discipline. The research activity develops generally from 'we knew' from the prior research to 'we hypothesized' before conducting the experiment, and then to 'we saw/observed' in the present experiment, and finally to 'now we know' from the findings. An example of reasoning from the Discussion stage is shown in Table 5.2. The sequence of reasoning is realized through interactions of connexions and positions; both depictions and principles are realized through figures. Implicit positions are shown in brackets.

Developing activities of reasoning is salient in the investigation report poster as it allows the student to situate his own study as part of a broader research field. It is facilitated by the prior research, and in turn facilitates what can be done for the next step.

Table 5.2 Sequence of reasoning in the Discussion stage.

Activity of reasoning		Depiction in the experiment	Scientific principle
Connexion	Position	Figure	Figure
	From the results gathered it is seen that the hypothesis is supported		that garlic is effective at inhibiting *E. coli*
because	(we saw)	its zone of inhibition (ZoI) had a radius of 5.714 mm (Graph.2) whilst the blank disc had a ZoI of 0 mm (Graph.1).	
	It is seen in the results	that garlic was the most effective (ZoI 5.714 mm), cloves and cinnamon were second most effective (ZoI 2.25 mm) and turmeric was the least effective (ZoI 0.25 mm).	
	From these results it can be inferred		that certain spices and herbs do have an effect on the inhibition of *E. coli*
As	(we saw)	each had a ZoI whilst the negative control (blank disc) had no ZoI (Graph.1).	
therefore	(we conclude)	the spices and herbs used were effective at inhibiting bacterial growth.	

Textual perspective

Finally, from a textual perspective we can consider the ways in which positioning through showing verbs interacts with the periodicity or waves of information flow in a text. At the scale of smaller waves interacting with figures, positions initiate figures, while the research phenomena they show are New information, as set out in Table 5.3. We will refer to the pattern of positions initiating figures as *launching*. In this pattern, research phenomena are 'launched' by research activities.

At the scale of a larger wave carrying phases of register, positions can preview the axiological values of a phase. In (14), *infer* is used to launch the concluding phase, construing it as negotiable. However, the subsequent language choices of high modality, *do have an effect,* and causal connexions *as, therefore*, contract the dialogic space.

Table 5.3 Positions launching phenomena.

Theme		New	
Connexion	Position	Figure	Figure
	From the results gathered it is seen that the hypothesis is supported		that garlic is effective at inhibiting *E. coli*
because	(we saw)	its Zone of Inhibition (ZoI) had a radius of 5.714 mm (Graph.2) whilst the blank disc had a ZoI of 0 mm (Graph.1).	
	It is seen in the results (Graph.2)	that garlic was the most effective (ZoI 5.714 mm), cloves and cinnamon were second most effective (ZoI 2.25mm) and turmeric was the least effective (ZoI 0.25 mm).	

(14) From these results it can be inferred [expand] that certain spices and herbs **do have an effect** [contract] on the inhibition of E. coli **as** [contract] each had a ZoI whilst the negative control (blank disc) had **no** [contract] ZoI (Graph.1), **therefore** [contract] the spices and herbs used were effective at inhibiting bacterial growth. Garlic was effective at this concentration, cinnamon and cloves were slightly effective at this concentration and turmeric had **little/no** [contract] effect at this concentration.

The interaction here between launching with expansion and concluding with contraction enacts a dynamic 'persuasive' voice in 'objective' scientific writing (Hood, 2010).

In summary, our metafunctional exploration shows that construing logical and persuasive discourse is indeed critical in the investigation report found in Alden's poster, in both the Introduction and Discussion stages. 'Showing' verbs play a critical role in enacting evaluations, as the syllabus advice suggests. Importantly, however, they also offer experiential meanings in construing disciplinary activities as well as intricate textual interactions with periodicity. It is the multifunctional features embodied in this resource that make an investigation report successful.

Designing pedagogies for reading and writing scientific discourse: Curriculum genres

The discourse semantic analysis in the section above re-instantiates features of Alden's investigation report in a different knowledge genre, a *linguistic description*, that configures a different set of register variables, including a different technical field, less charged tenor and more abstract mode. In Bernstein's (2000) terms, these features are *recontextualized*, 'which removes (de-locates) a discourse from its substantive practice and context and relocates that discourse according to its principles of selective reordering and focusing' (2000, p. 173). However, the investigation report is itself a recontextualization. It re-instantiates features from a series of curriculum genres, including the experiment it reports on, and lessons on the scientific field that underlies it. In this section we will bring this recontextualization full circle, by designing a lesson series that brings together the knowledge of biology research in the investigation report with the knowledge about language in our linguistic description. Our goal is to illustrate how language teaching can be effectively embedded in curriculum learning in school and further education.

We earlier described curriculum genres as configuring a curriculum register of knowledge and values with a pedagogic register of activities, modalities and teacher/learner relations. In this instance, the curriculum knowledge includes scientific research and the language resources for reporting it. Its values include the validity of prior research, the student's investigation and its social applications. This knowledge and these values are exchanged through a series of lessons that constitute a curriculum macro-genre. One of its constituent genres is explicitly named 'practical investigation', but the other curriculum genres through which the field and language are learnt generally remain implicit. A fundamental principle of visible pedagogies, such as genre pedagogy, is that such implicitness contributes to inequality of outcomes in school learning (Hattie, 2009; Rose & Martin, 2012). Hence, genre pedagogy attempts to make the structuring of both curriculum and knowledge genres explicit, and designs curriculum genres to explicitly teach language resources.

Two of the curriculum genres designed in genre pedagogy are *preparing for reading*, which supports learning of curriculum knowledge by reading together, and *joint construction*, which supports writing of assessment tasks by deconstructing model texts and writing new texts together. In a secondary science unit, *preparing for reading* may be used to study the scientific field, and *joint construction* may be used to prepare for assessment tasks such as the investigation report here. Two further curriculum genres are *detailed reading* and *joint rewriting*, which are designed to support learners to control the language patterns of written texts through guided practice with instances. These and other curriculum genres designed in the 'Sydney School' tradition of genre pedagogy are described in Martin and Rose (2005, 2013), Rose and Martin (2012, 2013) and Rose (2008, 2015, 2016).

In this section we illustrate how these curriculum genres can be used to support students to control the language of investigation reports and the research fields on which they report. Writing of an investigation report may be modelled with joint construction, using a well-written instance of the genre as a model. However, this assessment task culminates a curriculum macro-genre that begins with studying the research field, followed by the practical investigation. Preparing for reading can be used to support all students in studying the field. This practice involves joint reading of curriculum texts, followed by independent reading.

The teacher first prepares with an overview of how the field is sequenced through a text, which is then read paragraph by paragraph. The overview may include oral, visual and written modalities that are used to build the new field on learners' prior knowledge. Each paragraph in turn is then briefly previewed, read aloud, and its key meanings identified and discussed. Notes of these key meanings may then be jointly scribed on the class board and further discussed. This joint practice in reading for meaning, identifying key information and making notes is highly effective in enabling all students to practice these activities independently. Crucially, it embeds scaffolding of reading skills in study of the curriculum, which makes it a practical pedagogy for secondary curriculum teaching. These activities may be observed in practice in a secondary science lesson at NESA (2018).

Ideally, the model that will be used for joint construction should be introduced early in the lesson sequence, so that students can see the assessment task that will be required of them, and its elements can be practiced as time allows in the curriculum program. This iterative practice builds students' repertoires of language resources, so that they are well prepared for the assessment task at the end of the lesson sequence. Detailed reading and joint rewriting can be used to practice the language resources we have described above, using extracts from a well-written model such as Alden's investigation report. Detailed reading enables all students to comprehend a passage of text in depth and detail, and to recognize the language choices that its author has made. Joint rewriting provides a high level of support for all students to practice using these language choices themselves, to write about a field they have been studying. Detailed reading is illustrated in the following section, with an extract from Alden's report, to show how students are guided to identify its pertinent language patterns. Rewriting is then illustrated, using the same language patterns to write about another field.

Detailed reading

Detailed reading is a carefully designed interactional practice, in which students are guided to identify elements of meaning in each sentence of a text passage. These tasks are prepared with semantic cues, so that students themselves do the semiotic labour of identifying particular wordings in the text from these cues. Ideally, students are asked in turn to say the identified wording, so that authority and affirmation are distributed around the whole class. Students typically use highlighters to mark each wording as they go. Once identified, their meanings may be elaborated in more depth.

Rather than discussing detailed reading in the abstract, it is illustrated here by constructing a possible discussion, which shows concretely how such a designed interaction unfolds. The illustration discusses the *confirming* phase in Alden's Introduction. These sentences introduce the pattern of 'launching' a research activity with its source, which recurs throughout the text. They also illustrate the use of grammatical metaphor for presenting research activities, and the use of positions of figures for expanding and contracting negotiability.

The pedagogic activity of detailed reading consists of a series of learning cycles, in which students either identify wordings or propose responses from their own knowledge. Tables 5.4–5.7 illustrate a series of such learning cycles, with the two sentences from Alden's confirming phase. In Table 5.4, the teacher reads these sentences aloud, but first previews their function in the text, *prior research*, and rephrases them in congruent wordings that all students would comprehend. This preview enables all students to follow with general comprehension as the sentences are read. The task of identifying the first wording is then prepared with its location, *these sentences start*, and its general type of meaning, *the source of the research*. The identifying task is focused by asking one student to read, who is then affirmed. This cycle is repeated for the next wording, and the class is directed to highlight the identified words. The functions of each phase in these learning cycles are labelled to the right, along with speaker roles that enact the learning cycles as exchanges.[3]

In Table 5.5, the task of identifying the research activity is focused with *what they investigated*. Once identified, the nominal group *effects of ampicillin on E. coli growth* is elaborated by asking the class what it means, implicitly asking them to unpack

Table 5.4 Detailed reading of the confirming prior research phase.

Sp		Role	Cycle phases
T	This section is about prior research. The first two sentences are about research on an antibiotic that stops E. coli from growing, called ampicillin. *One report (Chopra, Dale and Blackwood, 1963) investigated the effects of ampicillin on E. coli growth. It was found that the ampicillin was effective at inhibiting growth of E. coli.* Inhibit means slow something down or stop it.	K1	Prepare sentence
	These sentences start with the source of the research.	K1	Prepare wording
	S1, can you read that to us?	dK1	Focus wording
S1	*One report (Chopra, Dale and Blackwood, 1963)*	K2	Identify wording
T	Excellent.	K1	Affirm
T	And what's the process they did?	dK1	Focus wording
S1	They *investigated*.	K2	Identify wording
T	Perfect.	K1	Affirm
	Can we highlight all of that, up to *investigated*.	A2	
Ss	[highlight text]	A1	

Table 5.5 Elaboration of launching structure.

T	S2, can you tell us what they investigated?	dK1	Focus wording
S2	*effects of ampicillin on E. coli growth*	K2	Identify wording
T	Yes	K1	Affirm
	Let's highlight *effects of ampicillin on E. coli growth*.	A2	Direct marking
Ss	[highlight text]	A1	
T	What do you think that means?	dK1	Focus metaphor
Ss	[hands up]	A2	
T	S3?	A1	
S3	How it stops *E. coli* growing?	K2	Propose activity
T	Exactly	K1	Affirm
	That's what they researched. The sentence starts by telling who researched it and ends with what they researched.	K1	Elaborate sentence structure

the grammatical metaphor. As this is a senior secondary class, students are able to interpret the activity it construes, and one student is selected to do so. The teacher then elaborates by directing their attention to the launching structure of the sentence.

Identifying tasks are directed to individual students by name, to ensure that all students are engaged and affirmed in turn. Elaborating tasks, such as unpacking metaphors, are directed to the whole class so that confident students may propose from their knowledge.[4] Alternatively, the teacher may elaborate with new knowledge.

In Table 5.6, the same pattern is repeated for the next two learning cycles. A wording is prepared with its location, *the next sentence ends*, and its type of meaning, *results of the research*. It is focused on a more exact location, *what they found*. Again, the identified wording is elaborated by inviting the class to unpack the grammatical metaphor.

Table 5.6 Elaboration by unpacking grammatical metaphor.

T	Now the next sentence ends with the results of the research.	K1	Prepare wording
	S4, can you read what the research found?	dK1	Focus wording
S4	*ampicillin was effective at inhibiting growth of E. coli*	K2	Identify wording
T	Yes.	K1	Affirm
	Let's highlight that.	A2	
Ss	[highlight text]	A1	
T	What do you think effective at inhibiting growth means?	dK1	Focus metaphor
Ss	[hands up]	A2	
T	S5?	A1	
S5	Ampicillin stopped *E. coli* from growing?	K2	Propose activity
T	Exactly right.	K1	Affirm

Table 5.7 Explaining evaluative function

T	How does the sentence start?	dK1	Focus wording
	S6?	K2	
S6	*It was found*?	K1	Identify wording
T	That's right.	A2	Affirm
Ss	[highlight text]	A1	
	Let's highlight that.		Direct marking
T	When we say *It was found,* it means they saw the results, as though they were there to be found. The results confirm that ampicillin inhibits *E. coli*, so they can't be argued with. This is important because it will be the control in the experiment, that other results will be measured against. If the experiment can repeat the same result, that will show the method was correct.	K1	Elaborate field

The goal of the final learning cycle in Table 5.7 is to explain the evaluative function of *it was found*, to contract the negotiability of the results, and its broader rhetorical function, to construe the research as confirmed.

Similar pedagogic strategies are repeated for each sentence and phase of the text. The class is guided to identify each wording, which is then elaborated. Patterns at the scale of sentences and phases are then discussed in culminative elaborations, as in Table 5.7. As similar patterns recur, they can be first discussed and named in elaborations, and then used to prepare and focus identifying tasks, reinforcing their recognition. For example, the sentence level pattern of launching followed by the research activity or results is repeated with variations through the text. Similarly, recurring patterns of expanding and contracting can first be discussed and named in elaborations, and then used to prepare and focus tasks. To this end, metalinguistic terms such as *launching, positioning, expanding* and *contracting* can be useful, along with instantial terms like *confirming* and *unconfirmed* research.

Discourse patterns under focus in detailed reading

For the linguistic description, we constructed a typology of discourse semantic resources that were instantiated in Alden's text. Linguistic descriptions such as this take a system-oriented perspective on language resources. Curriculum genres such as detailed reading have a different orientation to these resources, from the perspective of their instantiation in texts. In this perspective, the focus is on the instantial patterns in which language resources are coupled together to construct text. This approach reverses the traditional formal language teaching method that starts with features in systems that learners are then expected to instantiate in exercises. Instead, features are encountered as instances in context, and accumulated through repeated experience, as in natural language learning (Halliday, 1993; Painter, 1984, 1999). Genre pedagogy accelerates this instantial accumulation by preparing learners to recognize features in context and elaborating their recognition with a functional metalanguage.

Some of these recurrent instantial patterns in Alden's text may be discussed in detailed reading as follows. For example, the unconfirmed research is launched by expanding negotiability with *It is believed,* as well as counter-expectant *however,* to compare *herbs/spices* with *ampicillin.* The next sentence is launched with a similar pattern as the confirming research, *One study ... found,* but its negotiability is expanded with *could inhibit.* A taxonomy is implicitly constructed here, on the criteria of *antibacterial properties*, in which ampicillin is *certainly effective at inhibiting growth of E. coli,* while herbs and spices *could* do so. This implicit typology could be made explicit in elaborations, by naming it as 'E. coli inhibitors' or 'antibacterial agents'.

The negotiability of the unconfirmed research is further expanded by launching the *application* phase with the condition *If this is true.* This phase serves to justify the experiment in two ways. Firstly, it will test the prior research on herbs and spices, and secondly its potential application is very strongly valued with numbers of people who could avoid food poisoning and who currently die from it. These larger-scale rhetorical functions would again be explored in elaborations of learning cycles.

In the Introduction, discourse resources such as positioning are used primarily to expand negotiability. This serves to construe the field as a dialogue around the issue of *E. coli* poisoning and its solution, with researchers and their findings as voices that vary in authority. Highest authority is accorded to facts stated by the WHO, next is the research that found ampicillin was effective, and less authoritative is the research that found herbs and spices <u>could</u> inhibit *E. coli*. This expanding dialogue opens a space for the experiment to respond by testing the effectiveness of herbs and spices. In the detailed reading lesson, this pattern of engagement would emerge as each resource is identified and elaborated, culminating in an elaborating discussion of the whole pattern.

Turning to the Discussion stage, positioning is used to contract negotiability in the *findings* phase, *From the results gathered it is seen … It is seen in the results*. The results are construed here as authoritative, amplified by referencing the graphs and their values, as researchers were referenced in the Introduction. These contracting devices construe the results as confirming the hypothesis. Conversely, the *conclusion* phase is positioned by expanding *it <u>can be inferred</u>*. The reasoning interacts with contraction to construe the results as logically validating the prior research, *that certain spices and herbs <u>do have</u> an effect … therefore the spices and herbs used <u>were effective</u>*.

Making visible the intricacies of these instantial patterns in detailed reading supports students to recognize and deploy them. Few students can do so simply by encountering these language resources as systems. Reading with comprehension involves recognizing, not just the resources, but how they are deployed to achieve the rhetorical goals of a text. Detailed reading accelerates these reading skills for all students, by guiding their conscious recognition in actual texts.

Joint rewriting

Conscious recognition of instantial patterns also enables students to deploy the resources in their own writing. Rewriting is a supportive step towards autonomy in these writing skills, as it uses the language patterns of the reading text as a scaffold. It shows students how to appropriate the language resources of well-written texts into their writing, while reducing the semiotic labour of constructing a new text.

Rewriting typically begins jointly, with the teacher guiding the class, using the detailed reading text as the model. This joint practice affords further opportunities to identify and deploy delicate language features, such as tense and deixis choices that serve to distinguish general and specific fields. There is not the space here to illustrate the pedagogic activity of joint rewriting. Instead, it is illustrated with a possible writing product that re-instantiates the *findings* phase of Alden's Discussion.

In a biology curriculum unit, the passage from the model text used for detailed reading would be rewritten, following the same sentence patterns, but substituting the fields that the class has been investigating. For rewriting the *findings* paragraph, these fields include a hypothesis and results presented in graphs. Here we will illustrate rewriting with a completely different field, that is research on genre pedagogy. This will allow us to show how rewriting works, at the same time as concluding with an evaluation of the pedagogy.

In this substituted field, the hypothesis is that genre pedagogy can reduce the literacy achievement gap in schools. The results discussed are from a large-scale action research project, across school stages, in which students' writing was assessed before and after intervention (Rose & Martin, 2012, 2013). Figures 5.2 and 5.3 show average scores for low-, middle- and high-achieving student cohort in each school stage. Assessment criteria gave a total possible score of 40.

In the rewrite, this new field is substituted in similar instantial language patterns as the model passage in Alden's report, with some adjustments of the items instantiating appraisals and connexions.

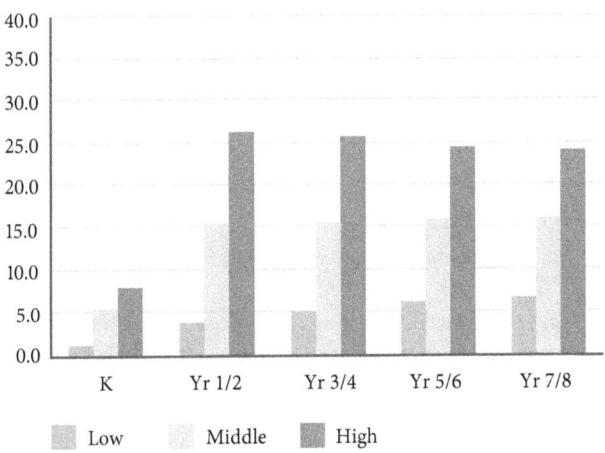

Figure 5.2 Pre-intervention scores.

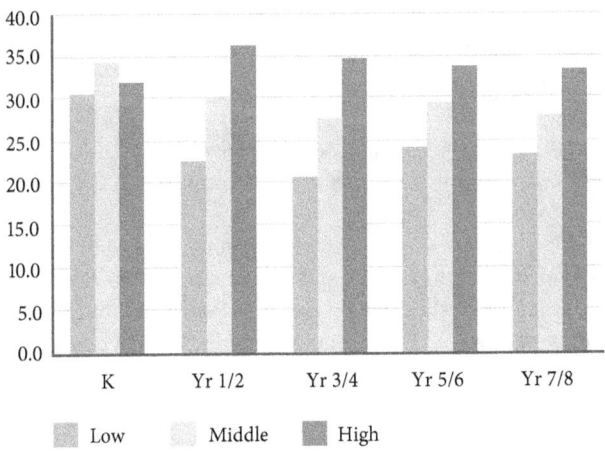

Figure 5.3 Post-intervention scores.

Detailed reading passage (findings phase in model text)

From the results gathered it is seen that the hypothesis that garlic is effective at inhibiting E.coli is supported because its Zone of Inhibition (ZoI) had a radius of 5.714mm (Graph.2) whilst the blank disc had a ZoI of 0mm (Graph.1). It is seen in the results (Graph.2) that garlic was the most effective (ZoI 5.714mm), cloves and cinnamon were second most effective (ZoI 2.25mm) and turmeric was the least effective (ZoI 0.25mm).

Rewrite (findings from new research field)

From the results presented above, it is evident that the hypothesis that genre pedagogy is effective at narrowing the literacy gap is supported, as pre-intervention scores showed a gap of 50% between low and high cohorts from Year 1 (Graph 1), whilst the gap in post-intervention writing scores is reduced to an average 25% in all school stages (Graph 2). It can be seen in the post-intervention data (Figure 5.3) that high achieving students improved above standard growth rates (~15%), middle band students improved faster (~25%), and lower achieving students had the fastest growth (~35%).

In the rewrite, much of the instantial language patterning is kept constant, while items instantiating the field, tenor and mode are varied. As flagged above, positioning is used in this phase to contract negotiability. Its instantiation in the model is adjusted in the rewrite, to practice manipulating degrees of contraction (italics below), as well as metadiscourse for relating this phase to the preceding results (underlined below).

> From the results gathered it is seen -> From the results <u>presented above</u>, *it is evident*
> It is seen in the results -> It *can be seen* in <u>the post-intervention data</u>

In addition, force of causality is graded down from *because* to *as*, 'showing' is used to relate the data to findings, *pre-intervention scores showed a gap*, and graduation is manipulated *improved faster ... had the fastest growth*. Furthermore, complex couplings of lexical relations and identification are also practiced in the rewrite, to compare pre- and post-intervention results.

> *pre-intervention scores showed a gap of 50% between low and high cohorts from Year 1*
> *the gap in post-intervention writing scores is reduced to an average 25% in all school stages*

In the joint rewriting lesson, a variety of such resources would be canvassed for each instance, from students and the teacher, and may be listed on the class board. Particular options would be chosen by the class for the joint rewrite, with the teacher's guidance, and other options may be used by students for their individual practice.

Given the diversity of these language resources, and the complexity of their instantial patternings, the advantages of repeated guided practice are evident. If detailed reading and rewriting are practiced each week of a curriculum unit, on various extracts from model texts, students accumulate valuable experience with relevant language resources to participate actively in the joint construction that culminates the unit, in preparation for their assessment task. The effectiveness of this practice, for all student groups, is evidenced in the writing results shown in Figure 5.3, and interpreted in the rewrite above (see also Rose & Martin, 2012, 2013).

Envoi

Along with the curriculum values exchanged in curriculum genres are values associated with pedagogic registers, including degrees of authority in curriculum knowledge, access to pedagogic modalities, inclusion and success in pedagogic relations and autonomy in pedagogic activities. The pedagogic research we have described in this chapter is deeply committed to these values, informed by Jim Martin's knowledge and practice, but also inspired by the principles he applies to his work in research and teaching. The research we have reported is part of the continuing project to democratize access for all students through genre-based pedagogies. This project is informed by Jim's towering authority in social semiotic fields, but his goal has always been to hand authority to learners, whether these are linguists, teacher educators, teachers or students in schools. His practice has always been designed to build autonomy for learners, to become successful practitioners in their chosen fields. In the process a community of practice has grown around him that includes scholars from many backgrounds across the world. For us it has been an ongoing pleasure and privilege to belong to that community.

Funding

This research was supported by the Australian Government through the Australian Research Council's *Linkage Projects* funding scheme (project LP160100263).

The views expressed herein are those of the authors and are not necessarily those of the Australian Government or Australian Research Council.

Notes

1. Other discourse semantic elements, including qualities and occurrences, are set aside in this paper. For the description of these meanings, see Hao (2015, 2020), cf. Martin (1992) and Halliday and Matthiessen (1999).
2. Following Hao (2015, 2020), the term 'connexion' is used to substitute Martin's (1992) use of 'conjunction' in referring to discourse semantic relations between figures. This terminology separates the discourse semantic choices from the 'conjunctions' in lexicogrammar discussed in Halliday and Matthiessen (2014).
3. Learning cycles are structures of pedagogic activity at the level of register. They are enacted in discourse semantics by speakers' roles in exchanges (Martin, 1992, 2000; Martin & Rose, 2007; Rose & Martin, 2012). Exchange roles here include primary knower (K1), delayed primary knower (dK1), secondary knower (K2), primary actor

(A1) and secondary actor (A2). As K1, the teacher presents knowledge and evaluates learners, and focuses the task as dK1. Learner roles are K2 as they are followed by K1 evaluations. A2 roles solicit actions, A1 roles perform them (Rose, 2018).

4   Students' [hands up] gesture is an A2 role as it solicits permission, which the teacher provides as A1.

References

Bernstein, B. (2000). *Pedagogy, Symbolic Control and Identity: Theory, Research, Critique*. Oxford: Rowman and Littlefield.

Christie, F. (2002). *Classroom Discourse Analysis*. London: Continuum.

Christie, F., & Cléirigh, C. (2008). On the importance of 'showing'. In C. Wu, C. M. I. M. Matthiessen & M. Herke (Eds.), *Conference Proceedings of the International Systemic Functional Linguistics Congress on Voices around the World* (pp. 13–18). Macquarie University: ISFC Organizing Committee.

Christie, F., & Martin, J. R. (Eds.) (1997). *Genre and Institutions: Social Processes in the Workplace and School*. London: Cassell.

Christie, F., & Martin, J. R. (Eds.) (2007). *Language, Knowledge and Pedagogy: Functional Linguistic and Sociological Perspectives*. London: Continuum.

Doran Y. J., & Martin, J. R. (forthcoming). Field relations: Understanding scientific explanations. In K. Maton, J. R. Martin, & Y. J. Doran (Eds.), *Studying Science: Language, Knowledge and Pedagogy*. London: Routledge.

Dreyfus, S., Humphrey, S., Mahboob, A., & Martin, J. R. (2016). *Genre Pedagogy in Higher Education: The SLATE Project*. Houndmills, Basingstoke, Hampshire, UK: Palgrave Macmillan UK.

Halliday, M. A. K. (1993). Towards a language-based theory of learning. *Linguistics and Education*, 5(2), 93–116.

Halliday, M. A. K. (1998). Things and relations: Regrammaticising experience as technical knowledge. In J. R. Martin & R. Veel (Eds.), *Reading Science: Critical and Functional Perspectives on Discourses of Science* (pp. 185–235). London: Routledge.

Halliday, M. A. K., & Matthiessen, C. M. I. M. (1999). *Construing Experience through Language: A Language-Based Approach to Cognition*. London: Cassell.

Halliday, M. A. K., & Matthiessen, C. M. I. M. (2014). *An Introduction to Functional Grammar, 4th Edition*. London: Routledge.

Hao, J. (2015). *Construing Biology: An Ideational Perspective*. Unpublished PhD thesis. The University of Sydney.

Hao, J. (2017). The discourse semantic meanings of 'showing' in scientific texts. in P. Chappell & J. S. Knox (Eds.), *Transforming Contexts: Papers from the 44th International Systemic Functional Congress* (pp. 102–8). Wollongong: The Organising Committee of the 44th International Systemic Functional Congress.

Hao, J. (2020). *Analysing Scientific Discourse from a Systemic Functional Linguistic Perspective: A Framework for Exploring Knowledge Building in Biology*. New York and London: Routledge.

Hao, J., & Humphrey, S. (2012a). The role of 'coupling' in biological experimental reports. *Linguistics and the Human Sciences*, 5(2), 169–94.

Hao, J., & Humphrey, S. (2012b). Burnishing and tarnishing in academic literacy. In J. S. Knox (Ed.), *To Boldly Proceed: Papers from the 39th International Systemic*

Functional Congress (pp. 15–20). Sydney: The Organising Committee of the 39th International Systemic Functional Congress.

Hao, J., & Humphrey, S. L. (2019). Reading nominalizations in senior science. *Journal of English for Academic Purposes*, 42, 100793.

Hattie, J. A. C. (2009). *Visible Learning: A Synthesis of Over 800 Meta-Analyses Relating to Achievement*. London: Routledge.

Hood, S. (2010). *Appraising Research: Evaluation in Academic Writing*. New York: Palgrave Macmillan.

Humphrey, S. (1996). *Exploring Literacy in School Geography*. Sydney: Metropolitan East Disadvantaged School Program.

Humphrey, S. (2016). *Academic Literacies in the Middle Years*. New York: Routledge.

Humphrey, S., & Hao, J. (2013). Deconstructing written genres in undergraduate biology. *Linguistics and Human Sciences*. [Special Edition of the SLATE project], 7, 29–53. Equinox.

Hyon, S. (1996). Genre in Three Traditions: Implications for ESL. *TESOL Quarterly*, 30(4), 693–722. doi: 10.2307/3587930.

Martin, J. R. (1992). *English Text: System and Structure*. Amsterdam: Benjamins.

Martin, J. R. (2000). Grammar meets genre: Reflections on the 'Sydney School'. *Arts: The Journal of the Sydney University Arts Association*, 22, 47–95.

Martin, J. R. (2008). Incongruent and proud: de-vilifying 'nominalization'. *Discourse & Society*, 19(6), 801–10.

Martin, J. R., & Rose, D. (2005). Designing literacy pedagogy: Scaffolding asymmetries. In R. Hasan, C. M. I. M. Matthiessen, & J. Webster (Eds.), *Continuing Discourse on Language* (pp. 251–80). London: Equinox.

Martin, J. R., & Rose, D. (2007). *Working with Discourse: Meaning beyond the Clause* (1st ed.). London: Continuum.

Martin, J. R., & Rose, D. (2008). *Genre Relations: Mapping Culture*. London: Equinox.

Martin, J. R., & Veel, R. (Eds.) (1998). *Reading Science: Critical and Functional Perspectives on Discourses of Science*. London: Routledge.

Martin, J. R., & White, P. R. R. (2005). *The Language of Evaluation: Appraisal in English*. London: Palgrave.

New South Wales Education Standards Authority (NESA) (2018). *Learning through Reading and Writing*. Sydney: NSW Education & Standards Authority. http://educationstandards.nsw.edu.au/wps/portal/nesa/k-10/learning-areas/english-year-10/learning-through-reading-and-writing/stage-1-preparing-for-reading. Last accessed 15 April 2020.

Painter, C. (1984). *Into the Mother Tongue: A Case Study in Early Language Development*. London: Frances Pinter.

Painter, C. (1999). *Learning through Language in Early Childhood*. London: Cassell.

Painter, C., Martin, J. R., & Unsworth, L. (2013). *Reading visual narratives: Image analyses of children's picture books*. London: Equinox.

Rose, D. (2008). Writing as linguistic mastery: The development of genre-based literacy pedagogy. In R. Beard, D. Myhill, J. Riley & M. Nystrand (Eds.), *Handbook of Writing Development* (pp. 151–66). London: Sage.

Rose, D. (2015). New developments in genre-based literacy pedagogy. In C. A. MacArthur, S. Graham & J. Fitzgerald (Eds.), *Handbook of Writing Research, 2nd Edition* (pp. 227–42). New York: Guildford.

Rose, D. (2016). Genre, knowledge and pedagogy in the 'Sydney School'. In N. Artemeva & A Freedman (Eds.), *Genre Studies around the Globe: Beyond the Three Traditions* (pp. 299–338). Ottawa: Inkwell.

Rose, D. (2018). Pedagogic Register Analysis: Mapping choices in teaching and learning. *Functional Linguistics*, 5(1), 1–33. Springer Open Access.

Rose, D. (2020). Building a pedagogic metalanguage I: Curriculum genres and Building a pedagogic metalanguage II: knowledge genres II. In J. R. Martin, K. Maton & Y. J. Doran (Eds.), *Accessing Academic Discourse: Systemic Functional Linguistics and Legitimation Code Theory* (pp. 236–302). London: Taylor & Francis.

Rose, D., & Martin, J. R. (2012). *Learning to Write, Reading to Learn: Genre, Knowledge and Pedagogy in the Sydney School*. London: Equinox.

Rose, D., & Martin, J. R. (2013). Intervening in contexts of schooling. In J. Flowerdew (Ed.), *Discourse In Context: Contemporary Applied Linguistics Volume 3* (pp. 447–75). London: Continuum.

Swales, J. (1990). *Genre Analysis: English in Academic and Research Settings*. Cambridge: Cambridge University Press.

Unsworth, L., Tytler, R., O'Halloran, K., Humphrey, S., & Love, K. (2016). *Multiliteracies for Addressing Disadvantage in Senior School Science*. Australian Research Council Linkages Grant 2016–2018. LP160100263.

Victorian Curriculum and Assessment Authority [VCAA] (2017). VCE Study Designs Advice for Teachers – Biology. Retrieved 9 August 2019, from www.vcaa.vic.edu.au

Zappavigna, M., & Martin, J. R. (2018). *Discourse and Diversionary Justice: An Analysis of Youth Justice Conferencing*. London: Palgrave.

6

Familiarity for the unfamiliar: Thailand, kinship, culture and language

John S. Knox
Macquarie University

Introduction

This chapter takes one small part of language used in Thailand – kinship terms for the first and second generations above the speaker (i.e. the speaker's parents' generation or G+1, and grandparents' generation or G+2). It investigates the kinship terms in Thai as typically spoken in Thai families, the kinship terms in Teochew as widely spoken in Chinese-Thai families, and compares these with the kinship terms in English as widely spoken in Australia. English is widely used in Thailand, but the point of comparing the Thai and Teochew terms with those used in Australian English is to give an 'external' point of reference in this English-language paper, and to provide a perspective on learning an additional language. This chapter does not seek to identify English-language categories in the other languages (see Martin, 1983).

The approach taken in this chapter takes inspiration from the scholarship of Jim Martin in several ways. First, the chapter 'starts systemic', meaning that it approaches kinship terms from a systemic perspective, which is unique in the literature on kinship terms (see discussion below). Secondly, it 'starts high' in stratal terms. That is, kinship terms are taken as indexical of tenor (Martin, 2001), and the systemic mapping of one small area of tenor relations in Thailand provides a point of departure for further studies on interpersonal meaning as enacted in discourse in Thailand, including work on individuation (e.g. Martin, 2010). Thirdly, it builds on the work of Martin (e.g. 1992) and Poynton (e.g. 1989) on power,[1] work which requires further exploration in SFL scholarship (Martin & White, 2005, pp. 29–30). Finally, it draws on Martin's (e.g. 2010) notion of commitment to explain the phylogenetic emergence of differences in meaning potential across languages.

Thailand, Thai and Teochew

There are more than seventy languages spoken in Thailand (Premsrirat, 2007). At the top of the language hierarchy, Standard Thai is spoken in Bangkok and is the language of government, the media and education throughout the nation (Premsrirat, 2007). On the second level of the hierarchy, other major languages/dialects are Northern Thai, Northeastern Thai, Southern Thai and Central Thai. Premsrirat identifies two 'town languages' on the third level of the hierarchy, which are spoken in urban areas of Thailand: Chinese and Vietnamese (2007, p. 78). In this classification, Teochew would be included under, or as, 'Chinese'. This is because Chinese immigrants arrived in Thailand for hundreds of years prior to the 1930s, and as a result most large Thai cities have relatively large populations of Teochew speakers (Draper, 2019, p. 230, citing Smalley, 1994). Chinese-Thai families with Teochew heritage increasingly speak Thai, but Teochew kinship terms are still widely used even where Teochew is not commonly used (Morita, 2007a, p. 51).

The objects of study in this chapter are Thai kinship terms, and Teochew kinship terms *as widely used in Thailand*. These are likely to differ from Teochew kinship terms used in other cultural contexts. Therefore, throughout the chapter, implications for English-L1 learners of Thai and Thai-L1 learners of English are considered, since Teochew kinship terms have become part of the linguistic environment of Thailand in various contexts.

My own interest in Thai and Teochew kinship terms comes from my experience in Thailand, learning and using both sets of terms in negotiating my own sets of relations. Kinship terms are crucial to understanding, establishing and maintaining successful relations in Thailand, where an elaborate and complex network of terms of address (including kinship terms, pronouns and title nouns) play a central role in the ongoing negotiation of interpersonal relations in formal and informal spoken discourse.

Kinship and interpersonal meaning

For the purpose of this chapter, studies of kinship terms appear to be classifiable into two extremely broad groups. One is studies that look for ways to classify or categorize kinship terms across languages. Such studies take a wide variety of disciplinary and methodological approaches (e.g. Bennardo, 2016; Kemp & Regier, 2012; Kronenfeld, 2006; Murdock, 1968; Read, 2013; Shapiro, 2009). A study that falls into this group is Benedict's (1943) account of kinship terms in proto-Thai, which aims to identify commonalities across 'Thai languages' and to show that 'the basic affinities of Thai are with Indonesian rather than with Sino-Tibetan' (p. 168). The terms he identifies are consistent with those of Prasithrathsint (2001) and Rusmeecharoen (2017) as discussed below.

The second broad group identified here includes studies that aim to describe kinship terms in a specific language. Of these, a number are of direct relevance to this chapter. In addition to Benedict (1943 – as mentioned above), Prasithrathsint (2001) aims to provide a methodologically documented, componential account of Thai kinship terms. Rusmeecharoen (2017) explores pronominal reference in Thai, and accounts for kinship terms because they are widely used as terms of address and for reference in

Thai (cf. Martin, 1992, pp. 109–11). Both Prasithrathsint (2001) and Rusmeecharoen (2017) identify five points of contrast in Thai kinship terms: generation, lineality, age, sex and parental side.

For Teochew kinship terms, there is some non-peer-reviewed information online, but I was unable to locate any peer-reviewed studies of Teochew kinship terms.[2] There are, however, two peer-reviewed studies of Hokkien kinship terms, and these terms are extremely similar to Teochew kinship terms as used in Thailand, at least for the subset of terms examined in this chapter. Ngo (2017) looks specifically at the kinship terms of the first- and second-generation Hokkien community in Surabaya, Indonesia. As is done in this chapter (see discussion below), the terms for maternal and paternal relatives at G+1 are presented separately. There is some difference between prefixes (when used) between the Hokkien terms identified by Ngo and the Teochew terms identified in this paper, but for G+1 and G+2 the terms are overall remarkably consistent. These terms are also consistent with those identified in Weller's (1981) research, which was conducted in Northern Taiwan and was the most 'complete list of Hokkien kinship terms [to be] published in English' at the time (p. 17).

Studies of kinship terms commonly provide lists of terms, and some cases identify the 'components', or oppositions of the different terms. However, they do not draw on the architecture of a stratified theory of language and context (e.g. Martin, 1992). Approaching kinship terms from an SFL perspective, the identification of oppositions (systems) and the choices in such systems necessitates following the convention of naming SYSTEMS, **choices** and *realisations* in SFL scholarship. Therefore, the system networks require an explicit account of what is at stake (in the naming of the system), what options are available (in the naming of the choices) and how these paradigmatic meanings are realized linguistically (in the identification of the realizations). These requirements in turn require specification of the relations between the terms, including dependency relations at different levels of delicacy within a system, and co-occurrence in simultaneous systems. Furthermore, the system networks provide a means of comparison of the meaning potential in the three languages.

This chapter, then, contributes to the existing research on kinship terms by providing a systemic perspective on English, Thai and Teochew G+1 and G+2 kinship terms, and relating this to a theory of tenor, more particularly power.

> For power, [Poynton] considers 'reciprocity' of choice to be the critical variable. Thus, social subjects of equal status construe equality by having access to and taking up the same kinds of choices, whereas subjects of unequal status take up choices of different kinds. Terms of address are one obvious exemplar in this area. (Martin & White, 2005, p. 30)

This chapter also contributes to the body of SFL scholarship on languages spoken in Thailand (e.g. Jitpranee, 2018; Knox & Patpong, 2008; Knox et al., 2010; Patpong, 2006a, 2006b, 2009, 2013, 2016; Vail, 2006; Wijiyewardene, 2012, 2017).

From a systemic perspective, two papers discuss kinship terms as part of a broader consideration of interpersonal meaning. In the first, Shin (2018) looks at the interpersonal resources in the lexicogrammar of Korean. Of most relevance to this chapter is his system of VOCATION, and its interaction with the systems of ADDRESSEE DEFERENCE and POLITENESS. The interplay between these systems illustrates the complexity of systems underlying the choices instantiated in interaction on the lexicogrammatical stratum, and is an illustration of how Hasan's (2015) 'grammarian's dream' of 'lexis as most delicate grammar' could be applied to kinship terms.

In the second paper, Rose (2018) examines the discursive negotiation of kinship relations among Pitjanjara speakers. While kinship terms are described and explained, Rose's aim is not to systematize the lexis. He points out that we learn kinship not only through the lexis of kinship terms, but through the 'experience of social interactions' (p. 131) which are social and discursive, drawing on linguistic systems at the strata of phonology, lexicogrammar and discourse-semantics (cf. Poynton, 1989). Nonetheless, Rose (2018, p. 130) explains that kinship terms

> function interpersonally as vocatives, but they can also function textually to identify people, typically with possessive deixis ('my brother', 'Cecily's son'). In this respect kin terms function similarly to personal names, but identify people by relationship rather than uniquely. ... These principles ideationalise kin relations, reconstructing tenor relations as roles of participants.

While not a study of kinship terms, Poynton's (1989) brief consideration of personal titles in English is also relevant to the current study (pp. 41–3). For the purposes of the current chapter, Poynton illustrates the 'direct' relation between the lexis of personal titles (and related vocatives and kinship terms) on the one hand, and tenor relations in specific cultural contexts on the other:

> From a purely grammatical perspective, no clause is ungrammatical simply because it does not contain a vocative. In practice, however, many utterances are certainly regarded as impolite (= socially unacceptable) or even insubordinate (= dangerously unacceptable) if they contain no vocative. (Poynton, 1990, p. 245)

This is because, as Martin (2001, p. 160) points out: 'One of the clearest indexical realisations of tenor is found in the choice of vocatives or address terms.' Whether or not they are used as terms of address (and many of the terms discussed in this chapter are widely used thus), kinship terms represent lexis that is indexical of tenor relations and therefore provide a delimitable and identifiable 'access point' for a systemic study of tenor, which can in turn be applied to the teaching and learning of a second language and culture.

Turning then to tenor systems, in her TENOR network, Poynton (1989) has two simultaneous systems under POWER (directly comparable to Hasan's STATUS) at initial delicacy, the first of which has choices of **equal** or **unequal**, and the second of which has choices of **force**, **authority**, **status** or **expertise**. The relevant choices for the kinship terms studied in this chapter would be **unequal** and **authority**, the latter of which 'is a function of socially-legitimated inherently unequal role relationships such as parent-child, teacher-child, employer-employee, or ruler-ruled' (Poynton, 1989, pp. 76–7; see Figure 6.1).

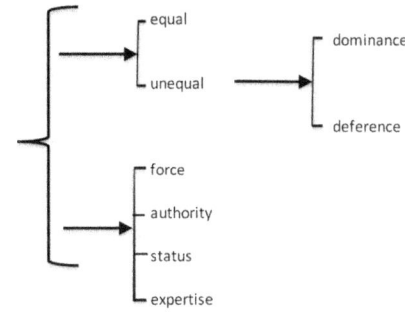

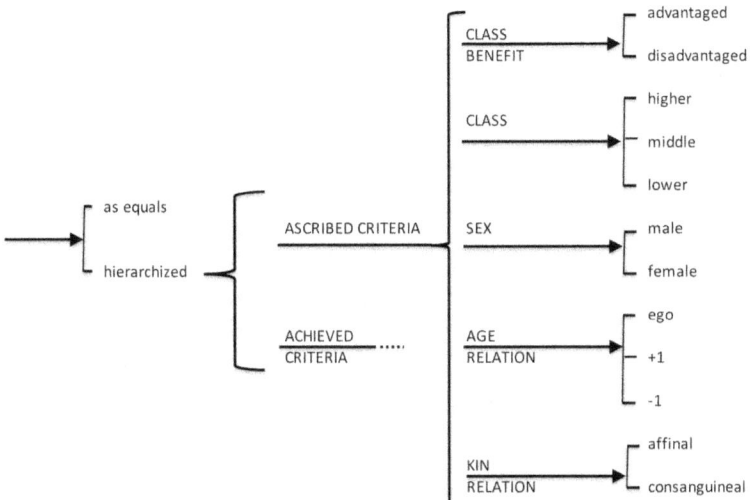

Figure 6.1 Subsystems of tenor: Detail of Poynton's (1989) subsystem of power (top) and detail of Hasan's (2014) subsystem of status (bottom).

In comparison, Hasan's (2014, p. 33) tenor network has, under status (directly comparable to Poynton's POWER), a more delicate option of **as equals** or **hierarchized**, with a subsystem of ASCRIBED CRITERIA (directly comparable to Poynton's **authority**), itself with simultaneous subsystems including SEX (**male, female**), AGE RELATION (**ego, +1, -1**) and KIN RELATION (**affinal** or marriage, **consanguineal** or blood) among others (Figure 6.1).

As will be seen below, the distinctions identified in this chapter are relatively consistent with these systems. The delicate choices show the differences in tenor relations in different cultural groups, and the way that different languages provide different options for speakers 'as we move from the community as whole, through master identities (generation, gender, class, ethnicity, dis/ability) and sub-cultures to the personas that compose individual members', on what Martin calls the individuation hierarchy (Martin, 2010, p. 24).

The perspective taken in this chapter shows that lexis for kinship terms can vary between languages (as widely acknowledged and to be expected), but also that the systems at play, and how they operate, can vary widely within languages from one generation to another, and even from one gender to another in the same generation. This means that, consistent with SF theory, systemic choices at the stratum of lexicogrammar (e.g. Hasan, 2014; Shin, 2018) are made in the context of choices at the stratum of context of situation such as those proposed below. However, this does not discount the observations made by both Poynton (1989) and Rose (2018), that for titles, kinship terms and terms of address, all metafunctions and all strata are implicated in language use.

Methodology

Kinship terms were sourced as follows. For English, the author's experience as a speaker of English was used. For both Thai and Teochew, three speakers of Thai were consulted as informants: (1) a Thai who grew up using basic Teochew in the family home and still uses Teochew kinship terms with family; (2) a Thai who speaks Teochew and Mandarin, grew up using Teochew in the family home and still uses Teochew with family; and (3) a Thai who is a teacher of Mandarin, speaks Teochew and Mandarin, grew up using Teochew in the family home and still uses Teochew with family.

In addition, as mentioned earlier, a number of published sources were consulted for Thai (Benedict, 1943; Prasithrathsint, 2001; Rusmeecharoen, 2017), and a number of published sources on Hokkien were compared (Ngo, 2017; Weller, 1981), since peer-reviewed literature on Teochew kinship terms is extremely limited and largely inaccessible, and Teochew and Hokkien appear to be extremely similar in the relevant kinship terms.

Finally, the terms were checked by a Thai scholar of translation who has Teochew-speaking kin.

Thai terms are presented first in Thai, then romanized following the Current Royal Institute Romanization System (Kanchanawan, 2006, p. 838).[3] Teochew terms are likewise presented first in Thai – since the object of study is Teochew kinship terms *as used in Thailand* as already noted – and are then romanized.

Kinship terms in three languages

The subsections that follow set out kinship terms in English, Thai and Teochew as widely used in Thailand. These are delimited to:

- Direct G+2 (i.e. direct line, and two generations above ego,[4] or grandparents)
- Direct G+1 (i.e. direct line, and one generation above ego, or parents)
- Indirect G+1 (i.e. indirect line, and one generation above ego, or siblings of parents and their spouses, or aunts and uncles).

The reasons for these particular delimitations are three. Firstly, the number of kinship terms in Thai and Teochew (see Benedict, 1943; Weller, 1981) is considerable, and addressing them all systemically is beyond the scope of a single chapter. Secondly, seniority is an important interpersonal value in Thailand, often marked discursively by the requirement to use kinship terms or title nouns as terms of address with people senior to ego (e.g. พี่ [*pi*] or 'elder'; น้า [*na*] or 'maternal aunt/uncle') but not with people junior to ego (e.g. น้อง [*nong*] or 'junior'; หลานสาว [*lan sao*] or 'niece'). So senior kinship terms are in common use as terms of address in everyday spoken discourse, whereas the junior kinship terms are less commonly (in most cases rarely or never) used as terms of address. Thirdly, the differences between the terms for direct G+2 (grandparents) and direct G+1 (parents) kinship terms in the three languages are relatively straightforward, but this provides an accessible point of intercultural comparison, and therefore a 'way in' to the abstract notion of paradigmatic meaning, and the complexity of kinship terms and the relations they construe for language teachers and learners.

G+2 Direct

Table 6.1 compares the terms across the three languages for direct G+2 kinship terms (i.e. for grandparents). The tables in this chapter adapt the format used by Boonsawasd (2013), and Table 6.1 shows that English has two terms, whereas Thai and Teochew have four terms.

Beginning with English, as illustrated in Table 6.1, at two generations above ego, direct kinship terms (i.e. for grandparents) are distinguished by gender only. This gives a basic system with two choices (Figure 6.2).

In contrast, both Thai and Teochew have distinctions based on gender, and on side (whether the grandparent is on ego's maternal or paternal side of the family), giving system networks as shown in Figure 6.3.

As illustrated in Figure 6.3, the two systems are almost identical. However, the choices in the system of SIDE are not identical. Both systems distinguish between maternal and paternal, but in Teochew there is a meaning which can be translated

Table 6.1 Kinship terms in three languages: second generation above ego, direct (G+2).

Relation to ego	English	Thai	Teochew
Mother's mother (MM)	Grandmother	ยาย Yai	อั๋วม่า ua ma
Mother's father (MF)	Grandfather	ตา ta	อั๋วกง ua kong
Father's mother (FM)	Grandmother	ย่า ya	ไหล่ม่า lai ma
Father's father (FF)	Grandfather	ปู่ pu	ไหล่กง lai kong

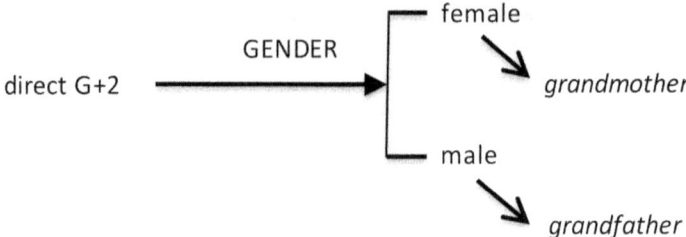

Figure 6.2 System English G+2.

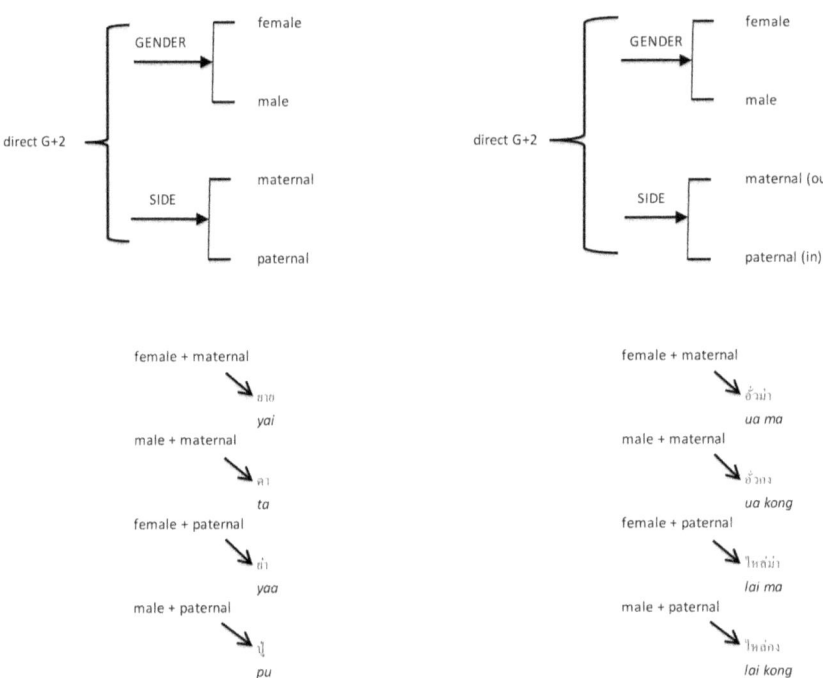

Figure 6.3 Systems for Thai G+2 (left) and Teochew G+2 (right).

as 'out' or 'outside' for maternal, and as 'in' or 'inside' for paternal. This out-and-in distinction becomes more evident when the indirect G+1 terms are considered (see following subsection), but as the terms suggest, the paternal (or 'in') side of the family is more highly valued than the maternal (or 'out') side.

The implication of the three systems is that children who grow up in families using Thai and Teochew kinship terms also grow up with an inherent knowledge of whether they are related to their respective grandparents on their maternal or paternal side of the family. In contrast, in cultures where English has emerged, the distinction between parental and maternal grandparents has not emerged as significant enough to be lexicalized. It is possible to make this distinction by using the Classifiers *paternal* and *maternal*, but in everyday spoken Australian English these Classifiers are not commonly used. More common is that English terms of address are personalized (e.g. *grandma, nana, grandad, pa*). But unlike Thai and Teochew, Australian English does not distinguish grandparents' family side in G+2 direct kinship terms.

This approach shows systemic consistencies between Thai and Teochew, and differences with English. With this degree of complexity, G+2 terms provide a good starting point for understanding some of the potential systems in kinship terms (namely GENDER and SIDE) and provide an initial point of comparison for English-speaking learners of Thai and/or Thai-speaking learners of English. Not only do the systemic choices become apparent, but the respective valeurs (e.g. the difference between **paternal/maternal** and **in/out**, whether these are in the L1 or L2) become potential resources for teaching and learning language and culture.

G+1 Direct

Table 6.2 compares the terms across the three languages for direct G+1 kinship terms (i.e. for parents). The basic distinction between 'mother' and 'father' is consistent across the three languages. In addition to these traditional family roles, terms for carers/guardians who are not the biological parents of ego are important to consider as family structures evolve internationally, and particularly for this chapter, in Thailand and Australia in the twenty-first century (OECD, 2011, pp. 23–30; Peek et al., 2015).

Although historical figures are difficult to discern, step families and blended families have become more common in Australia since the mid-twentieth century (Forster-Jones, 2007; see also de Vaus, 2004; Hayes et al., 2010).[5] Figures on step and blended families in Thailand are not available or difficult to locate, but divorce and remarriage have been common in Thailand (Limanonda, 1995, p. 75), and ongoing change in social and family practices and structures could lead to the use of the terms for step- and blended-family parents/carers in Thai becoming more common (cf. Yoddumnern, 1992). The *use* of such terms is likely to be different to the use of traditional terms across all three languages. For example, in Australian English, the use of *step mum as a term of address would be highly marked, and step mothers are far more likely to be addressed by first name, or as *mum*, depending on a range of factors. Similarly, in Thai, the terms แม่เลี้ยง [*mae liang*] and พ่อเลี้ยง [*pho liang*] are extremely unlikely to be used as terms of address, with G+1 indirect terms (see below), or simply แม่ [*mae*] or พ่อ [*pho*] likely to be used depending on a range of factors. Also in Teochew in Thailand, the term เอ่าบ๊อ [*ao bo*] or 'step mother' is extremely unlikely to be used as a term of address, with อาอี๊ [*a i*] or 'maternal aunty' being a much more likely choice. Furthermore, the term เอ่าแป๋ [*ao pae*] is rarely even used since it is uncommon for women in this community to re-marry (cf. Mak & Chan, 1995; Morita, 2007b).

Regardless of terms of address, the dimension of 'birth/marriage' in direct G+1 kinship terms is of much greater relevance in the twenty-first century than in the twentieth. These terms instantiate modern tenor relations, and approaching them systemically contributes to mapping the contemporary social and linguistic terrain, and to opening up such social and familial changes, and their interaction with culture and language, for language teachers and learners (cf. Poynton, 1989, pp. 41–3). Terms of address – and the variations in their consistency with kinship terminology – are an additional resource for language teachers to draw on in teaching language and culture.

Table 6.2 shows the direct G+1 kinship terms in English, Thai and Teochew.

As with direct G+2 kinship terms, the systemic oppositions in direct G+1 kinship terms (i.e. parental terms) across Thai and Teochew are consistent with one another. These same oppositions also apply to English. There is a basic distinction for GENDER, and another one for BLOOD (i.e. whether ego's parent is related to ego by blood, or by marriage). The system network for these terms is shown in Figure 6.4 and provides a potential starting point for language teaching tasks around linguistic and cultural similarities and differences between speakers of the three languages for learners of English and Thai.

Having dealt with the relatively straightforward systems for direct G+2 and direct G+1 relations, we now turn to the more complex systems for indirect G+1 relations.

Table 6.2 First generation above ego (G+1), direct.

Relation to ego	English	Thai	Teochew
Mother (M)	Mother	แม่ mae	ม่าม้า mama
Mother's husband – not ego's father (MH)	Step father	พ่อเลี้ยง pho liang	เอ่าแป๋ ao pae
Father (F)	Father	พ่อ pho	ป่าป๊า papa
Father's wife (FW) – not ego's mother	Step mother	แม่เลี้ยง mae liang	เอ่าบ๊อ ao bo

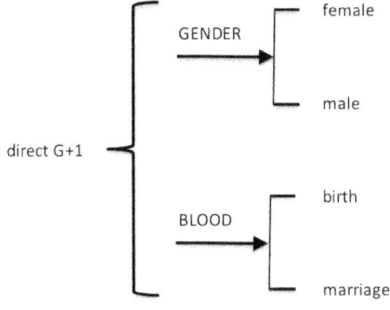
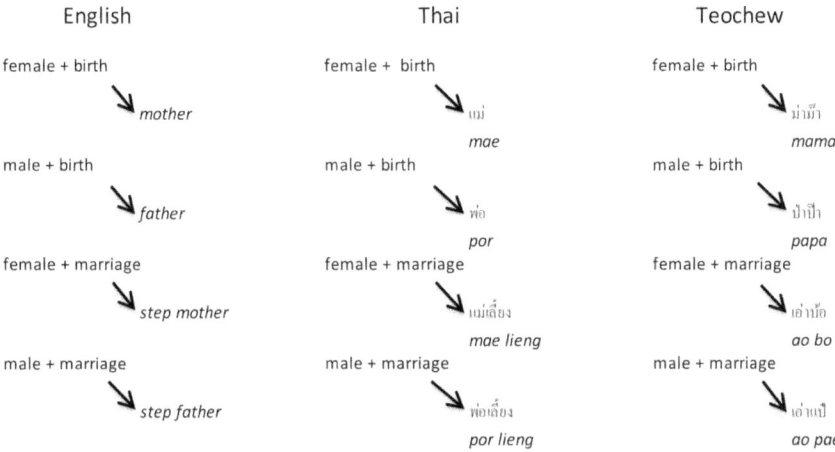

Figure 6.4 Direct G+1 kinship terms across the three languages.

G+1 Indirect

Indirect kinship terms at G+1 show much greater difference across the three languages than the G+2 direct or G+1 direct terms already considered. The terms in the three languages are listed in Table 6.3.

Beginning with English indirect G+1 kinship terms, the only distinction made is gender (Figure 6.5). This construes a relatively homogeneous set of relations between children and the indirect (i.e. non-parental) generation above ego. The wife of the eldest brother of your father is your aunt. Your mother's younger sister is your aunt. Children raised in families using English kinship terms can and often do grow up not knowing whether ego's aunts and uncles are related to ego by birth or by marriage; not knowing whether they are related on ego's maternal or paternal side; not knowing their seniority to ego's parents.

Table 6.3 First generation above ego (G+1), indirect.

Relation to ego	English	Thai	Teochew
Mother's elder sister (M+Z)	Aunt	ป้า pa	อาอี้ a i
Mother's elder sister's husband (M+ZH)	Uncle	ลุง lung	อาเตี่ย a tia
Mother's younger sister (M-Z)	Aunt	น้า na	อาอี้ a i
Mother's younger sister's husband (M-ZH)	Uncle	น้า na	อาเตี่ย a tia
Mother's elder brother (M+B)	Uncle	ลุง lung	อากู๋ a ku
Mother's elder brother's wife (M+BW)	Aunt	ป้า pa	อากิ้ม a kim
Mother's younger brother (M-B)	Uncle	น้า na	อากู๋ a ku
Mother's younger brother's wife (M-BW)	Aunt	น้า na	อากิ้ม a kim
Father's elder sister (F+Z)	Aunt	ป้า pa	อาโกว a ko
Father's elder sister's husband (F+ZH)	Uncle	ลุง lung	อาเตี่ย a tia
Father's younger sister (F-Z)	Aunt	อา a	อาโกว a ko
Father's younger sister's husband (F-ZH)	Uncle	อา a	อาเตี่ย a tia
Father's elder brother (M+B)	Uncle	ลุง lung	อาแปะ a pae
Father's elder brother's wife (M+BW)	Aunt	ป้า pa	อาอึ้ม a uem
Father's younger brother (M-B)	Uncle	อา a	อาเจ็ก a chek
Father's younger brother's wife (M-BW)	Aunt	อา a	อาซิ่ม a sim

The implication is that, on a phylogenetic timescale, it has been relatively unimportant in cultures where English is spoken to signify marriage versus blood relations, family side or seniority with indirect G+1 kinship terms. It may be the case that in some Englishes, these kinship terms are modified (e.g. *first aunty*, *birth uncle*) and/or that culturally significant modifications are emerging or will emerge (see Fang, 2019; cf. Schmied, 2006, p. 196; Sharifian, 2006, p. 15; Völkel, 2016). Thus, while Classifiers can be used, in Standard Australian English, such distinctions are not lexicalized and therefore are neither linguistically nor culturally signified unless families make an explicit effort to do so by using Classifiers.

In Thai, the primary distinction is SENIORITY (Figure 6.6). This means that children raised in families using Thai kinship terms grow up knowing whether ego's indirect G+1 are senior or junior to ego's parents. As in English, marriage relations are not distinguished, so those same children can grow up not knowing whether ego's 'aunts' and 'uncles' are related to ego by birth or by marriage.

The question of gender is secondary to seniority in Thai indirect G+1 kinship terms. For parents' older siblings, terms are distinguished by gender. Thus, ป้า [*pa*] can be translated into English as something like 'senior aunty', and ลุง [*lung*] as something like 'senior uncle'. However, for parents' younger siblings, kinship terms do not mark for gender. Rather, they distinguish whether the relation is on the mother's or father's side. So น้า [*na*] can be translated into English as something like 'junior aunty or uncle on my mother's side', and อา [*a*] as something like 'junior aunty or uncle on my father's side'.

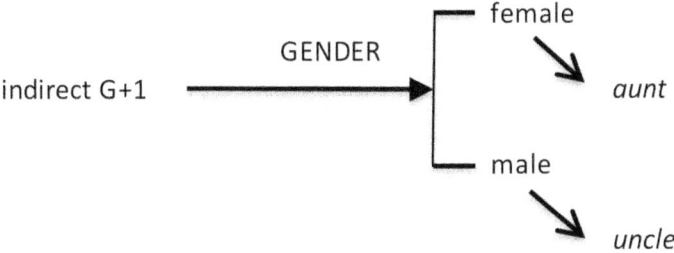

Figure 6.5 System network of English indirect G+1 kinship terms.

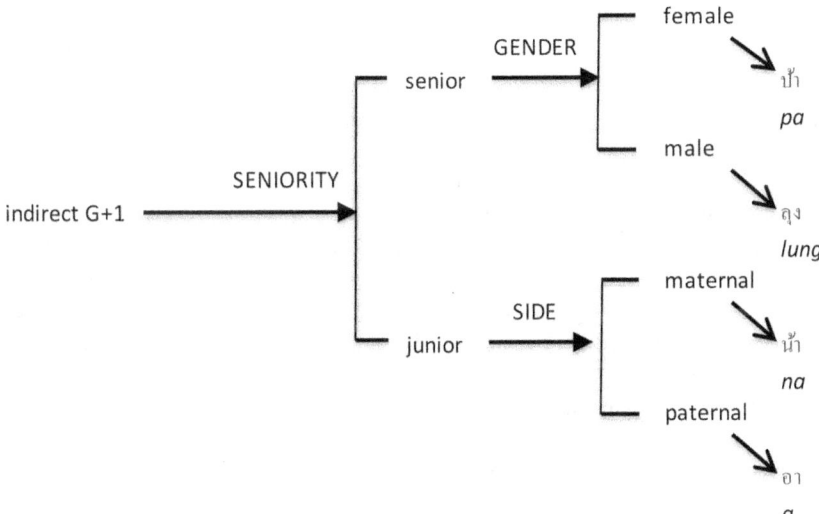

Figure 6.6 System network of Thai indirect G+1 kinship terms.

As in English, these kinship terms do not distinguish whether the relation to ego is by blood or marriage. Systemically, in comparison to English, Thai has emerged to construe seniority as a primary distinction, with gender and family side more delicate to and dependent upon the initial choice of seniority. For English-speaking learners of Thai, the lack of distinction of gender with junior aunts and uncles is likely to be an unusual naming practice to come to terms with. For Thai speakers learning English, the lack of distinction of seniority is, likewise, likely to be unusual.

Turning now to Teochew as used in Thailand, the situation is more complex again. The primary distinction in indirect G+1 kinship terms in Teochew as used in Thailand is GENDER. A system network can be drawn with this initial distinction, and if the system is drawn this way, the more delicate systems under both choices (i.e. **female** or **male**) involve the systems of BLOOD, SIDE and SENIORITY.

However, these more delicate systems of BLOOD, SIDE and SENIORITY are in completely different configurations for females and males. As a consequence, the preference here is to model the G+1 Teochew kinship terms as two separate systems, with entry conditions of **G+1 indirect female** and **G+1 indirect male**, respectively, in order to: (1) avoid duplication of systems and choices in the same system network, (2) capture the degree of difference in the meaning potential for female and male G+1 kinship terms, and (3) capture the extent to which they differ from both English and Thai terms, where GENDER can be integrated unproblematically into the respective system networks.

Turning to the Teochew networks, Figure 6.7 shows the system for Teochew G+1 indirect female kinship terms. At initial delicacy, there are parallel systems for SIDE and BLOOD. In addition, if the choices **paternal** and **marriage** are made, the system of SENIORITY is entered.

The ramification of this is that children raised in families using Teochew kinship terms grow up knowing whether ego's indirect female G+1 relatives (or in English, aunts) are related to ego on ego's mother's or father's side of the family, and also whether they are related to ego by marriage or blood. Thus, อาอี้ [*a i*] can be translated into English as something like 'maternal aunty by birth' (mother's sister), and อากิ้ม [*a kim*] as something like 'maternal aunty by marriage' (mother's brother's wife). Likewise, อาโกว [*a ko*] can be translated into English as something like 'paternal aunty by birth' (father's sister).

None of these choice sets (i.e. **maternal + birth**, **maternal + marriage**, **paternal + birth**) select for SENIORITY. However, when the choice set **paternal + marriage** is selected, the system of SENIORITY is entered. This means that children raised in families using Teochew kinship terms grow up knowing whether ego's indirect G+1 who are related by marriage on ego's father's side (i.e. who are related through male kin – father and father's brothers) are married to a brother who is older than or younger than their father. Thus, อาอึ้ม [*a uem*] can be translated into English as something like 'senior paternal aunty by marriage' (father's elder-brother's wife), and อาซิ่ม [*a sim*] as something like 'junior paternal aunty by marriage' (father's younger-brother's wife). The effect of this is to ascribe significance to women in ego's G+1 who are related to ego by means of marriage to ego's father's brothers (the kin relation is through males only), with greater intricacy applied in naming the male-connected females for indirect G+1.

Thailand, Kinship, Culture and Language   123

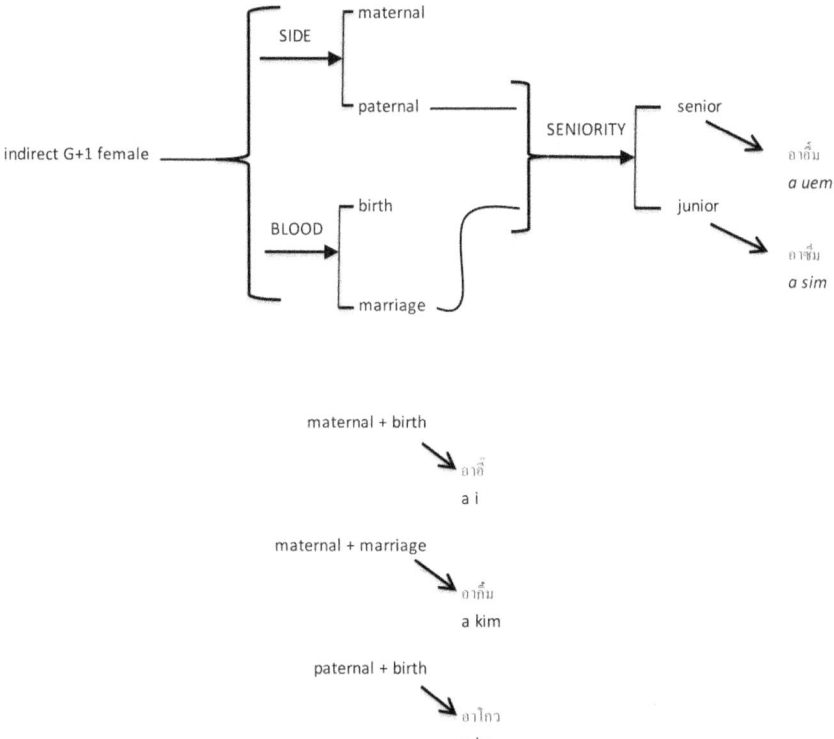

Figure 6.7 System network for Teochew G+1 indirect female kinship terms as commonly used in Thailand.

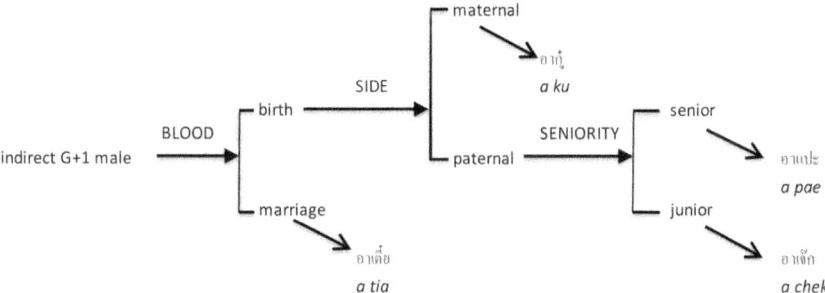

Figure 6.8 System network for Teochew G+1 indirect male kinship terms as commonly used in Thailand.

As mentioned above, the configuration of kinship terms is systemically different for Teochew indirect G+1 male kinship terms, as shown in Figure 6.8. The system at initial delicacy is BLOOD. Any indirect male G+1 related to ego by marriage is known to ego as อาเตี้ย [*a tia*]. If related by birth, the system at the next level of delicacy is SIDE. Any indirect MALE G+1 related to ego by birth on the maternal side is known to ego as อากู๋ [*a ku*]. If **birth** and then **paternal** are selected, the next system is SENIORITY.

Thus, children raised in families using Teochew kinship terms grow up knowing whether ego's indirect male G+1 (or in English, uncles) are related to ego by blood or marriage. If by marriage, the relation is through female kin (through either parent's sister) and they are identified by a single term regardless of family side or seniority. If related by blood, ego knows whether the relation is on ego's mother's or father's side of the family. If related by blood on the maternal side, the relation is through ego's mother (again, through female kin) and they are identified by a single term regardless of seniority. If related by blood on the father's side, the relation is through the father (male kin) and the kinship terms distinguish whether they are senior or junior to ego's father. Thus, อาเตี่ย [*a tia*] can be translated into English as something like 'uncle by marriage' (father's or mother's sister's husband), อากู๋ [*a ku*] as something like 'maternal uncle by birth' (mother's brother), อาเจ็ก [*a chek*] as something like 'younger paternal uncle by birth' (father's younger brother) and อาแปะ [*a pae*] as something like 'older paternal uncle by birth' (father's older brother).

Men related to ego indirectly at G+1 by birth on the male side (i.e. a father's brother) are distinguished by seniority, as are their wives (see Figures 6.7 and 6.8). Other indirect kinship relations at G+1 in Teochew signify GENDER, BLOOD and SIDE. These systemic choices in the language mark the direct male side of the family, and those females who marry into it, distinctly from ego's other indirect kinship relations at G+1, by selecting for SENIORITY.

For language teachers and materials developers, the information provided here shows that the four systems of GENDER, BLOOD, SIDE and SENIORITY are signified in Teochew indirect G+1 kinship terms, but that after the primary distinction of GENDER, the other systems are in different configurations. Such knowledge can be the basis of an informed exploration of cultural differences, with learners exploring the relevant terms in each language according to their own family and taking a cross-cultural perspective on the meanings at stake, and the tenor relations that each language construes in this specialized lexis. Armed with such knowledge, language teachers can provide informed instruction on cultural contexts for which they do not have 'insider' status, employing and imparting language expertise by means of a model where the relations between context and language are explicitly theorized.

Discussion

The systems above demonstrate that POWER is a complex and dynamic subsystem of meaning, where relations vary according to 'master identities' related to ethnicity, gender, generation and so on, but also according to how they interact in culturally and situationally specific configurations of power relations. This is illustrated in kinship terms in this chapter, but there is no reason to expect that tenor relations become less complex or less dynamic in contexts where relations are not expressed in indexical lexis such as kinship terminology.

Many of the terms discussed above are used as terms of address in discourse, sometimes as presented here, sometimes without prefixes or with different prefixes (e.g. อากง [*a kong*] or 'grandfather' rather than อั๋วกง [*ua kong*] or 'maternal (outside) grandfather'). Sometimes the tenor relations construed in the lexical sets analysed above are routinely avoided as terms of address (e.g. with stepparents in all three languages). The Teochew indirect G+1 terms can also take numbers as prefixes (to indicate birth order), adding further intricacy to the systemic choices indicating relative status.[6] The Teochew and Thai indirect G+1 terms can be used in conjunction with names to personalize them, as is done in English (e.g. Aunty June). Thus, while the lexical sets analysed above are indexical of POWER relations in tenor, in discourse they also instantiate SOLIDARITY relations in tenor in the associated lexical choices and in the ways that they are used, all of which reflect and contribute to constructing the tenor relations in a particular family. As both Poynton (1989) and Rose (2018) show, a range of systems at different strata are implicated in what Poynton calls 'the politics of address'.

In Thailand, it is common to hear parents tell their children:

ไป เรียก อา กง
bai riak a kong
go call grandfather
'Go and pay respect to your grandfather'

ไป สวัสดี ลุง
bai sawasdi lung
go call senior uncle
'Go and greet your uncle'.

An essential part of any greeting involving senior family members and important others is for the junior family member to initiate the greeting and to เรียก [*riak*] or 'call' the senior family member by their appropriate term of address.

Such terms are not only used in greetings. They are regularly used when initiating an address to the senior family member in conversation and/or in performing other speech acts such as thanking or requesting, depending on the circumstances. The kinship terms analysed above set out the tenor relations as construed in indexical lexis in each language. The terms of address, which draw on these terms heavily but not exclusively, instantiate these relations and play a crucial role in maintaining the social fabric. For most learners of Thai as a second language, such kinship terms will rarely be crucial in terms of family interactions.[7] Kinship terms more broadly however are used in social discourse as pronouns and as terms of address (e.g. when referring to a friend's grandparent, you are likely to use the same term of address as your friend; senior friends may be given titles such as น้า [na] or 'junior maternal aunt or uncle'; older interactants may be given titles such as ป้า [pa] or 'senior aunt'), including sometimes Teochew terms where the addressee is of Chinese heritage. So an awareness and understanding of these terms is important for learners of Thai. Likewise, for Thai learners of English, it is important to learn that such titles are not as widely used or easily bestowed as in Thailand.

All of this is also knowledge about language that language teachers can usefully employ with their learners to teach who is warranted to speak, when, and what they are and are not warranted to say. The kinship terms analysed above begin this work, but further research investigating the discourse of address as enacted in spoken Thai from a systemic functional perspective is clearly warranted (cf. Poynton, 1989; Rose, 2018; Shin, 2018).

Conclusion

According to Martin and White (2005, p. 29): 'In post-colonial societies the five most general factors which position us in relation to tenor are generation, gender, ethnicity, capacity and class', and these factors 'condition access to the various hierarchies we encounter beyond domestic life'. We may also ask about the hierarchies of domestic life, and about the role of these factors and others therein, since '[o]ur positioning begins at birth in the home' (ibid.).

In terms of kinship, ethnicity figures at a very indelicate level to determine which set or sets of kinship terms (i.e. from which language(s)) we draw on to construe our familial relations (cf. Vail, 2006). Kinship lexis varies between languages in terms of positioning factors (e.g. GENDER in English versus GENDER and SIDE in Thai and Teochew at direct G+2) and varies even between generations within languages.

The differences in kinship terms as illustrated in this chapter can be viewed from the perspective of what Martin calls **commitment**, which 'refers to the degree of specificity of the meaning instantiated in a text; this has to do with how many optional choices for meaning are taken up and how generally the choices a text subscribes to are instantiated' (Martin, 2010, p. 20). Martin (2010) approaches commitment from a logogenetic perspective.

However, if we consider commitment on a phylogenetic timescale, different languages emerge with different degrees of commitment in different areas of their meaning potential. In interpersonal terms, we can compare, for example, the valeurs in G+1 indirect kinship terms in Teochew to those in English and demonstrate that different languages require different degrees of commitment in tenor relations of their speakers. For language teachers and learners, awareness of this fact is already a step towards greater intercultural understanding. Further steps can be made with explicit instruction in, for example, kinship terms at the system end of the cline, and terms of address and vocation at the instance end of the cline by using learners' knowledge of their L1 and bringing that into an understanding of the similarities and differences with the target language.

Such an approach is consistent with SFL genre-based approaches to language teaching (see Rose & Martin, 2012), where culture is modelled as a system of genres. Much of the SFL-based work done in the Australian Adult Migrant English Program was aimed at helping learners with the genres required for everyday life (e.g. Burns et al., 1996; Hammond et al., 1992). Similarly, understanding tenor relations in families is an important window into the target culture for language learners, and a possible first step into an understanding of the use of terms of address in negotiating the genres of everyday life.

In second- and foreign-language education, questions of the relations between language and culture are often dealt with in ways that treat the two as separate phenomena. By applying SFL theory, kinship in different cultures can be understood 'on its own terms', and this knowledge can be used to make the unfamiliar familiar for language learners, providing opportunities for genuine intercultural understanding.

Acknowledgements

I would like to thank J. R. Martin for teaching me and befriending me – thanks Jim. I owe you a debt that goes beyond language. I would like to thank Michele Zappavigna for her professionalism, and saint-like patience far above and beyond, and both Michele and Shooshi Dreyfus for valuable feedback on an earlier draft of this chapter. I would like to thank Dr Nutthaporn Owatnupat and the Thai/Teochew informants without whom this chapter would not have been possible.
ขอบคุณครับอาเฮียอาซ้ออาหมีและครอบครัวทุกคน. Any inaccuracies or errors are mine.

Notes

1. The term 'power' is used here (following Martin & White, 2005) to refer to Poynton's (1989) 'power', Martin's (1992) 'status' and Hasan's (2014) 'status'. The term 'solidarity' is used here (following Martin & White, 2005) to refer to Poynton's (1989) 'contact', Martin's (1992) 'contact' and Hasan's (2014) 'social distance'.
2. I was unable to access a relevant unpublished Master thesis (Xue, 2016).
3. This romanization system is not unproblematic; however, the options also have drawbacks (see Kanchanawan, 2006), and for the purposes of this chapter, it provides a standardized, readable system.
4. 'Ego' refers to the person from whom kinship relations are traced. It is widely used in the kinship literature and in related fields (cf. Figure 6.1).
5. Census data on the 'Family Blending classification variable' in Australia was only collected from 2006. The Australian Bureau of Statistics defines a step family as one that has 'at least one resident step child, but no child who is the natural or adopted child of both partners', and a blended family as one that has 'two or more children; at least one child who is the natural or adopted child of both partners, and at least one who is the step child of one of them'.
6. These could be drawn as a simultaneous system of RANK.
7. One obvious exception is those marrying into Thai families.

References

Benedict, P. K. (1943). Studies in Thai kinship terminology. *Journal of the American Oriental Society*, 63(2), 168–75.
Bennardo, G. (2016). Space in kinship: Frames of reference and kinship terminology systems. *Structure and Dynamics*, 9(2), 16–32.

Boonsawasd, A. (2013). Chinese influence on Bouyei basic kinship terms. *Dialectologia*, 11, 67–84.

Burns, A., Joyce, H., & Gollin, S. (1996). *'I See What You Mean', Using Spoken Discourse in the Classroom: A Handbook for Teachers*. Sydney: National Centre for English Language Teaching and Research (NCELTR).

de Vaus, D. (2004). *Diversity and Change in Australian Families: Statistical Profiles*. Melbourne: Australian Institute of Family Studies.

Draper, J. (2019). Language education policy in Thailand. In A. Kirkpatrick & A. J. Liddicoat (Eds.), *The Routledge International Handbook of Education Policy in Asia* (pp. 229–42). London: Routledge.

Fang, N. (2019). Chinese-Australian cultural conceptualisations of ancestor worship, death and family. *World Englishes*, 38(4), 644–658.

Forster-Jones, J. (2007). Family diversification in Australia – The increasing share of blended and step families. *People and Place*, 15(4), 9–19.

Hammond, J., Burns, A., Joyce, H., Gerot, L., & Brosnan, D. (1992). *English for Social Purposes*. Sydney: National Centre for English Language Teaching and Research (NCELTR).

Hasan, R. (2014). Towards a paradigmatic description of context: Systems, metafunctions, and semantics. *Functional Linguistics*, 1(9), 1–54.

Hasan, R. (2015). The grammarian's dream: Lexis as most delicate grammar. In C. Cloran, D. Butt, & G. Williams (Eds.), *Ways of Saying: Ways of Meaning: Selected Papers of Ruqaiya Hasan* (pp. 73–103). London: Bloomsbury.

Hayes, A., Weston, R., Qu, L., & Gray, M. (2010). Families then and now: 1980–2010. *Journal of the Home Economics Institute of Australia*, 17(2), 33–40.

Jitpranee, J. (2018). A study of systemic functional linguistics phenomena in Thailand. *Proceedings of 1st HUNIC Conference* (pp. 1883–99). Surin, Thailand: Faculty of Humanities and Social Sciences, Surindra Rajabhat University.

Kanchanawan, N. (2006). Romanization, transliteration, and transcription for the globalization of the Thai language. *The Journal of the Royal Institute of Thailand*, 31(3), 832–41.

Kemp, C., & Regier, T. (2012). Kinship categories across languages reflect general communicative principles. *Science*, 336(6084), 1049–54.

Knox, J. S., & Patpong, P. (2008). Reporting bloodshed in Thai newspapers: A comparative case study of English and Thai. In E. Thomson & P. R. R. White (Eds.), *Communicating Conflict Multilingual Case Studies of the News Media* (pp. 173–202). London: Continuum.

Knox, J. S., Patpong, P., & Piriyasilpa, Y. (2010). ข่าวหน้าหนึ่ง (Khao naa nung): A multimodal analysis of Thai-language newspaper pages. In M. Bednarek & J. R. Martin (Eds.), *New Discourse on Language: Functional Perspectives on Multimodality, Identity, and Affiliation* (pp. 80–110). London: Continuum.

Kronenfeld, D. B. (2006). Issues in the classification of kinship terminologies: Towards a new typology. *Anthropos*, 101(1), 203–19.

Limanonda, B. (1995). Families in Thailand: Beliefs and realities. *Journal of Comparative Family Studies*, 26(1), 67–82.

Mak, A. S., & Chan, H. (1995). Chinese family values in Australia. In R. Hartley (Ed.), *Families and Cultural Diversity in Australia* (pp. 70–95). St Leonards: Allen & Unwin.

Martin, J. R. (1983). Participant identification in English, Tagalog and Kâte. *Australian Journal of Linguistics*, 3(1), 45–74.

Martin, J. R. (1992). *English Text: System and Structure*. Philadelphia: John Benjamins.

Martin, J. R. (2001). Language, register and genre. In A. Burns & C. Coffin (Eds.), *Analysing English in a Global Context: A Reader* (pp. 149–66). London: Routledge.
Martin, J. R. (2010). Semantic variation: Modelling realisation, instantiation and individuation in social semiosis. In M. Bednarek & J. R. Martin (Eds.), *New Discourse on Language: Functional Perspectives on Multimodality, Identity, and Affiliation* (pp. 1–34). London and New York: Continuum.
Martin, J. R., & White, P. R. R. (2005). *The Language of Evaluation: Appraisal in English.* Hampshire: Palgrave Macmillan.
Morita, L. (2007a). Discussing assimilation and language shift among the Chinese in Thailand. *International Journal of the Sociology of Language*, 186, 43–58.
Morita, L. (2007b). Religion and family of the Chinese and Thai in Thailand and influences. *Studies in Language and Culture (言語文化論集)*, 28(2), 125–42.
Murdock, G. P. (1968). Patterns of sibling terminology. *Ethnology*, 7(1), 1–24.
Ngo, J. (2017). *An Exploration of Kinship Terms of Hokkien Chinese-Indonesians in Surabaya. Proceedings of the 3rd Doing Research in Applied Linguistics and 19th English in South-East Asian Conference* (pp. 105–14). Bangkok: School of Liberal Arts, King Mongkut's University of Technology Thonburi.
OECD. (2011). *Doing Better for Families*. Paris: OECD Publishing.
Patpong, P. (2006a). *A Systemic Functional Interpretation of the Grammar of Thai*. PhD thesis, Macquarie University, Sydney.
Patpong, P. (2006b). A corpus-based study of the conjunction ko:3 in Thai: An exploration of textual resource. In G. Thompson & S. Hunston (Eds.), *System and Corpus: Exploring Connections* (pp. 226–47). London: Equinox.
Patpong, P. (2009). Thai persuasive discourse: A systemic functional approach to an analysis of amulet advertisements. *Revista Alicantina de Estudios Ingleses*, 22, 195–217.
Patpong, P. (2013). Thematic progression of Thai Song Dam folktales. *Journal of the Southeast Asian Linguistics Society*, 6, 189–215.
Patpong, P. (2016). Construing the ecological perspective of the Tai Dam as seen in 'Sen Huen' ritual manuscripts. *Functional Linguistics*, 3(11), https://doi.org/10.1186/s40554-016-0031-3.
Peek, C., Im-em, W., & Tangthanaseth, R. (2015). *The State of Thailand's Population 2015: Features of Thai Families in the Era of Low Fertility and Longevity*. Bangkok: United Nations Population Fund Thailand Country Office and the Office of the National Economic and Social Development Board of Thailand.
Poynton, C. (1989). *Language and Gender: Making the Difference* (2nd ed.). Oxford: Oxford University Press.
Poynton, C. (1990). *Address and the Semiotics of Social Relations: A Systemic-functional Account of Address Forms and Practices in Australian English*. PhD thesis, University of Sydney, Sydney.
Prasithrathsint, A. (2001). A componential analysis of kinship terms in Thai. In M. R. K. Tingsabadh & A. S. Abramson (Eds.), *Essays in Tai Linguistics* (pp. 261–76). Bangkok: Chulalongkorn University Press.
Premsrirat, S. (2007). Endangered languages of Thailand. *International Journal of the Sociology of Language*, 2007(186), 75–93.
Read, D. W. (2013). A new approach to forming a typology of kinship terminology systems: From Morgan and Murdock to the present. *Structure and Dynamics*, 6(1). Retrieved from https://escholarship.org/uc/item/0ss6j8sh. Last accessed 15 April 2020.
Rose, D. (2018). Sister, shall I tell you? Enacting social relations in a kinship community. *Functions of Language*, 25(1), 97–134.

Rose, D., & Martin, J. R. (2012). *Learning to Write, Reading to Learn: Genre, Knowledge and Pedagogy in the Sydney School*. Sheffield: Equinox.

Rusmeecharoen, T. (2017). Pronominal reference in standard Thai: Mirror of interpersonal relationships and socio-cultural perspective in Thai society. *Vacana*, 5(2), 70–103.

Schmied, J. (2006). East African Englishes. In B. B. Kachru, Y. Kachru, & C. L. Nelson (Eds.), *The Handbook of World Englishes* (pp. 188–202). Oxford: Blackwell.

Shapiro, W. (2009). A. L. Kroeber and the new kinship studies. *Anthropological Forum*, 19(1), 1–20.

Sharifian, F. (2006). A cultural-conceptual approach and World Englishes: The case of Aboriginal English. *World Englishes*, 25(1), 11–22.

Shin, G.-H. (2018). Interpersonal grammar of Korean: A Systemic Functional Linguistics perspective. *Functions of Language*, 25(1), 20–53.

Smalley, W. A. (1994). *Linguistic Diversity and National Unity: Language Ecology in Thailand*. Chicago: University of Chicago Press.

Vail, P. (2006). Exploring codeswitching in systemic functional linguistics: Languages and meaning-making among Lao speakers in Northeastern Thailand. *Linguistics and the Human Sciences*, 2(1), 133–64.

Völkel, S. (2016). Tongan-English language contact and kinship terminology. *World Englishes*, 35(2), 242–58.

Weller, R. P. (1981). Affines, ambiguity, and meaning in Hokkien kin terms. *Ethnology*, 20(1), 15–29.

Wijeyewardene, I. (2012). Transitivity/ergativity in Thai political science texts. In J. S. Knox (Ed.), *To Boldly Proceed: Papers from the 39th International Systemic Functional Congress* (pp. 129–34). Sydney: Organising Committee of the 39th International Systemic Functional Congress.

Wijeyewardene, I. (2017). The representation of social actors in debates on the 2006 Thai coup. In P. Chappell & J. S. Knox (Eds.), *Transforming Contexts: Papers from the 44th International Systemic Functional Congress* (pp. 47–53). Wollongong, Australia: Organising Committee of the 44th International Systemic Functional Congress.

Xue, W. (2016). *The Semantics of 'Uncle'-type Kinship Terms in Cantonese (Guangzhou) and Teochew (Jieyang)*. Master thesis, Australian National University, Canberra.

Yoddumnern-Attig, B. (1992). Thai family structure and organization: Changing roles and duties in historical perspective. In B. Yoddumnern-Attig, K. Richter, A. Soonthorndhada, C. Sethaput, & A. Pramualratana (Eds.), *Changing Roles and Statuses of Women in Thailand: A Documentary Assessment* (pp. 8–24). Salaya: Mahidol University at Salaya, Institute for Population and Social Research.

7

Intermodal relations, mass and presence in school science explanation genres

Len Unsworth
Australian Catholic University

Introduction

The discourse of science and science education has been a significant arena for Jim Martin's theoretical work on genre and discourse semantics and for the contributions to disciplinary literacy pedagogy made by Jim and his colleagues through their work in educational semiotics (Halliday & Martin, 1993; Martin & Rose, 2012; Martin & Veel, 1998). Within this work one key aspect has been the theorization of explanation genres – and early recognition of the integral role of images in science explanations and their occurrence within complex multimodal macro-genres (Martin, 1994; Martin & Rose, 2008; Rose & Martin, 2012). This chapter explores a theoretical trajectory for advancing a multimodal perspective on the accounts by Martin and his associates of the semiosis of school science explanations (Halliday & Martin, 1993; Martin, 1989; Martin & Rose, 2008, 2012; Martin & Veel, 1998). The focus is on the ongoing recontextualization of canonical verbal explanation genres in multimodal texts, and how verbiage and image share the work of building the field of the text. The theoretical basis for this exploration is the work deriving from Martin's dialogue with Legitimation Code Theory (LCT) (Maton, 2013, 2016). Specifically, it is based on Martin's formulation of what he calls *mass* and *presence* (Martin, 2017; Martin & Matruglio, 2013). Mass is a cover term for Martin's metafunctional re-working of systemic functional linguistics (SFL) accounts of meaning condensation, which he developed in response to the LCT concept of semantic density. Presence is a cover term for Martin's metafunctional re-working of SFL approaches to context dependency, which he developed in response to the LCT concept of semantic gravity. The work reported here draws on the emerging adaptation of mass and presence to images and their annotations, captions and integrated verbiage (Martin et al., in press).

This research was supported by the Australian Government through the Australian Research Council's *Linkage Projects* funding scheme (project LP160100263). The views expressed herein are those of the authors and are not necessarily those of the Australian Government or Australian Research Council.

In the first section of this chapter the work to be presented will be contextualized in relation to the publications on school science explanations by Martin and his associates, and the key variables in mass and presence will be briefly outlined. The second section introduces the different kinds of infographic explanations of mitosis in four science textbooks for year 10 students that form the data set for analysis. The third section describes comparative analyses of the four mitosis explanations. The emphasis is on mass and in particular on detailed comparative analyses of the construal of the field dimensions of compositional relations and activity; however, the analyses also draw attention to the significance of presence in the construal of field. The concluding section summarizes the variability in the intermodal construal of field in the four textbook infographics and draws implications for evolving infographic explanation design.

Explanation genres and re-contextualization as multimodal texts

The four main types of explanations theorized by Martin and his colleagues are succinctly explained and exemplified in *Genre Relations* (Martin & Rose, 2008). Sequential explanations involve a series of events in which an obligatory causal relation is implied between each event and the next. Examples provided by Martin and Rose include: the formation of wetlands, the formation of DNA in cell nuclei and how sound travels. Factorial explanations deal with events that may be explained by two or more contributing factors, such as how the *Acacia* tree species, Mulga, survives long droughts by reference to its shape, colour and the food source in its own leaves. In consequential explanations a single event may have two or more consequences, each following independently from the causal event. The example provided sets out the three independent consequences of the clearing of the woodlands of southern Australia: death of remaining trees, erosion of land and destruction of habitat. Conditional explanations construe effects as contingent on variable factors, such as the effects on animal populations under three conditions: if predators are absent, if prey are too few, and if numbers of both predator and prey fall and build up again. Another example is the explanation of buoyancy in which the upthrust on an object in a liquid depends on the density of the object relative to the liquid. The explanation specifies two possible conditions: the object's density is either greater or less than that of the liquid, causing two possible buoyancy effects – sinking or floating.

Among the multiple examples of the various types of explanation discussed in *Genre Relations*, three include images. A complex activity image is included with the sequential explanation of DNA formation; however, although it is noted that 'the technical density of the text makes it difficult to follow without the accompanying diagram' (p. 154), the role of the diagram is not discussed further. Similarly, a technological sequential explanation of the function of a brassert in cooling a blast furnace is accompanied by a series of diagrams that 're-expressed' the composition of the gas cleaning system realized in the explanation, but again the role of the images in relation to the written explanation is not pursued (p. 165). The images included in the factorial explanation of the survival of the Mulga tree (Figure 7.1) are discussed in some detail in *Genre Relations* and in other publications (Martin, 2013; Martin & Dreyfus, 2015; Martin & Rose, 2012).

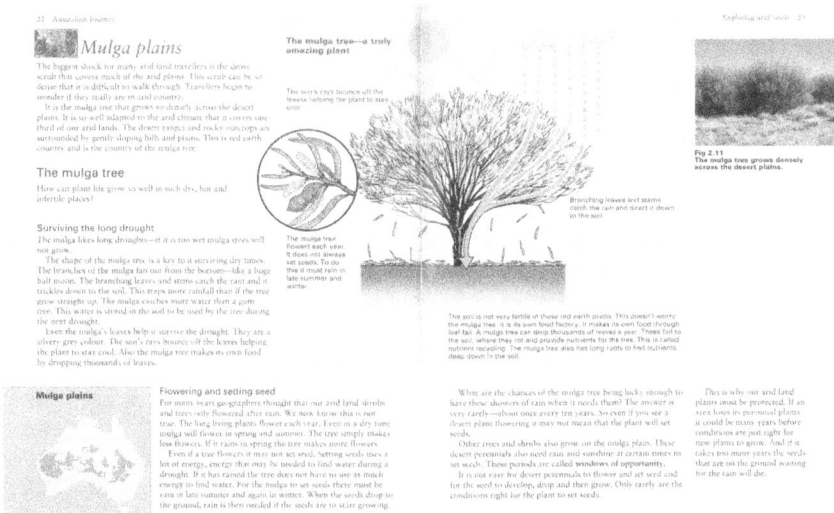

Figure 7.1 Mulga tree text (Scott & Robinson, 1993).

In *Genre Relations* (Martin & Rose, 2008) the various images related to explanation of the Mulga tree's survival are discussed in terms of the logical relations between visual and verbal texts as being elaborating (re-stating, summarizing, specifying or repeating). This and subsequent discussion of the explanation of the survival of the Mulga tree intimate future theorization to further address 'trajectories along which the canonical structure of genres may be re-contextualised in macro-genres and multimodal texts' (Martin & Rose, 2012, p. 10). The Mulga tree explanation is a part of an image-centred page layout entailing complex interrelationships among main text explanations, images and caption texts, which 'comprise a macro-explanation, pictorially supported by the action vectors in the diagram' (Martin & Rose, 2012, p. 10). This kind of intermodal explanatory portrayal, described by Bateman (2008) as page flow and as increasingly occurring in science trade books, has also become prominent in science textbooks (Bezemer & Kress, 2010; Danielsson & Selander, 2016; Peterson, 2016) and as a form of public communication of science understanding, referred to as infographics (Gebre & Polman, 2016; Polman & Gebre, 2015).

These forms of intermodal explanations impel the need to theorize the nature of meaning-making at the intersection of image and language, beyond the notion of logical relations. The prescience of the discussion of a number of intermodal aspects of the Mulga tree explanation by Martin and Rose (2012) can now be appreciated in relation to that theory development. Firstly, they recognized that the contribution of the image depicted vectors from schematized clouds to branches to ground involved more than 'restating' the activity realized in the verbiage. In terms of Martin's later theorizing, this concerned differences in *commitment* of meaning from the potential of the meaning-making systems of image and verbiage (Painter & Martin, 2011; Painter et al., 2013). (Commitment refers to the amount of meaning potential activated in a particular process of instantiation. For example, verbally, 'a large, hairy funnelweb spider' commits more meaning than 'a spider', and visually, a full colour photograph of a Mulga tree commits more meaning than an outline pencil drawing.) Secondly, the significance for this kind of imagic meaning commitment of the superimposition of the vectors representing water flow onto the generic drawing of the Mulga tree would later be taken up in the adaptation to images of Martin's metafunctional reworking of SFL models of context dependency as *presence* (Martin, Unsworth & Rose, in press). In images, presence involves *congruence* (to what extent is an image a naturalistic representation of the activity, items and properties that it depicts), *explicitness* (to what extent does an image retain or omit descriptive detail) and *appeal* (to what extent does an image invite some kind of engagement from the viewer in terms of an aesthetic response, amusement, awe, etc.). Thirdly, Martin and Rose drew attention to the image simultaneously depicting a complex activity as well as the components of the Mulga tree relevant to that activity, whereas systemic functional semiotic approaches to analysis of such images had tended to focus on structures portraying either narrative (activity) or analytic (compositional or classificational) meanings (Kress & van Leeuwen, 2006). Martin and Rose also drew attention to the intermodal condensation of meaning where the main text explanations were abbreviated and segmented into the several image annotations which required their joint reading with the image for interpretation. These matters would later be further developed in the adaptation to images of Martin's conceptualization of *mass* (Martin et al., in press). In images, from an ideational perspective, the key variable in mass is *technicality* (to what extent does an image involve multiple moments and/or tiers of activity, broader and/or deeper classification and composition or multiple and/or gauged properties); interpersonally the key variable is *iconization* (to what extent does an image invoke bonds constelling a community of social practice (e.g. genetics, nuclear energy, climate change activism, peace movements); and textually the key variable is *aggregation* (to what extent are activity, classification, composition and properties combined in an integrated image-language portrayal, including images, captions, annotation and aligned text). The theorizing of mass and presence alongside commitment, and the application of these ideas intermodally, have created new frameworks for investigation of the trajectory of recontextualization of the canonical structures of explanation in contemporary school science textbooks as infographic portrayals with images as the rhetorical locus.

Infographic explanations in school science textbooks

The analysis of the Mulga tree text by Martin and Rose drew attention to the building of the field in the image-focused infographic as being shared work by both the verbiage and the image. They discussed the adaptation of verbal elemental genres in this context as captions and noted that their interpretation depended heavily 'on images and/or related verbal texts' (2012, p. 10). They also noted that in some textbooks the construal of field occurred only in infographic portrayals of images and captions and that unabbreviated instances of canonical genres, such as explanation and report genres, were not included. This now appears to be very common in junior secondary school science textbooks (Danielsson & Selander, 2016). It is therefore important to understand the nature and the extent of the construal of field knowledge in infographics and how this varies in different infographic formats in different textbooks. The next section of the chapter explores the construal of field in different infographic explanations of mitosis (cell division) in four contemporary year 10 science textbooks in current wide use in Australian schools (Chidrawi et al., 2013; Linstead et al., 2012; Lofts, 2015; Silvester, 2016).

Three of the four textbooks rely entirely on the annotated images and captions of their infographic portrayals to explain mitosis (Chidrawi et al., 2013; Lofts, 2015; Silvester, 2016). Each includes very minimal co-text which does not explain the process, so only the infographics will be analysed here. The first of these texts (henceforth 'Nelson') includes a series of annotated images and tabular presentation of verbiage as 'dot points', with each column of the table aligning with an image segment above (Figure 7.2).

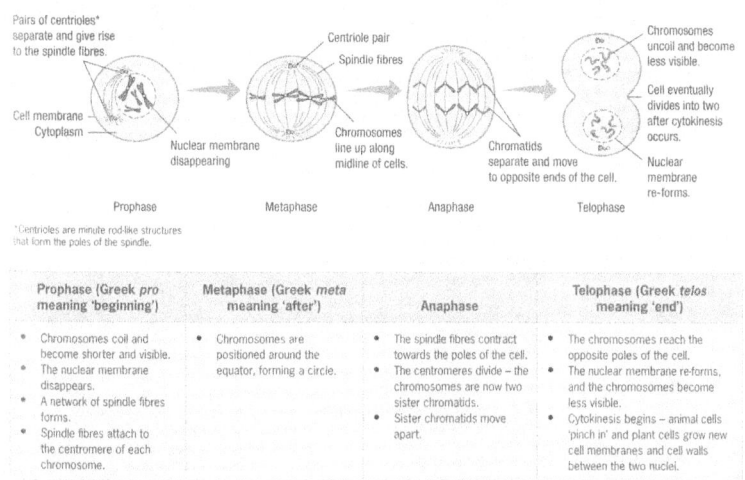

Figure 7.2 Infographic explanation of mitosis – Nelson (Chidrawi et al., 2013, p. 19).

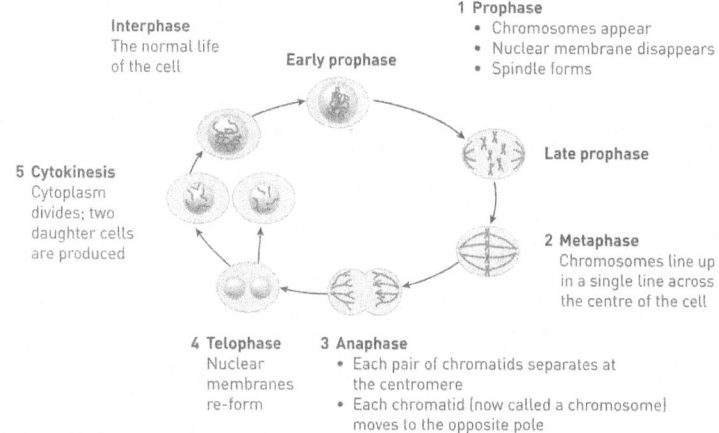

Figure 7.3 Infographic explanation of mitosis – Oxford (Silvester, 2016, p. 10).

136   Discourses of Hope and Reconciliation

In each of the next two texts the explanation relies entirely on two images, each presented as discrete figures. In the first of these texts (henceforth 'Oxford') one image is an annotated diagram representing mitosis as cycle (Figure 7.3) and the second image shows a photograph of mitotic cells at different stages in the process of mitosis, which have been stained to show the separation of DNA (Figure 7.4).

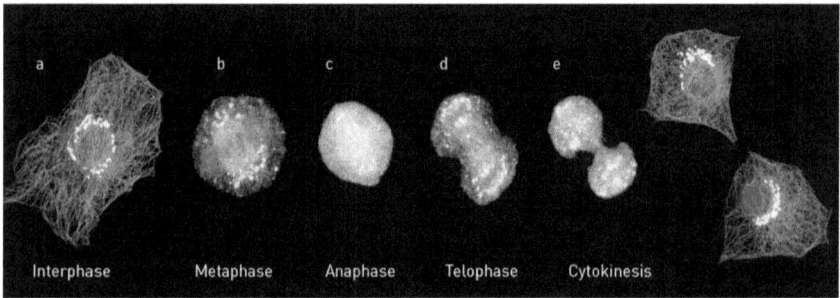

Figure 7.4 Stages of mitosis – Oxford (Silvester, 2016, p. 11).

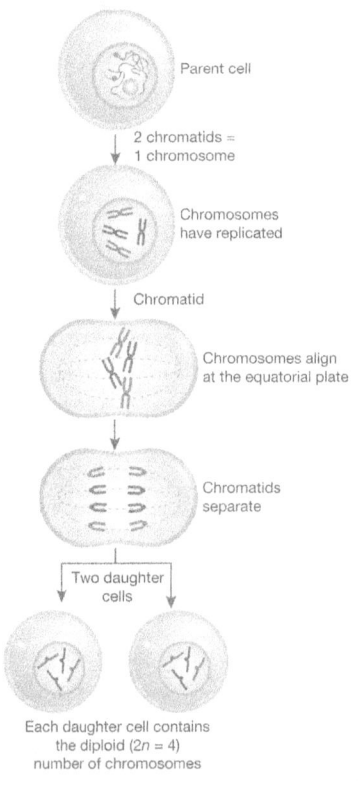

Figure 7.5 Diagram of mitosis – Jacaranda (Lofts, 2015, p. 28).

School Science Explanation Genres   137

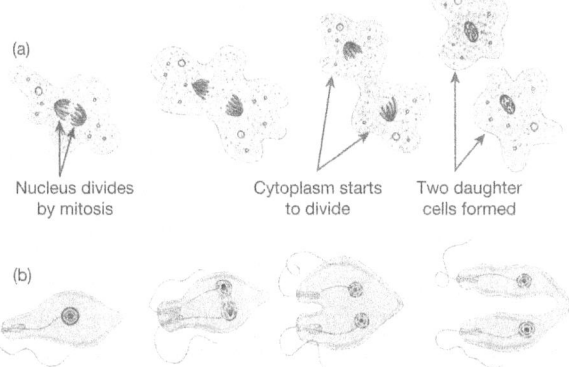

Figure 7.6 Image of unicellular organisms undergoing mitosis (Lofts, 2015, p. 28).

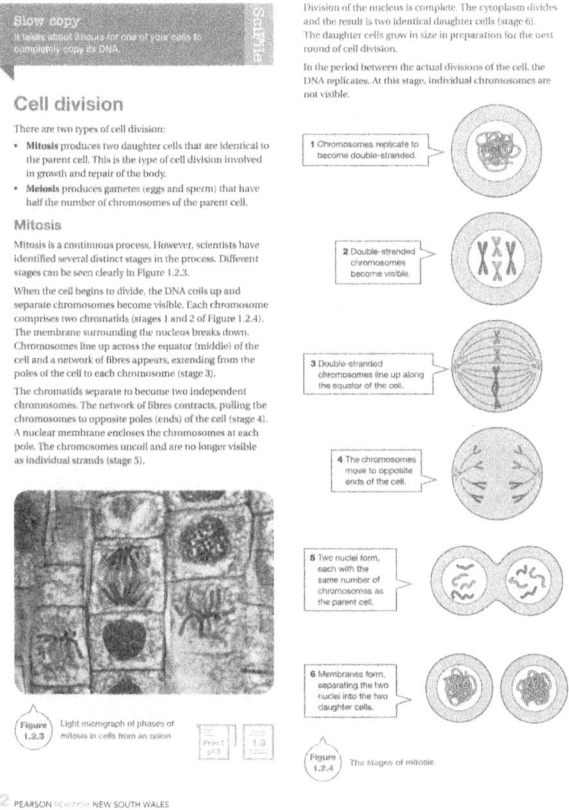

Figure 7.7 Multimodal explanation of mitosis – Pearson (Linstead et al., 2012, p. 12).

The third text (henceforth 'Jacaranda') also relies entirely on two figures for the explanation of mitosis. The first figure is a vertical diagram of the process (Figure 7.5) and the second is an image of two different unicellular organisms dividing by binary fission involving mitosis (Figure 7.6).

The fourth year 10 textbook (henceforth 'Pearson') is the only one in which the mitosis infographic is accompanied by a co-text that is an explanation of the process of mitosis. The full page of this textbook is provided here as Figure 7.7.

The intermodal construal of field in infographic explanations in school science textbooks

To establish the field knowledge of mitosis that might normally be included in a range of year 10 textbooks, the mitosis infographics in the corresponding senior secondary school textbooks, produced by the publishers of the four year 10 textbooks, were added to the year 10 corpus (Borger, 2015; Kinnear, 2016; Armstrong et al., 2018; Huxley & Walter, 2019). All of the ideational meanings realized by the images and verbiage in the eight infographics were compiled to form comprehensive composite representations of the compositional relations and of the activity construed in those texts. The composite taxonomy of compositional relations for the cell derived from the compilation of ideational meaning is shown in Figure 7.8.

The activity of mitosis is part of the cell cycle. While phenomena such as 'the cell cycle' or 'evaporation' or 'condensation' may be construed lexicogrammatically as if each were a single undivided activity, they are actually composed of many interconnected activities. In explaining such phenomena, it is common for the single undivided activity to be reconstrued as a series of smaller activities. This reconstruing is referred to as 'momenting' (Doran & Martin, forthcoming). The cell cycle is momented as a series of smaller activities: interphase and mitotic phase (mitosis). The interphase is in turn momented, but this momenting did not appear in the mitosis infographics. The activity of mitosis is also momented as a series of smaller activities: prophase, metaphase, anaphase and telophase. The prophase can be further momented – as chromosomes condense, the nucleolus breaks down, two centriole pairs move apart, microtubules radiate from

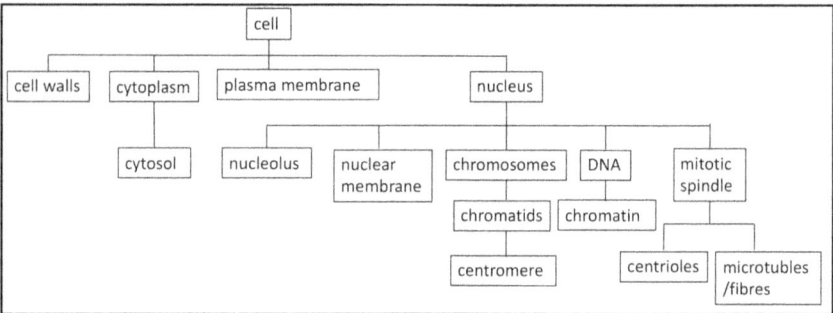

Figure 7.8 Composition taxonomy for the cell derived from the eight-textbook corpus.

School Science Explanation Genres 139

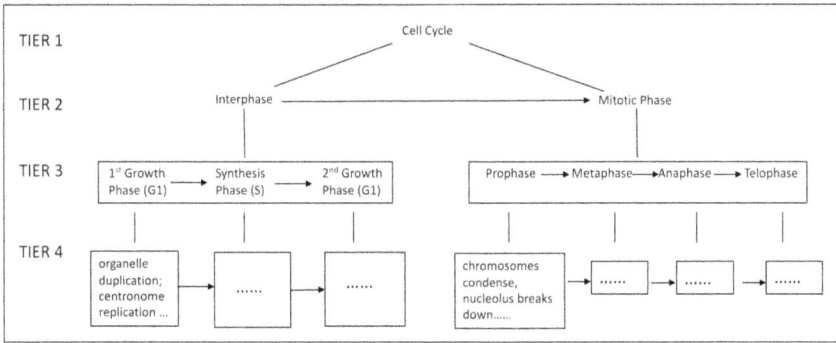

Figure 7.9 Momenting and tiering of activity in the cell cycle.

the centrioles, the microtubules attach to the centromere of the chromosomes and so on. These tiers of momented activity are outlined in Figure 7.9.

All of the realizations of the tiered activity of mitosis in the verbiage and the images of all eight of the infographics were mapped to derive a comprehensive composite representation. In order to refer to activity, readily accessible phrasing based on similarities in the lexicogrammatical construal of mitosis in the corpus was adopted. While the activities of the interphase and cytokinesis within the cell cycle are not considered part of the activity of mitosis in biology, five of the eight textbooks include these in their infographics. For this reason, they have been included in the composite representation of the tiered activity of mitosis (Table 7.1).

Most infographics moment the activity of mitosis as prophase, metaphase, anaphase and telophase; however, some also include early prophase and late prophase or transition to metaphase, while one includes late anaphase. There does not seem to be consistency in this further momenting, so this has been acknowledged by including the vertical arrowed lines in Tier 2 in Table 7.1.

To indicate the extent of the realization of compositional relations in the images only, in each of the four year 10 infographics, those compositional relations that are depicted in the images in each text were mapped in turn against the taxonomy of compositional relations in Figure 7.8. While abducing (inductively inferring) the interpretation of the cell components relies on knowledge of the field accessed from elsewhere, aspects of presence are also significant in this interpretation. Some images make use of a wider range of colour with more vibrancy and greater explicitness in depiction of detail, so that components are readily discernible, whereas in other cases components do not seem to be depicted or are extremely difficult to discern.

There is some commonality, but significant variation in the compositional relations of the cell that can be abduced from the images in each of the four infographics as shown in Table 7.2. Three of the cell components derived from the eight-text corpus do not appear in any of the images as shown by the dark shading in Table 7.2. None of the images construe cell walls (which occur only in plant, bacteria and algae) so it can be assumed the images are construing animal cells – and none of the images include cytosol or chromatin. Four of the cell components were depicted in some infographics but not in others, as indicated by the light shading in Table 7.2.

Table 7.1 Composite representation of the tiered activity of mitosis.

Tier 1	Tier 2	Tier 3
Mitosis	Interphase	Chromosomes replicate
	Prophase	Chromosomes condense/become visible
	Early	Nucleolus disappears
		Nuclear membrane disappears
	↕	Pairs of centrioles separate
		Fibres extend from centrioles
	Late/transition	The spindle fibres attach to centromere
	Late prophase/ transition to metaphase	A network of spindle fibres forms
	Metaphase	Chromosomes line up along the equator of the cell
	Anaphase	Spindle fibres (microtubules) contract
		Each centromere divides
	↕	Chromatids separate
	Late	Chromatids move to the opposite ends of the cell
	Telophase	Chromosomes uncoil and become less visible
		The nuclear membranes re-form
		Spindle fibres disappear
	Cytokinesis	Cytoplasm divides
		New cell membrane forms
		Two daughter cells are formed

Table 7.2 Composition in the year 10 textbook infographics on mitosis.

			Pearson	Jacaranda	Oxford	Nelson
Cell			X	X	X	X
	Cell walls					
	Plasma membrane		X	X	X	X
		Cytoplasm	X	X	X	X
		Cytosol				
	Nucleus		X	X	X	X
		Nuclear membrane	X	X	X	X
		Nucleolus		X		

Table 7.2 Composition in the year 10 textbook infographics on mitosis. *(Continued)*

		Pearson	Jacaranda	Oxford	Nelson
Chromosomes		X	X	X	X
	Chromatids	X	X	X	X
	Centromere				X
DNA		X	X	X	
	Chromatin				
Mitotic spindle		X	X	X	X
	Centrioles	X			X
	Spindle fibres	X	X	X	X

The nucleolus appears only in the Jacaranda text and is not mentioned in the verbiage in this text or in any of the other three texts. What is more contentious is the variation of presence in the images across the four texts. The centromere is clearly depicted in the Nelson text only. This is the centre point of the double-stranded chromosomes through which the spindle fibres are attached and is the point at which the double-stranded chromosomes divide into two identical chromatids. As well as being depicted in the image in the Nelson text only, the centromere is mentioned in the verbiage in this text and in the verbiage of the Oxford and the Pearson texts. Of similar concern is the clear depiction of the centrioles in the Nelson and the Pearson texts, but not in the other two. The centrioles are the pairs of rod-like structures that give rise to the spindle fibres and form the poles of the spindle. The centrioles are mentioned in the verbiage of the Nelson text only. Neither the centromere nor the centrioles are shown in the images in either the Jacaranda or the Oxford texts. From the perspective of presence this lack of explicitness also constrains the construal of compositional relations and activity in these texts. The Nelson text provides the most functionally comprehensive visual depiction of the relevant compositional relations, with the Pearson text approximating this, but with significant omissions in the other two texts.

Confirmation of the abduction of compositional relations from the images requires the verbal naming of the visually depicted components and their positioning within the composition taxonomy. In the Pearson, Nelson and Oxford infographics, some compositional relations are explicitly construed lexicogrammatically, but this is not the case in the Jacaranda text. In the Pearson text (Figure 7.7) one such confirmation occurs in the annotations: *Two nuclei form, each with the same number of chromosomes*; three occur in the co-text: *Each chromosome comprises two chromatids*; *The membrane surrounding the nucleus* ... and *a nuclear membrane encloses the chromosomes*. In the Nelson text (Figure 7.2) some compositional relations are realized by Classifier^Thing structures (Halliday & Matthiessen, 2004, p. 378): *spindle fibres, cell membrane* and *nuclear membrane*. In the first column of the aligned text in the Nelson infographic the compositional relation between the centromere and the chromosome is explicitly stated (... *the centromere of each chromosome*), and in the final column the relation between walls and cells is specified (as *cell walls*). Another form of confirmation in the

Nelson text is provided by the asterisked note about centrioles in the lower left-hand corner of the infographic, which explicitly constructs centrioles as part of the mitotic spindle (*Centrioles are minute rod-like structures that form the poles of the spindle*). As well as these explicit lexicogrammatical construals, in the Nelson text the annotations naming items in the images are directly linked to the corresponding image elements by connecting lines. The seven instances of these connectors directly support abductions about composition that might be drawn from the images. There are no such connectors in the other infographics. In the Pearson infographic the verbiage in the 'call outs' construes activity and affords inferred naming of chromosomes and nuclei only (Figure 7.7). In the Oxford infographic there are also no connecting lines linking the annotations to image elements (Figure 7.3). All of the annotations positioned above, beside or below the images focus on activity. But these include the Classifier^Thing structure *nuclear membrane*, indicating the membrane as part of the nucleus, and the activity, *each pair of chromatids separate at the centromere*, indicates that the centromere is part of the chromatid pairing. In addition, some compositional relations may be inferred by relating the verbal realization of activity to the depiction of activity in the image segment. For example, reading the metaphase activity (*Chromosomes line up in a single line across the centre of the cell*) in relation to the image in that micro-group, it is possible to relate the visual and verbal representations of the chromosomes from the concurrent visual and verbal realizations of segments located across the centre of the cell – and hence to confirm a compositional relationship between the chromosomes and the cell. It may then be possible to read back to the prophase and work out what the visual representation of *spindle* is in that image. However, the *1 Prophase* annotation, which has no corresponding image, indicates that the nuclear membrane has disappeared; but comparing the early prophase image with the late prophase image does not make clear what precisely it is from the former that is meant to represent the nuclear membrane. In the Oxford text then, none of the abductions of compositional relations are confirmed by connectors to verbiage in the micro-groups, but two are construed lexicogrammatically and some may be inferred from the annotations positioned in proximity to the images. In the Jacaranda infographic (Figure 7.6) three annotations juxtaposed with images construe activity: *Chromosomes have replicated*; *Chromosomes align at the equatorial plate*; *Chromatids separate*. From these juxtapositions, it is possible to infer the naming of the relevant components. Explicit naming occurs in only two instances: the topmost image is labelled as *Parent cell*, and the bottom images are labelled as *Two daughter cells*. The other two annotations are very confusing. To the right of the downward arrow between the top and second image the juxtaposed annotation reads: *2 chromatids = 1 chromosome*. This may indeed construe a compositional relation, but it is not at all clear what it means when located alongside this arrow. A novice reader may infer that two chromatids in the form of one chromosome is transferred from the top to the second image. Similarly, it is not at all clear what is meant by the positioning of the annotation in the form of a single word label, *Chromatid*, to the right of the downward arrow between the second and third images. Very limited confirmation and significant obfuscation of compositional relations occurs in the annotations in the Jacaranda infographic. The contribution of the images and the different forms of verbiage to the construal of compositional relations in the four infographics is summarized in Table 7.3. The greyed-out columns indicate the absence of 'aligned text'.

Table 7.3 The contribution of the images and the different forms of verbiage to the construal of compositional relations in the four infographics.

	Oxford 10								Nelson 10				Jacaranda 10				Pearson 10				
	Fig. 1.16				Fig. 1.17																
	Caption	Aligned Text	Annotations	Image	Caption	Aligned Text	Annotations	Image	Caption	Aligned Text	Annotations	Image	Caption	Aligned Text	Annotations	Image	Co-text	Caption	Aligned Text	Annotations	Image
Cell			X	X	X						X	X			X	X	X			X	X
Cell walls										X										X	
Plasma membrane				X						X	X	X				X	X				X
Cytoplasm				X							X	X			X	X					X
Cytosol																					
Nucleus				X				X		X	X	X			X	X	X			X	X
Nuclear membrane			X	X	X					X	X	X			X	X	X			X	X
Nucleolus																X					
Chromosomes			X	X	X			X		X	X	X	X		X	X	X			X	X
Chromatids			X	X	X			X		X	X	X			X	X	X				X
Centromere			X		X					X		X									
DNA				X				X	X							X	X				X
Chromatin																					
Mitotic spindle			X	X				X		X	X	X				X	X			X	X
Centrioles				X							X	X									X
Microtubules				X	X			X		X	X	X				X	X				X

Table 7.4 Summary of the distribution across image and verbiage of the construal of composition.

	Oxford	Nelson	Jacaranda	Pearson
Image or verbiage	10	12	11	11
Image + verbiage	7	11	5	10
Verbiage only	1	1	0	0
Image only	2	0	6	1

As an indication of the extent of the explicit construal of compositional relations, it is useful to consider the number of compositional relations construed by both image and verbiage compared with the number construed by image only. Table 7.4 shows in the top row the number of compositional relations construed by either image or verbiage; the second top row shows the number construed by both image and verbiage, followed by those construed by verbiage only and then by image only.

Clearly, the verbiage in the Nelson and Pearson texts provides much more confirmation of the abduction of componential relations from the images than the other two texts. In the Nelson text, reference back to Table 7.3 shows that the verbal construal of composition is quite consistent across the annotations (nine instances) and the aligned text (eight instances). In contrast, in the Pearson text the co-text provides much more confirmation (nine instances) than the 'call-out' annotations (four instances). Although the Nelson co-text does not deal with the explanation of mitosis, the infographic itself is at least as explicit in the construal of compositional relations as the Pearson text, which is the only year 10 text in this corpus where the co-text does deal with the explanation of mitosis. From the perspective of mass, the intermodal construal of composition confirms deeper taxonomic relations in the Nelson and Pearson texts, and this is significantly facilitated by presence due to the greater explicitness of depiction in these texts compared with the Oxford and Jacaranda texts.

The activity of mitosis is construed very differently in each of the four infographics. These differences will be discussed in relation to the affordances of the overall shape of the images; the extent of the tiering of the activity; the construal of activity in the images alone; the construal of activity in the annotations, the aligned text (where present) and the captions; and the concurrence of the construal of activity in image and verbiage. The only infographic that is accompanied by a co-textual explanation of mitosis is in the Pearson text. The construal of activity in this co-text and its relationship to construal in the infographic will also be discussed.

As indicated in relation to Figure 7.9, the cell cycle is usually construed as activity momented firstly as interphase and mitotic phase (mitosis), with both interphase and mitosis further momented. Only the Oxford text (Figure 7.3) includes the interphase and depicts the images of the activity of mitosis as a circle affording its construal as part of the cell cycle. The Nelson infographic (Figure 7.2) depicts mitosis as a horizontal line of images and hence construes the activity as a sequence with start and end points, rather than cyclic. The Pearson (Figure 7.7) and Jacaranda (Figure 7.6) infographics depict mitosis as a vertical line of images and hence also construe the activity as a sequence with start and end points. Both Oxford and Nelson moment mitosis as prophase, metaphase, anaphase and telophase, with Oxford further momenting prophase as early prophase and late prophase. However, this second tier of momented activity is not indicated at all in the Jacaranda text, while in the Pearson text mitosis is momented into six stages but these are not named.

The images and connecting arrows construing mitosis as a sequence in the Nelson and Jacaranda texts and as a cycle in the Oxford text afford the interpretation of successive images as transformations of the prior images. Arguably these connecting arrows are the only examples in these infographics of activity represented by vectors or action lines (Kress & van Leeuwen, 2006). However, action can also be inferred as having occurred in successive images when items depicted in one image recur in subsequent images but are configured differently – that is, it is inferred that some action has brought about this change in configuration (Painter et al., 2013). An example is the depiction of centrioles (the small cylinder/circle depictions) in the first image in Figure 7.10 and their recurrence in the second image in a different position; we can infer from this that they have moved apart. This is the means by which the tier 3 momented activity of mitosis is imagically realized in the infographics examined here.

The imagic construal of the activity of mitosis at tier 3 exemplifies the multiple tiering of activity that reflects a core aspect of what Martin is calling mass, but this construal of tiered activity is significantly influenced by presence, particularly explicitness. While the construal of activity relies on a great deal of abduction from the visual depiction, drawing on prior knowledge and/or information conveyed in the verbiage, aspects of presence such as the omission and/or problematic discernibility of detail in the images obviate the construal of some aspects of activity. For example, Nelson is the only infographic that consistently and clearly depicts the centrioles and the centromere, so activities like *pairs of centrioles separate*, *fibres extend from the centrioles* and *spindle fibres attach to the centromere* can only be readily abduced from the Nelson images.

The construal of tier 3 momented activity in each of the four infographics was mapped against the nineteen tier 3 activities listed in the composite representation of activity from our corpus shown in Table 7.1. The results of this mapping are summarized in Table 7.5.

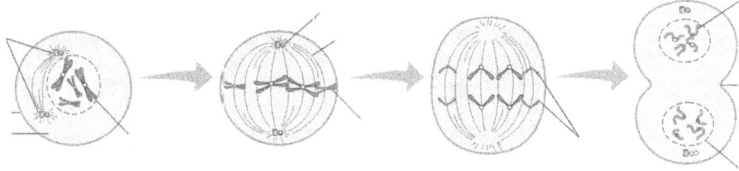

Figure 7.10 Image only depiction of mitosis from the Nelson infographic.

Table 7.5 The construal of momented activity in mitosis in four year 10 infographics.

	Oxford 10								Nelson 10				Jacaranda 10				Pearson 10				
	Fig. 1.16				Fig. 1.17																
	Image	Annotations	Aligned Text	Caption	Image	Annotations	Aligned Text	Caption	Image	Annotations	Aligned Text	Caption	Image	Annotations	Aligned Text	Caption	Image	Annotations	Aligned Text	Caption	Co-text
Interphase	X							X													
Chromosomes replicate	X	X								X								X			
Prophase																					
Chromosomes condense/become visible	X	X						X	X	X	X	X	X			X	X	X		X	X
Nucleolus disappears																					
Nuclear membrane disappears	X	X						X	X	X	X	X	X			X	X			X	X
Pairs of centrioles separate	X								X	X	X	X									
Fibres extend from centrioles	X								X	X	X	X									
Spindle fibres attach to centromere	X	X						X	X	X	X	X									
A network of spindle fibres forms	X	X							X	X	X	X					X	X		X	X
Metaphase							X														
Chromosomes line up along equator of the cell	X	X			X			X	X	X	X	X	X	X		X	X	X		X	X
Anaphase		X				X		X													
Spindle fibres (microtubules) contract								X	X	X	X	X	X	X		X				X	X
Each centromere divides								X	X	X	X	X	X	X		X				X	X
Chromatids separate	X	X						X	X	X	X	X	X	X		X				X	X
Chromatids move to the opposite ends of the cell	X	X						X	X	X	X	X		X		X	X	X		X	X
Telophase	X					X															
Chromosomes uncoil and become less visible								X	X	X	X	X					X			X	X
Nuclear membranes re-form	X	X						X	X	X	X	X	X	X		X	X			X	X
Spindle fibres disappear	X								X		X	X	X								
Cytokinesis						X		X													
Cytoplasm divides	X	X				X		X	X	X	X	X		X		X	X	X		X	X
New cell membrane forms								X	X		X	X						X		X	X
Two daughter cells are formed	X	X						X	X	X	X	X	X	X		X	X	X		X	X

Table 7.6 Summary of the distribution across image and verbiage of the construal of activity.

	Oxford	Nelson	Jacaranda	Pearson
Image or verbiage	11	16	11	15
Image + verbiage	8	11	3	9
Verbiage only	1	4	2	5
Image only	2	1	6	1

In a similar approach to the investigation of compositional relations, in seeking an indication of the extent of the explicit construal of activity, it is useful to consider how much of the activity is construed by both image and verbiage compared with the construal by image only. In Table 7.6 the first row shows the extent to which the tier 3 momented activity shown in Table 7.5 is construed in the images or the verbiage or both in the four infographics. The second row shows the concurrence of the construal of the momented activity in the images and the verbiage. The subsequent rows show the construal in verbiage only and image only.

The most comprehensive and explicit construal of activity occurs in the Nelson (Figure 7.2) and Pearson (Figure 7.7) infographics. In these infographics the only activity that is construed by image only is *spindle fibres disappear*. There is a good deal of concurrence in the construal of activity in image and verbiage and the remainder are primarily construed explicitly in language.

While the Oxford infographic (Figures 7.3 and 7.4) has less commitment to activity in either image or verbiage than the Nelson and Pearson texts as indicated in the first row of Table 7.6, there is a good deal of concurrence in what is committed in Oxford as shown in row 2. The Jacaranda infographic (Figure 7.6) has the same overall level of commitment to activity as Oxford, but little concurrence, with a significant proportion of the activity committed in images only. As the Pearson text is the only one where the co-text deals with the explanation of mitosis, it is significant to note that much more of the confirmation of the imagic construal of activity by the verbiage occurs in the co-text rather than the 'call-out' annotations. This can be seen in Table 7.6 with eleven construals of activity in the co-text verbiage and six in the call-out annotations for the Pearson text. On the other hand, Table 7.6 shows that the confirmation of imagic construal of activity in the Nelson infographic occurs much more evenly between the verbiage in the annotations (ten instances) and in the aligned text (fourteen instances). Hence, the Nelson infographic alone with no co-text explanation of mitosis seems to provide a more comprehensive and explicit construal of activity than the Pearson infographic with accompanying co-text explanation. From the perspective of mass, the intermodal construal of activity confirms the most extensive tier 3 activity in the Nelson and Pearson texts. This was more limited in the Oxford and Jacaranda texts with aspects of presence such as the problematic discernibility of image detail obviating the construal of some tier 3 activity.

Variability in the intermodal construal of field: Implications for evolving infographic explanation design

This analysis has shown the substantial variation from the perspectives of both mass and presence in the nature of the recontextualizations of mitosis provided by different textbook publishers for the year 10 science curriculum. The fact that three of the four most prominently used year 10 science textbooks in Australia rely solely on infographic portrayals for the construal of field with no unabbreviated canonical explanation genres included confirms a trajectory of recontextualization of such genres that warrants investigation of the emergence of new canonical forms. The distinctiveness of the Nelson text in relation to technicality and aggregation within mass and explicitness and appeal within presence are suggestive of an approach to infographic design that is highly facilitative pedagogically.

From the perspective of the construal of field, two of the texts examined here, the Nelson and Pearson texts, demonstrate greater meaning commitment in terms of the compositional relations and activity involved in mitosis. What characterizes these texts is the greater concurrence in the construal of compositional relations and activity in the images and verbiage as indicated in Tables 7.4 and 7.6. The greater technicality of the Nelson text is reflected in the deeper compositional taxonomy – it was the only text that construed centromeres and centrioles in both image and verbiage. The momenting of the activity in the Nelson text is named technically as Prophase, Metaphase, Anaphase and Telophase, whereas in the Pearson text this tier 2 momenting is not named technically and is simply referred to as numbered stages. Tier 3 of the momented activity is more detailed in the Nelson text (Table 7.5). For example, the further momenting of the Prophase includes the following activities construed in both image and verbiage: *pairs of centrioles separate, fibres extend from the centrioles* and *spindle fibres attach to the centromere*. These activities are not included in the Pearson text. The mass of the Nelson text, in terms of technicality with deeper composition and more technical momented and tiered activity, and in terms of its aggregation of meaning as an intermodal synoptic 'eyeful', suggests that consideration of the intermodal design of this text may inform the creation of more effective infographic explanation genres.

The first issue for consideration is mass – what field knowledge is to be included in terms of the depth of taxonomies of compositional relations of items and the extent of momenting and tiering of the activity in which they are involved. The Nelson text has the closest approximation to the composite representation of compositional relations in mitosis infographics derived from the corpus of the four publishers' junior and senior high school science textbooks (Figure 7.8). None of the year 10 texts included cytosol or chromatin and only one included the nucleolus in an image. Clearly, this indicates consensus about the compositional relations required at year 10. The only one of the remaining items in this consensus taxonomy not included in the Nelson text was DNA. This contrasted with the other texts which variously omitted centromeres and centrioles (Table 7.3). Similarly, the Nelson text most closely approximated the composite representation of activity derived from the eight-text corpus (Figure 7.9). The only year 10 text that indicated the nucleolus disappeared was the Jacaranda text that included it in one image but not the next image. Apart from that, all of the activities on the composite representation were included in at least two of the four year 10 texts. The only activity not included in the Nelson text is the Interphase activity of *chromosomes replicate*. As indicated in Table 7.5, this is in contrast to the omission of several of the activities across the other texts.

The second design factor to be considered is presence. The Nelson text surpasses the others in explicitness in clear and consistent depiction of cell components such as the centromere and centrioles and in the detailed imagic tiering of activity such as the spindle fibres emerging from the centrioles and forming the mitotic spindle and the disappearing of the nuclear membrane (indicated by its representation as a circular dotted line). The absence of such detailed depiction in the other texts impedes the construal of compositional relations and activity. Thirdly, the itemizing of the cell components and the construal of activity in the verbiage of the annotations in the Nelson infographic are directly linked to the relevant aspects of the images by connecting lines, which facilitates the intermodal construal of composition and activity. Notwithstanding these positive dimensions of the Nelson text, there remain some problematic aspects of design. These aspects concern the linear rather than a circular macro-grouping principle for the annotated image as a whole. Rather than affording the construal of mitosis as part of the cell cycle the linear choice affords construal as a discrete sequence with a start and end point. This might have been ameliorated by including the Interphase at each end of the linear portrayal, hence implying, if not depicting, a cyclic process. The linear design choice may have influenced the omission of DNA in the construal of mitosis in image and verbiage. Nevertheless, from the perspective of the construal of field and the intermodal aggregation of ideational meaning in knowledge building, this analysis indicates that infographics such as the Nelson example may well become sufficiently developed to provide teachers and students with a highly accessible resource for learning, independent of an accompanying unabbreviated canonical explanation genre. As infographics are already highly prominent in the public dissemination of scientific knowledge and are increasingly investigated and advocated as resources for knowledge building in schools (Gebre & Polman, 2016; Polman & Gebre, 2015), they appear to be a clear example of how

> genres flexibly adapt themselves to co-textual, inter-modal and contextual environments as needs arise; and some adaptations, if recurring often enough, give rise to new genres as a culture evolves. (Martin & Rose, 2012, p. 19)

The robust genre theory developed by Jim Martin and his colleagues, and Martin's ongoing seminal theorizing of social semiotics through concepts such as mass and presence, continues to provide educators with a highly effective means of optimizing for pedagogic purposes the relationship between a culture's system of genres and their instantiation in emerging new forms of actual texts.

Science textbooks

Armstrong, Z., Deeker, W., Madden, A., McMahon, K., Naughton, K., Siwinski, S., & Wheeler, A. S. (2018). *Pearson Biology 12: New South Wales Student Book*. VIC: Pearson Australia.

Borger, P. (2015). *Nelson Biology VCE Units 1 & 2* (3rd ed.). South Melbourne, VIC: Nelson Cengage Learning.

Chidrawi, G., Davis, A., Farr, R., Lampman, K., Matchett, B., & Young, P. (2013). *Nelson Iscience 10*. Melbourne: Nelson Cengage

Huxley, L., & Walter, M. (2019). *Oxford Biology for Queensland Units 1 and 2*. Melbourne: Oxford University Press.

Kinnear, J. (2016). *Nature of Biology. 1: VCE Units 1 and 2* (5th ed.). Milton, QLD: John Wiley & Sons Australia Ltd.

Linstead, G., Clarke, W., Devline, J., Madden, D., Rickard, H. C., & Spenceley, M. (2012). *Pearson Science. 10: S.B.* Port Melbourne, VIC: Pearson Australia.

Lofts, G. (2015). *Science Quest 10: Australian Curriculum* (2nd ed.). Milton, QLD: Jacaranda.

Silvester, H. (2016). *Oxford Science 10: Victorian Curriculum*. Melbourne: Melbourne Oxford University Press Australia.

References

Bateman, J. (2008). *Multimodality and Genre: A Foundation for the Systematic Analysis of Multimodal Documents*. London: Palgrave Macmillan.

Bezemer, J., & Kress, G. (2010). Changing text: A social semiotic analysis of textbooks. *Designs for Learning*, 3, 10–29.

Danielsson, K., & Selander, S. (2016). Reading multimodal texts for learning – a model for cultivating multimodal literacy. *Designs for Learning*, 8(1), 25–36.

Doran, Y. J., & Martin, J. R. (forthcoming). Field relations: Understanding scientific explanations. In K. Maton, J. R. Martin, & Y. J. Doran (Eds.), *Studying Science: Knowledge, Language, Pedagogy*. London: Routledge.

Gebre, E. H., & Polman, J. L. (2016). Developing young adults' representational competence through infographic-based science news reporting. *International Journal of Science Education*, 38(18), 2667–87.

Halliday, M. A. K., & Martin, J. R. (Eds.) (1993). *Writing Science: Literacy and Discursive Power*. London: Falmer Press.

Halliday, M. A. K., & Matthiessen, C. (2004). *An Introduction to Functional Grammar* (4th ed.). London: Arnold.

Kress, G., & van Leeuwen, T. (2006). *Reading Images: The Grammar of Visual Design* (2nd ed.). London: Routledge.

Martin, J. R. (1989). *Factual Writing: Exploring and Challenging Social Reality*. Oxford: Oxford University Press.

Martin, J. R. (1994). Macro-genres: The ecology of the page. *Network*, 21, 29–52.

Martin, J. R. (2013). Embedded literacy: Knowledge as meaning. *Linguistics and Education*, 24(1), 23–37.

Martin, J. R. (2017). Revisiting field: Specialized knowledge in secondary school science and humanities discourse. *Onomazein*, Special Edition SFL, 111–48.

Martin, J. R., & Dreyfus, S. (2015). Scaffolding semogenesis: Designing teacher/student interactions for facetoface and online learning. In S. Starc, C. Jones & A. Maiorani (Eds.), *Meaning Making in Text: Multimodal and Multilingual Functional Perspectives* (pp. 265–98). Basingstoke, UK: Palgrave Macmillan.

Martin, J. R., & Matruglio, E. (2013). Revisiting mode: Context in/dependency in Ancient History classroom discourse. In H. Guowen, Y. Zhu, Z. Delu, & Y. Xinzhang (Eds.), *Studies in Functional Linguistics and Discourse Analysis, 5* (pp. 72–95). Beijing: Beijing Higher Education Press.

Martin, J. R., & Rose, D. (2008). *Genre Relations: Mapping Culture*. London: Equinox Pub.

Martin, J. R., & Rose, D. (2012). Genre and texts: Living in the real world. *Indonesian Journal of Systemic Functional Linguistics*, 1(1), 1–21.

Martin, J. R., & Veel, R. (Eds.) (1998). *Reading Science: Critical and Functional Perspectives on Discourses of Science*. London: Routledge.

Martin, J. R., Unsworth, L., & Rose, D. (in press). Condensing meaning: Imagic aggregations in secondary school science. In G. Parodi (Ed.), *Multimodality: From Corpus to Cognition*. London: Bloomsbury.

Maton, K. (2013). *Knowledge and Knowers: Towards a Realist Sociology of Education*. London: Routledge.

Maton, K. (2016). Legitimation code theory: Building knowledge about knowledge-building. In K. Maton, S. Hood, & S. Shay (Eds.), *Knowledge-building: Educational Studies in Legitimation Code Theory* (pp. 1–24). London: Routledge.

Painter, C., & Martin, J. R. (2011). Intermodal complementarity: Modelling affordances across image and verbiage in children's picture books. In F. Yan (Ed.), *Studies in Functional Linguistics and Discourse Analysis* (pp. 132–58). Beijing: Education Press of China.

Painter, C., Martin, J. R., & Unsworth, L. (2013). *Reading Visual Narratives: Image Analysis of Children's Picture Books*. London: Equinox.

Peterson, M. O. (2016). Schemes for integrating text and image in the science textbook: Effects on comprehension and situational interest. *International Journal of Environmental and Science Education*, 11(6), 1365–85.

Polman, J. L., & Gebre, E. H. (2015). Towards critical appraisal of infographics as scientific inscriptions. *Journal of Research in Science Teaching*, 52(6), 868–93.

Rose, D., & Martin, J. R. (2012). *Learning to Write, Reading to Learn: Genre, Knowledge and Pedagogy in the Sydney School*. London: Equinox.

Scott, L., & Robinson, S. (1993). *Australian Journey: Environments and Communities*. Melbourne: Longman Cheshire.

8

Engaging readers and institutionalizing attitude: A social semiotic perspective on multimodal EFL pedagogic materials

Yumin Chen
Sun Yat-sen University

Introduction

The link between multimodality, social semiotics and pedagogy forms the nexus of this chapter. It aims to explore the ways linguistic and visual semiotic resources are deployed to engage readers and institutionalize attitude. While curriculum goals are typically construed as being ideational in orientation, there is a remarkable interpersonal underpinning in the curriculum goals in China (Ministry of Education of the People's Republic of China, 2001). The data drawn upon are a series of multimodal textbooks for teaching English as a foreign language (henceforth EFL). Given the evolving multimodal resources in educational settings, it is argued that these enable diversity in the realization of both interpersonal meanings and pedagogic goals. In the tradition of social semiotic studies of multimodal pedagogic discourse (Unsworth, 2001, 2017; Zhang, 2009, 2010, 2018) while extending this approach to cover primary and secondary English teaching in China, this chapter examines the multimodal construal of ENGAGEMENT and ATTITUDINAL meanings by drawing upon and extending the APPRAISAL system (Martin, 2000; Martin & White, 2005).

The interpersonal aspect of the curriculum standards

The choice to focus on the interpersonal dimension of pedagogic discourse has partially grown out of one of the recent developments in China's curriculum standards for primary and secondary education. As stipulated by the Ministry of Education, curriculum standards provide guiding principles for the editing and compiling of pedagogic materials for all school subjects. The eighth curriculum reform in 2001 has been recognized as 'an important milestone in the history of China's curriculum development' (Zhong, 2006, p. 373), because it has unprecedentedly highlighted an attitudinal dimension of developing students' positive emotions (Zhu, 2006, p. 193). This emotion and attitude goal is clearly articulated as one of the essential five aspects of the overall goal in EFL education. Nevertheless, the relative lack of research on how this emotion and attitude dimension is incorporated in primary and secondary textbooks has been identified as one of the drawbacks in textbook studies in China (Zhang, 2005, p. 11). As pointed out by Cheng (2002, p. 32), language teaching and learning, among other subject areas, is acknowledged as 'far more closely related to emotion and attitude education than other school subjects'. Given EFL textbooks frequently contain visual resources, one of the twofold concerns of the current study is to investigate how the attitudinal goals are realized through both their visual and their linguistic choices.

In addition to the attitudinal dimension, the interactive aspect of interpersonal management also calls for further exploration. Dialogic processes are advocated in classroom teaching, and the textbook is considered to be an essential component in this process (Chen & Ye, 2006; Zhong, 2006). Nonetheless, the way multimodal resources can be manipulated to mediate the heteroglossic space in EFL textbook discourse remains under-examined.

The aforementioned aspects of interpersonal meaning (i.e. editor-reader engagement and the attitudinal dimension) constitute the major pedagogic concerns of the present study. It is hoped that by making visible how linguistic and visual semiotic choices work in tandem to construe the dialogic setting and to hint at the intended evaluative stance, we can arrive at a better understanding of the functions fulfilled by multiple semiotic systems in the pedagogic context.

The APPRAISAL system

The theoretical framework drawn upon in the present study is the discourse semantic system of APPRAISAL (Martin, 2000; Martin & White, 2005), which covers three important semantic regions in evaluation, that is, the types, sources and degrees of attitude. As Martin and Rose (2007, p. 25) state, APPRAISAL is concerned with 'evaluation – the kinds of attitudes that are negotiated in a text, the strength of the feelings involved and the ways in which values are sourced and reader aligned'. There are thus three appraisal subsystems – ATTITUDE, ENGAGEMENT and GRADUATION – for exploring the attitudinal meanings realized in a text, the ways in which space can be opened up or closed down for different voices, and the resources for manipulating the strength of feelings or degree of alignment. Each of the subsystems has its own subcategories or options, and all these options are semantic ones that transcend diverse lexicogrammatical structures (Hood, 2004, pp. 13–14).

Among the three interacting dimensions, ATTITUDE covers three the semantic regions of AFFECT, JUDGEMENT and APPRECIATION, which are concerned with emotional responses, judgements of human behaviours and evaluations of products and processes. Linguistically, ATTITUDE can be realized through attitudinal lexis and mental processes of reaction. Besides its overt realization, ATTITUDE can also be indirectly invoked through a selection of ideational meanings that invoke evaluations of people and things (Martin & White, 2005, pp. 61–8).

AFFECT is considered to be at the heart in the semantic system of ATTITUDE, since it concerns feelings from which institutionalized JUDGEMENT and APPRECIATION later develop (Martin, 2000; Martin & White, 2005, p. 42; Painter, 2003). JUDGEMENT is concerned with positive or negative evaluative meanings that construe attitude towards human characters and behaviours. According to Martin (1997, p. 23), JUDGEMENT can be regarded as the institutionalization of feelings in the context of proposals. In other words, JUDGEMENT recontextualizes individual emotions in the realm of proposals about human behaviour. These proposals may be formalized ideationally as rules and regulations in a given culture and become part of field. JUDGEMENT covers two broad categories, that is, SOCIAL ESTEEM and SOCIAL SANCTION, which respectively deal with moral rules and legal implications. APPRECIATION encompasses evaluations of man-made or natural, concrete or abstract phenomena and processes, which can be further categorized into REACTION, COMPOSITION and VALUATION.

The ENGAGEMENT system draws on Bakhtin's (1981) notions of dialogism and heteroglossia, comprising networks of options for opening up or closing down the space for voices. ENGAGEMENT resources cover a wide range of devices construing a heteroglossic communicative setting, including alternative points of views and anticipatory responses from the audience. As Martin and White (2005, pp. 97–8) point out, the taxonomy of ENGAGEMENT meanings includes four main categories, that is, DISCLAIM, PROCLAIM, ENTERTAIN and ATTRIBUTE. The DISCLAIM and PROCLAIM resources are dialogically contractive, while those under the categories of ENTERTAIN and ATTRIBUTE are dialogically expansive.

Another subsystem within APPRAISAL is GRADUATION, which accommodates meaning-making resources for scaling attitudinal meanings and engagement values. GRADUATION is central to the whole system of APPRAISAL, for ATTITUDE and ENGAGEMENT can be regarded as domains of GRADUATION that differ only in terms of the nature of the meanings being scaled (Martin & White, 2005, p. 136). There are two axes along which the semantic system of graduation operates, that is, FORCE and FOCUS. The former grades meanings in terms of the intensity or amount of a scalable value, while the latter grades meanings according to the prototypicality and preciseness by which the categorical boundary is drawn. Hood and Martin (2007) further extend the graduation network, specifying FORCE as embracing INTENSITY (of a quality), QUANTITY (of a thing) and ENHANCEMENT (of a process), and FOCUS encompassing VALEUR and FULFILMENT.

Multimodal resources for engaging readers

The multimodal texts under examination are taken from seventeen EFL textbooks for primary, junior and senior secondary schooling, edited and published by People's Education Press (henceforth PEP) between 2002 and 2006. They constitute an entire series of the edition produced directly after the aforementioned curriculum reform in 2001. Altogether 118 teaching units are involved (i.e. 47 in the primary textbooks, 46 in the junior secondary ones and 25 in the senior secondary textbooks) and 1,398 visual images of different styles are employed. All teaching units contain visual images as well as verbal texts, ranging from those with a relatively small amount of language for primary school through to those with a greater proportion of language for secondary education.

In previous studies, three voices have been identified as constituting the heteroglossic backdrop of EFL textbook discourse: editor voice, reader voice and character voice (Chen, 2010a). In the present study we mainly focus on the multimodal resources for managing the heteroglossic space for the reader voice in relation to the editor voice and character voice. We concentrate particularly on the multimodal features of dialogue balloon and jointly constructed text in engaging the readers.

Dialogue balloon

The dialogue balloon is a common multimodal resource in EFL textbooks. This visual structure is 'projective' (Kress & Van Leeuwen, 2006, p. 68), since the utterance is not directly represented but mediated through a Sayer. In the EFL textbooks under examination, three types of dialogue balloon are identified, based on the functions they perform: lending support to the editor voice, explaining rules of games by demonstration, and giving directions to the reader (Chen, 2010a). Here we mainly focus on the two latter types because these are the ones that involve reader voice.

As shown in Figure 8.1, the dialogue balloon functions to explain the rules of a game through demonstration. Through the use of cartoons, it shows the reader (i.e. primary school student) how to practise commanding and offering by playing a game with pictorial cards. Although there is no verbal instruction, the image involving a dialogue between the cartoon characters demonstrates the way the students could perform this

Figure 8.1 Explaining rules of games by demonstration. Excerpted from PEP *Primary English Students' Book I for Year 3,* 2003, p. 53. Reproduced with permission.

kind of interaction. The dialogue balloons bring in character voice, encouraging the reader to act similarly. Visual demonstrations with dialogue balloons are frequently found in task-oriented teaching sections, such as *Let's play, Task time, Pair work* and *Group work*, where interaction between readers is required to fulfil the tasks. In this kind of multimodal text, at least one way to accomplish the task is demonstrated by the cartoon characters. The dialogue balloons thus actively make allowance for character voice, opening up the heteroglossic space and realizing the ENGAGEMENT meaning of ATTRIBUTE.

In most images in the EFL textbooks, the characters do not gaze at the reader. There are some cases where characters look directly at the reader and where eye contact is established. In this type of 'contact' image (Painter, 2007), directions are often given through imperative or interrogative clauses in dialogue balloons. This can be seen in Figure 8.2 for instance, in which a cartoon policeman looks directly at the reader. This gaze symbolically invites the reader to engage in an imaginary relation. Character voice, as indicated in the dialogue balloon, gives directions to the reader, and the utterance in the dialogue balloon (i.e. *Look, read and match*) clarifies what is required from the reader in completing the exercise (i.e. to match the traffic signs with their corresponding meanings). Through using the dialogue balloon as an ENGAGEMENT resource to attribute the demonstration or instruction to character voice, the textbook discourse fulfils the pedagogic goals.

Figure 8.2 Explaining rules of games by demonstration. Excerpted from PEP *Primary English Students' Book I for Year 6*, 2003, p. 12. Reproduced with permission.

Jointly constructed text

Jointly constructed text refers to any text that is intentionally unfinished and aims to involve the reader's participation in its ultimate completion (Chen, 2010a). Jointly constructed texts, which are essential in aligning the reader, have been widely used in EFL textbooks.[1] They take a great variety of forms, and the multimodal modes of communication further enrich the ways of engaging the reader voice. Figure 8.3 shows a jointly constructed drawing exercise.

The main part in Figure 8.3 is an unfinished picture of a human face, which is an analytical process (Kress & Van Leeuwen, 2006, p. 87) to be completed. In this analytical process, the human face picture is the carrier, while the eyes, ears, nose and mouth to be drawn by the reader are possessive attributes. The labels *eye, ear, nose* and *mouth* proclaimed by the editor voice indicate what should be drawn and where it should be drawn. The reader is thus required to follow the labels to complete this structured analytical process.

The strong, diagonal line of the pencil at the top-left corner forms a vector, indicating the presence of a narrative representation. In a transactional visual narrative process the vector links the Actor from which the vector departs and the Goal at which the vector is directed (Kress & Van Leeuwen, 2006, p. 59–63). The Actor can sometimes be fused with a vector. For example, the salient pencil in Figure 8.3, foregrounded with full colour saturation, plays the dual role of both Actor and vector. The Goal in this transactional action process is the unfinished drawing, and the vector formed by the oblique pencil encourages the reader to participate in co-constructing the multimodal text.

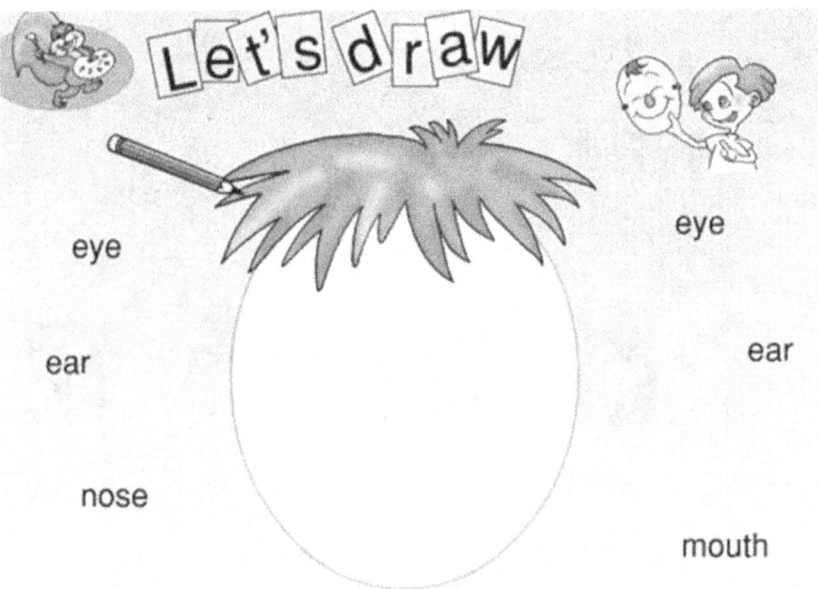

Figure 8.3 Jointly constructed text. Excerpted from PEP *Primary English Students' Book I for Year 3*, 2003, p. 16. Reproduced with permission.

In terms of visual composition, there is a smaller image at the top-right corner depicting a cartoon character holding a finished picture of human face. The upper-right position indicates that the smaller image is the Ideal and the New (Kress & Van Leeuwen, 2006, pp. 179–94). As compared with the upper smaller image, the larger unfinished human face is placed at the lower left position, which suggests its status as the Real and the Given. In other words, the unfinished drawing is presented as the practical, agreed-upon starting point, whereas the finished picture is the idealized and generalized information that is new to the reader. In light of the labels that indicate the possessive attributes and the contour of human face, the reader is supposed to achieve the distant, ideal goal as is indicated in the upper smaller image. In this multimodal text, the practice of labelling conveys editor voice, whereas the upper smaller image indicates character voice. The lack of completion or fulfilment in this multimodal jointly constructed text in effect opens up space for a reader voice to take part. The reader voice could engage with the editor voice and character voice through co-constructing the text. Owing to the fact that the answer to this multimodal exercise comes from the external source of reader voice, the meaning of the unfinished jointly constructed text can be expressed in the clause '*According to* the reader, the picture will be … '. Therefore, it may be inferred that jointly constructed text realizes the ENGAGEMENT meaning of ATTRIBUTE, expanding the heteroglossic space by bringing in the reader voice.

As analysed above, multimodal resources in textbook discourse facilitate engagement with readers and help achieve pedagogic goals. Another interpersonal aspect highlighted in the curriculum standards, that is, emotion and attitude, will be addressed in the following section.

Multimodal institutionalization of attitude

Inscribed happiness of English learning

As observed in the data, cartoons are widely used in primary and junior secondary EFL textbooks, with students and teachers/family members as the major cartoon characters who are learning English in a class or involved in community activities. For instance, Figure 8.4 depicts four school-age students conducting a group discussion. It contains two cartoons representing the scene where the students are discussing how they get to school. All characters demonstrate expressive countenances indicative of delight, which can be observed from their disproportionately large eyes with enlarged pupils implying great interest, their facial expression of laughing from side to side with their eyes closed, as well as their demonstrative and enthusiastic gestures. Positive AFFECT (i.e. happiness) is thus directly inscribed in the visual display, with the school-age cartoon characters as emoters (i.e. the conscious participants who experience the emotion) and the English-learning activities as the trigger (i.e. the phenomenon that is responsible for that emotion).

Figure 8.4 Inscribed happiness of English-learning. Excerpted from *PEP Primary English Students' Book I for Year 6*, 2003, p. 5. Reproduced with permission.

Following Martin and White's (2005, p. 46–52) framework for approaching linguistic AFFECT in terms of six factors (i.e. positive or negative, behavioural manifestations or internal mental processes, a reaction to an emotional trigger or an undirected ongoing mood, high or low value, realis or irrealis value, un/happiness, in/security or dis/satisfaction), we extend these categories to the analysis of visual affect in Figure 8.4 as follows (Chen, 2010b, p. 65):

Types of affect corresponding visual patterns

- positive affect cheerful facial expressions showing great interest
- behavioural surge exciting gestures indicative of active engagement
- reaction to other feelings directed at the ongoing English learning activity
- high value overtly expressed emotions and great merriment
- realis affect reaction to the existing stimulus, that is, group discussion
- happiness showing comfort and enjoyment
- security confident when expressing themselves
- satisfaction absorbed in the group work

When exploring the amount of meaning potential activated in a given text, Martin (2008, p. 45) proposes the concept 'commitment' to capture the degree of meaning instantiated. It could be inferred that the cartoons in Figure 8.4 commit positive AFFECT through a series of overt, direct visual patterns, that is, depictions of facial expressions and behavioural manifestations.

When examining Figure 8.4 inter-modally, we can see that its verbal texts are framed in four dialogue balloons, demonstrating two dialogues between four students. The language is mainly concerned with the students' experiences, namely how they usually go to school and the reasons for choosing certain means of transport. Attitude, however, is not indicated in the language, neither by inscription nor by invocation. It is hard to tell by reading the verbal texts alone what the students feel about the activity. In other words, the language commits no attitudinal meanings. In fact, it is through the visual images that the affective meanings are conveyed. The students are depicted as feeling excited, self-assured and engrossed.

The images also echo the section title *Group Work* by presenting the scene of a group of students working together in class, with a mood of happiness added via visual affective inscriptions. While the verbal text within the dialogue balloons explains to the reader the way they are supposed to perform the task by giving two model dialogues, the images imply the attitude that the reader is supposed to assume in undertaking the task and perhaps in learning English in a broader sense. The atmosphere of happy English learning is thus created visually. The language–image relation is complementary as far as the construal of evaluative stance is concerned (Chen, 2010b). As stated in the *Curriculum Standards for English* (Ministry of Education of the People's Republic of China, 2001, p. 1), it is a crucial task for EFL education to arouse and cultivate students' interest in English learning, as well as to build up their confidence in the learning process. As analysed above, visual meaning-making resources play an important role in the realization of this attitudinal orientation in the primary EFL pedagogic setting.

Logogenetic recontextualization in moral education

The cartoons in primary textbooks are mostly inscribed with a high degree of positive affectual meanings. Some of the cartoons also invoke an attitudinal response in the intended reader. In Figure 8.5, for instance, besides the explicitly inscribed affective meanings, the cartoon also invokes an attitudinal response in the reader through the way it represents the characters. In this figure, five family members are represented as connected with each other by the vectors of arms and/ or eye gaze lines. Specifically, the right arm of the grandfather forms an oblique line, hence generating a vector linking him with his granddaughter. On the other hand, the eyelines emanating from the granddaughter and the father relate them to the grandmother and the mother. This visual connection, together with the inscribed happiness, presents to the reader the scene of a harmonious and happy family get-together. The image thus 'invites' or 'affords' to be more precise (Martin & White, 2005, p. 67), a favourable evaluation of filial piety and parental responsibility from the putative reader (Chen, 2010b).

When examining the role of evaluation in the discourse of reconciliation, Martin (2002) proposes the notion of 'logogenetic recontextualisation' to reveal the reworking of evaluation from affect through JUDGEMENT to APPRECIATION. In Figure 8.5 the positive emotion is first 'reworked' as ethics, which is in turn recontextualized as 'politicised aesthetics' (Martin, 2002, p. 200), concerning the social value of the harmonious family that conforms to the standard, conventional principle advocated in the given educational and social context. In other words, what is supposed to be invoked in the reader is the positive APPRECIATION concerning the value of a family being united, and this moral education is achieved through the JUDGEMENT of the

Figure 8.5 Logogenetic recontextualization. Excerpted from *PEP Primary English Students' Book II for Year 3,* 2003, p. 15. Reproduced with permission.

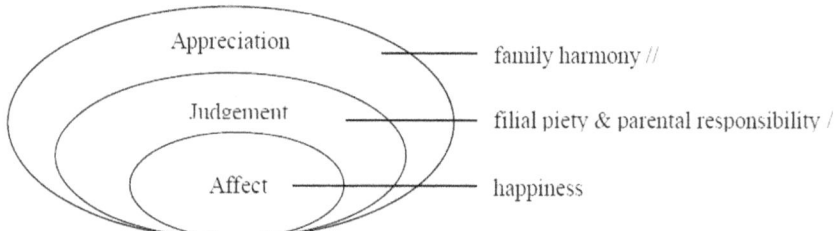

Figure 8.6 Recontextualizing feeling in Figure 8.5. Adapted from Martin, 2002, p. 199; Chen, 2010b.

ethical behaviour of filial piety and parental responsibility. Adapted from Martin's (2002, p. 199) model of the logogenetic recontextualization process, the attitudinal recontextualization in Figure 8.5 can be diagrammatically represented in Figure 8.6.

Accumulation of institutionalized feelings in EFL education

The accumulation of attitudinal meanings across educational levels with reference to the relationship between AFFECT, JUDGEMENT and APPRECIATION will now be discussed. AFFECT is taken as the core system among the three subsystems within

ATTITUDE, because it is concerned with the feelings we are born with, which are later developed into culturally specific emotional repertoires (Martin, 2000, p. 147). AFFECT is recontextualized or institutionalized into the uncommon sense realms of shared values in two directions: on the one hand, affect is recontextualized as judgement in relation to the evaluation of human behaviours that need to be controlled under social norms; on the other, affect is recontextualized as APPRECIATION with respect to the evaluation of things that need to be valued with reference to their social significance. JUDGEMENT and APPRECIATION can therefore be viewed as institutionalized affect. Based on Halliday's (1994) concepts of proposition and proposal, Martin (2000, p. 147) reveals that JUDGEMENT institutionalizes feelings as proposals (about behaviour), whereas appreciation institutionalizes feelings as proposition (about things). In other words, JUDGEMENT and APPRECIATION can be viewed as the institutionalizations of AFFECT in two different directions.

In developing an ontogenetic view of ATTITUDE in language development, Painter (2003) points out that at the protolinguistic stage, before first words are uttered, a child's initial semiotic system is essentially for sharing emotion or affect. The institutionalizations of AFFECT, that is, JUDGEMENT and APPRECIATION, occur 'only later with new semiotic steps on the child's part – either the adoption of mother tongue lexical words in lieu of protolinguistic symbols or a "meta" awareness of the sign itself' (Painter, 2003, p. 189). In other words, the growing capability of symbolizing enables the evaluations in terms of JUDGEMENT and APPRECIATION to emerge along with the direct expressions of emotions.

In extending the discussion beyond the early pre-school period to account for the construal of evaluation in primary and secondary education, we identify a gradual shift in terms of attitudinal orientation in the EFL textbooks considered in this chapter (Chen, 2010b). As analysed above, primary and junior secondary textbooks mainly adopt cartoons to describe human participants with explicit affective inscriptions and dialogue balloons. This tendency gradually diminishes and images of a more serious style (i.e. portraits and photographs) emerge in senior secondary textbooks (see Table 8.1).

As analysed in Chen (2010b), portraits and photos in textbooks are more institutionalized ways of expressing evaluation due to the lack of affective inscriptions. Table 8.1 shows that at primary school level, 97.9 per cent of the visuals are cartoons; however, by the time students are in senior secondary school, this decreases to 29.7 per cent. It could be inferred that as students advance through the school years from

Table 8.1 The distribution of different visual styles in EFL textbooks.

Visual style Type of textbook	Cartoon	Portrait	Photograph	Total numbers of images
Primary textbooks	839 (97.9%)	16 (1.9%)	2 (0.2%)	857 (100%)
Junior secondary textbooks	403 (89.6%)	5 (1.1%)	42 (9.3%)	450 (100%)
Senior secondary textbooks	27 (29.7%)	15 (16.5%)	49 (53.8%)	91 (100%)
Number of each visual style	1269	36	93	1398

Source: Y. M., Chen, *The semiotic construal of attitudinal curriculum goals: evidence from EFL textbooks in China.*

primary to secondary schooling, a personal way of expressing individual emotions gradually shifts to a more institutionalized way of evaluating people's behaviours and abstract concepts.

Conclusion

This chapter has explored how multimodal resources of dialogue balloons and jointly constructed text open up different degrees of heteroglossic space for the reader to engage with the editor and characters in EFL textbooks. It examined the explicit attitudinal inscriptions and the implicit attitudinal invocations in multimodal textbooks, with special reference to how the intended pedagogic goals are achieved. The study showed that a wide range of meaning-making resources, including non-verbal resources, can be brought together and considered systematically as realizing common evaluative meanings and are involved in constructing a global rhetorical orientation. A close reading of multimodal pedagogic materials through the lens of a semantically oriented framework like the APPRAISAL system enables a deep understanding of how semiotic resources interact to make meanings, which may in turn have implications for designing and utilizing pedagogic materials.

Note

1   The 'jointly-constructed text' referred to here (i.e. reader participation in completing an incomplete text in a textbook) differs from the teacher-led joint construction in genre pedagogy (i.e. the co-creation of a text through dynamic classroom interaction between the teacher and students).

References

Bakhtin, M. (1981). *The Dialogic Imagination: Four Essays*. In M. Holquist (Ed.), C. Emerson (Trans.). Austin, TX: University of Texas Press.
Chen, Y. M. (2010a). Exploring dialogic engagement with readers in multimodal EFL textbooks in China. *Visual Communication*, 9(4), 485–506.
Chen, Y. M. (2010b). The semiotic construal of attitudinal curriculum goals: Evidence from EFL textbooks in China. *Linguistics and Education*, 21(1), 60–74.
Chen, Y. R., & Ye, L. X. (2006). Textbook: The open discourse in dialogue. *Contemporary Educational Science*, 23, 34–6.
Cheng, X. T. (2002). Reflections on the curriculum standards for English. *Teaching Monthly (Middle School Edition)*, 11, 29–33.
Emerson, C., & Holquist, M. (Eds.) (1986). The problem of speech genres. In M. Bakhtin (Author) & V. W. McGee (Trans.), *Speech Genres and Other Late Essays* (pp. 62–105). Austin, TX: University of Texas Press.
Halliday, M. A. K. ([1984] 1994). *An Introduction to Functional Grammar*. London: Arnold.

Hood, S. (2004). *Appraising Research: Taking a Stance in Academic Writing* (Doctoral dissertation). Retrieved from The Appraisal Website. (http://www.grammatics.com/appraisal/suehoodphd/hoods-phd-links.htm). Last accessed 15 April 2020.
Hood, S., & Martin, J. R. (2007). Invoking attitude: The play of graduation in appraising discourse. In J. Webster, C. Matthiessen, & R. Hasan (Eds.), *Continuing Discourse on Language* (pp. 740–64). London: Equinox.
Kress, G., & Van Leeuwen, T. ([1996] 2006). *Reading Images: The Grammar of Visual Design*. London: Routledge.
Martin, J. R. (1997). Analysing genre: Functional parameters. In F. Christie & J. R. Martin (Eds.), *Genre and Institutions: Social Processes in the Workplace and School* (pp. 3–39). London: Cassell.
Martin, J. R. (2000). Beyond exchange: Appraisal systems in English. In S. Hunston & G. Thompson (Eds.), *Evaluation in Text: Authorial Stance and the Construction of Discourse* (pp. 142–75). Oxford: Oxford University Press.
Martin, J. R. (2002). Blessed are the peacemakers: Reconciliation and evaluation. In C. Candlin (Ed.), *Research and Practice in Professional Discourse* (pp. 187–227). Hong Kong: City University of Hong Kong Press.
Martin, J. R. (2008). Tenderness: Realisation and instantiation in a Botswanan town. In N. Nørgaard (Ed.), *Odense Working Papers in Language and Communication* (pp. 30–62). Special Issue of Papers from 34th International Systemic Functional Congress.
Martin, J. R., & Rose, D. ([2003] 2007). *Working with Discourse: Meaning beyond the Clause*. London: Continuum.
Martin, J. R., & White, P. R. R. (2005). *The Language of Evaluation: Appraisal in English*. London: Palgrave.
Ministry of Education of the People's Republic of China (2001). *Curriculum Standards for English*. Beijing: Beijing Normal University Press.
Painter, C. (2003). Developing attitude: An ontogenetic perspective on APPRAISAL. *Text – Interdisciplinary Journal for the Study of Discourse*, 23(2), 183–209.
Painter, C. (2007). Children's picture book narratives: Reading sequences of images. In A. McCabe, M. O'Donnell, & R. Whittaker (Eds.), *Advances in Language and Education* (pp. 40–59). London: Continuum.
Unsworth, L. (2001). *Teaching Multiliteracies across the Curriculum: Changing Contexts of Text and Image in Classroom Practice*. Buckingham: Open University Press.
Unsworth, L. (2017). Image–language interaction in text comprehension: Reading reality and national reading tests. In C. Ng & B. Bartlett (Eds.), *Improving Reading and Reading Engagement in the 21st Century* (pp. 99–118). Singapore: Springer.
Zhang, D. L. (2009). The application of multimodal discourse analysis and media technology in foreign language teaching. *Foreign Language Education*, 30, 15–20.
Zhang, D. L. (2010). Preliminary investigation into the concept of design and the selection of modalities in multimodal foreign language teaching. *Foreign Languages in China*, 7, 48–53.
Zhang, D. L. (2018). Exploring the teaching mode for cultivating foreign language majors' multiple competences. *Foreign Language World*, 1, 28–35.
Zhang, S. H. (2005). Review of the studies on primary and secondary school textbooks in China. *Educational Science Research*, 5, 9–12.
Zhong, Q. Q. (2006). Curriculum reform in China: Challenges and reflections. *Frontiers of Education in China*, 1(3), 370–82.
Zhu, X. M. (2006). Moral education and values education in curriculum reform in China. *Frontiers of Education in China*, 1(2), 191–200.

9

Uncovering 'The Story' behind meaningful texts: Bilingual students' intentions and linguistic choices

María Estela Brisk and Jasmine Alvarado
Boston College

In the 1980s Jim Martin and his team of linguists joined Australian educators in exploring the status of writing instruction and student work in primary schools. Their exploration revealed that current writing instruction was not beneficial for students getting an education. The need for change was 'an issue of social justice' (Martin, 2009). The *Writing Project* and *Language and Social Power* project brought to elementary schools the notion of teaching the genres of writing informed by systemic functional linguistics (SFL) theory. In the 1990s the work was extended to secondary schools in the project called *Write it Right* and finally, in the 2000s, *Reading to Learn* integrated reading and writing (Rose & Martin, 2012).

Jim Martin and his group considered it essential for writing instruction to include a variety of genres connected to various disciplines (Martin & Rose, 2008). In addition, Martin proposed that meaning is construed beyond the clause through 'semantic resources that lead us from one clause to another as a text unfolds' (Martin & Rose, 2007, p. 1). The Teaching and Learning Cycle (TLC) evolved as the approach to teaching writing, where students are apprenticed into the various genres of writing by developing the field, and deconstructing and joint constructing texts before independently writing (Callaghan, & Rothery, 1988; Rothery, 1996).

This work by Martin and his colleagues, especially Beverly Derewianka (2011, 2016) and Sally Humphrey (2012), became the inspiration and source of theoretical grounding for collaboration between Boston College researchers and the staff of a Boston public school, who were dedicated in their efforts to improve the writing instruction of the multilingual student population. The work with teachers in this school continued for ten years (Brisk, 2015; Brisk & Ossa-Parra, 2018). The impact of SFL-informed pedagogy on student writing was measured not only by State annual literacy tests but also by genre-specific analytic rubrics that assessed the purpose, stages and selected aspects of language (Brisk, 2015). To determine the writing improvements and challenges, each teacher chose for analysis the writing of two students who came from high and low writing proficiencies. Teachers experimented with a variety of genre units such as arguments (Brisk et al., 2018), fictional narratives (Brisk et al. 2016), scientific reports and explanations (Hodgson-Drysdale & Rosa, 2015) as well as a number of other genres, greatly expanding the breath of text types their students produced as well as enhancing students' discourse and language resources. Research shows that these teachers taught writing using genre pedagogy informed by SFL and the TLC, successfully connecting their writing instruction with the disciplines. All students actively participated in classroom activities regardless of level of English proficiency (Brisk & Kaveh, 2020).

This chapter highlights a new aspect of research from this school and university partnership. It examines fifth-grade bilingual students' writing packages consisting of first and last drafts as well as all the planning and writing done in between. In addition, this chapter explores the talking of students about their understandings of and intentions with writing, as they reviewed with the researchers the contents of their writing packet for the argument (exposition) unit. The argument units covered the purpose of arguments, discussions on topics worth writing about, the stages of argument texts and selected language features that help make arguments stronger, such as type of sentences, grammatical person, modality, evaluative language and graduation.

Relevant literature

Students' development in argument writing

Argument texts differ from the chronological genres more common in the elementary curriculum. Arguments have a rhetorical rather than chronological organization, and they require logical reasoning to support a point of view (Derewianka & Jones, 2016; Martin & Rose, 2008). Producing arguments that are logical, clear and persuasive is a difficult process for elementary school students due to the cognitive and linguistic demands of this kind of work (Christie, 2012; McCann, 1989; Nippold, Ward-Lonergan, & Fanning, 2005). Argument texts also require coherence among the thesis, reasons and evidence. Moreover, language resources for expressing evaluation, which is essential in argumentation, are not usually mastered until late childhood and early adolescence (Christie & Schleppegrell, 2018). However, Anderson (2008) believes that children beginning the third and fourth grades should be exposed to persuasive texts rather than waiting until middle and high school, and that they should be taught to write in this genre to establish the basis for successful performance in later school years.

Indeed, argument writing is a developmental skill that can be improved as a result of increased exposure of argument texts as well as classroom instruction and feedback from teachers (Nippold et al., 2005). The literature on teaching writing suggests multiple ways to teach this genre within the elementary grades. These strategies include, but are not limited to, scaffolding argumentative writing through oral discussion, choosing audiences and topics that are relevant to the students, exposing students to argument texts through literature and modelling the language of argumentation (Anderson,

2008; Brisk et al., 2016; Crowhurst, 1990; Derewianka & Jones, 2016; Humphrey & Macnaught, 2015; Rose & Martin, 2012).

Students' interpretations of their writing process

Embedded within the aforementioned instructional practices to build argument writing is the development of students' interpretations of their own language choices in relation to their argument writing goals. Research into students' identities as writers has made connections between students' writing development and their own interpretations of their choices and situational contexts throughout the writing process. Specifically, studies about writers' dialogically shaped perspectives (Gutiérrez et al., 1995; Knoeller, 2004; Landay, 2004) focus on the relation between the dialogic shaping of ideas and the ways these perspectives are expressed through different modes and genres. As Ferretti and Lewis (2013) assert, 'dialogic support is essential for the development of reflective argument writing' (p. 114). We argue that dialogic support extends opportunities for students to negotiate their understandings of contextually relevant topics and features of argument texts so they can confidently support and defend their stances.

Within this literature, several studies (Gillespie et al., 2013; Kinloch, 2008; O'Connor, 2017) have used interview data to gain a more nuanced understanding of bilingual students' process of writing and the characteristics of genre. Focusing on African-American students, Kinloch (2008) showcased interview data to advocate for the importance of teachers encouraging student writers' *choice and voice* in their teaching (p. 89). In O'Connor's (2017) study, interviews revealed how students understood the interpersonal relationship with their audience and the corresponding language choices related to tenor which they made based on their understandings. Additionally, O'Connor (2017) noted how factors related to audience awareness and the tenor of a text, particularly the continua of power, contact and affective involvement, are given greater clarity through analysis of student interviews. O'Connor (2017) asserts that educational stakeholders should analyse not only student writing but also student interviews because this approach provides valuable insights about students' understanding of audience, language choices and the specific purpose of the writing. From the perspective of research, student interviews provide important triangulation of findings of text analysis and themes. The incorporation of interviews prevents educators and researchers from having to guess or approximately interpret students' experiences and motivations when participating in argument writing projects and making language choices in response to audience (O'Connor, 2017). As such, we extend O'Connor's (2017) recommendations through our analysis of bilingual students' rationale behind their purpose, structure and language in their argument texts.

Context

As part of a ten-year school-university partnership to develop a genre-based, SFL-informed writing curriculum, teachers at one school learnt about the purpose, stages and linguistic features of genres to then tailor their focus of instruction to meet the linguistic needs of all students. This elementary school has a student population of 57 per cent Latino, 30 per cent Black, 10 per cent Asian and 3 per cent White, with 51 per cent of the students considered English Language Learners (ELLs).

By working with researchers from Boston College, the teachers acquired and adapted knowledge of SFL and the TLC to their multilingual context. All teachers at this school teach genre writing related to a variety of disciplines and work across grade levels to plan the entire school writing calendar. For each class, teachers chose two students from high and low writing proficiencies, determined from state and in-class writing assessments as the focus students for research purposes.

The students in this study were enrolled in two fifth-grade classrooms, where their classroom teachers planned together and shared resources with each other as they each implemented an argument unit informed by SFL and genre-based pedagogy. The argument writing unit was taught over a period of six weeks and was the second genre of the school year, the first being reports, where the students in both classes wrote about the positions of the candidates for president of the United States. The teachers planned to have students use their reports as the basis for their argument texts on who would make a better president. However, the report unit took longer than predicted. Consequently, the US presidential election took place as the students had begun their arguments, which they considered futile to complete. Both classes went on to search for other topics appropriate for argumentation.

The data for the study reported in this chapter included the writing packets for each student with all the written work for the unit, transcribed student interviews and transcribed teacher interviews with both teachers. The written work was analysed using the SFL informed writing rubric (Brisk, 2015) that includes the following items: purpose, thesis statement, reasons, evidence, reinforcement of statement of position, generalized participants, language choices, use of technical vocabulary, types of sentences, use of person, modality, evaluative vocabulary, graduation and cohesive paragraphs. These items in the rubric were chosen to reflect the structure of genres (Rose & Martin, 2012) and the language of appraisal (Martin & White, 2005). The students' interviews were analysed for comments related to decisions they made during the purpose and stages of their writing, the challenges they faced throughout the argument unit and references to teachers' curricular and pedagogical choices. The teacher interviews were reviewed for clarification on teachers' curricular resources, pedagogical choices, students' academic and cultural backgrounds, and classroom interactional dynamics.

The following section covers the experiences of four bilingual students from two different fifth-grade classroom. Within the findings section, each case begins with conclusions about the students' abilities to write arguments drawn from direct analyses of their final writing piece. Next, this subsection illustrates how drafts and materials produced before the final piece reflect the entire writing process, and finally, the section concludes with the students' commentary on their written work, further illuminating their choices in their writing of the argument genre.

Findings

Nebus composes and reflects on writing

Nebus's final piece showcases a clear thesis statement about whether late homework should be accepted by teachers. He previews the three reasons in his introduction:

> Late Homework acception is what I strongly Recommend. Some Kids Just Have other things going besides school. Just because Kids go to school six hours a day does not mean they should spend All their time on homework. Some Kids Just forget.

Despite having clear reasons, the evidence for these reasons did not refer to other texts or resources. Furthermore, Nebus shifts into narrative prose to present evidence for one of his reasons, how easy it could be for a student to forget to do homework:

> Some kids just forget. It was a beutiful (beautiful) sunny day out side. The birds were singing. The children were playing. But the little boy had homework to do. The little boy forgot all about His homework and went to play with his friends.

The language features were mostly aligned to the register and purpose of the argument genre. The argument text is mostly written in third person and with statements. He includes word such as *grueling, deliciose (delicious), worry* and *poor,* and words that show gradation, *strongly, all, enough* and *non-stop*. For example, in his final piece, Nebus writes, That leaves you with an <u>extremely</u> <u>tierd</u> kid, <u>definenataly not enough</u> energy to do all that homework. Further, he includes logical methaphors such as *another reason* and *the last reason but not least* in the topic sentences of his body paragraphs to introduce different reasons. Through his cohesive paragraphs and language features expected in an argument genre, Nebus produces a coherent argument text that showcases its purpose and stages.

Nebus's packet of drafts and graphic organizers that were written between the production of his first argument piece and his last argument text demonstrates his consistent understanding of thesis statements supported by reasons and evidence. In all his drafts and planners, Nebus includes his thesis statement with three supporting reasons. A major challenge that his graphic organizers and drafts demonstrate is the consistent integration of evidence that directly supports his reasons. Two graphic organizers from two projects about classroom parties and owning a pet lacked evidence for each reason that supported Nebus's thesis statements for these topics. His graphic organizer about the topic of his final piece, late homework acceptance, was missing evidence for his reason about *students' forgetting to do their homework.*

Although Nebus's graphic organizer for his argument piece about late homework acceptance contained limited evidence for his reasons, Nebus's drafts showcased how he included evidence for all his reasons. He includes more evidence for his reasons in his draft than in his final piece. In his draft, to support his reason about students not having enough time to do homework, Nebus discusses the implications on sleep quality and wellbeing when students are at home.

> *The student could start his or her homework at school. Then as soon as they get home, work on it non-stop and still not finish [until] 8:00. <u>Kids also need to be well-rested. If we don't get enough rest we won't be ready for that long grueling school day the next day.</u>*

In his final piece, Nebus does not include the sentence (underlined above) following the one about not being able to finish at 8.00. Additionally, Nebus's draft indicates that he continuously does not refer to other resources or texts in his evidence and includes the aforementioned evidence in narrative prose to support his reason for students forgetting to do homework. As such, the drafts disclose that some evidence was not included in the final argument piece, and continual insertion of the narrative prose as evidence for reasons.

The drafts of Nebus's argument piece also demonstrated the inclusion of more varied language features expected in an argument text than those featured in his final piece. For example, he used the resources of evaluative language, graduation and modality to strengthen his stance: *deliciose* (delicious), *well-rested and grueling*, and *tramendously* (tremendously), *absolutly* (absolutely) and *most Deffinenetely* (most definitely). For example, Nebus includes the following sentence in his draft but not in his final piece that includes multiple language features: *And that leaves you with a* <u>tramendously (tremendously) tierd (tired) kid</u> *who* <u>most deffinentely (definitely)</u> *does not have* <u>enough</u> *energy to do that* <u>big</u> *stack of homework.*

When reviewing and discussing the packet of the argument unit work with Nebus, he helped clarify questions, omissions and inconsistencies throughout his drafts, graphic organizers and final piece. Consistent with the inclusion of a thesis statement and reasons throughout his work, Nebus explained the stages and purpose of an argument piece: 'So depending on what the topic is we need to make up the thesis … and then after we found out the thesis, the reasons would be the main focus of each other paragraph that I'm going to write and the evidence would be the information in each paragraph.' He also revealed that he wished that he had included a conclusion in his final piece but disclosed his limited time to complete the text, 'If I had more time I think we would have written a conclusion but I don't think I had enough time for that.'

In terms of his evidence, Nebus explained how he included many pieces of evidence that were based on personal experiences in his drafts and graphic organizers. He pointed to the aforementioned narrative prose about a boy forgetting to do homework from his final piece and explained how he wanted to include a short story to make his reason relatable to his audience, 'It's like an example of a kid like being overwhelmed because like so much time to go outside and play but he has homework to do.' However, Nebus did not include an explanation in his body paragraph about how the story supported the reason. As such, the narrative seems disjointed from the paragraph's reason about students forgetting to do homework because there are no explicit explanations about the evidence.

When reviewing his work during the argument unit, Nebus was very conscious about the need to convince his audience about his stance expressed in his writing. He illustrated how his teacher would remind him of the intended audience of middle and high school students as he looked over his drafts about late homework acceptance, 'As we went and wrote each paragraph, he would remind us of our audience. I wanted to write for middle and high school students so I had to remember that.' Furthermore, Nebus described how his teacher, with the help of the class, would use a model argument text and revise sentences from the model text by including evaluative vocabulary and words that indicate grading, 'He would basically pull out a sentence that sounds boring and then he would go around asking us for the words and things that would make it sound better.' Nebus pointed to how he changed a sentence from first person in one of his body paragraphs from his drafts to third person in his final piece, *spend all our time on homework*, to third person, *they should spend all their time on homework*. Nebus illuminated how his inclusion of language features seems to have been guided by his teacher's pedagogical practices which highlighted language features as the class was introduced to the purpose and stages of argument texts. Lastly, he noted how the unit encompassed shifts in topics every one to two weeks. Despite Nebus's understanding of the unit structure and pace, Nebus did not know his teacher's rationale for the unit layout, 'I don't know, he didn't really say, he didn't say this is why we are doing this instead of that.'

Nebus's discussion about his work during the argument writing unit shows his perseverance in wanting to express his stance on an issue for his intended audience. He supports his understandings about the argument genre with descriptions of class lessons. While Nebus can take a stance with multiple reasons, his evidence was not composed of multiple sources and he did not clearly explain to the audience about how it supported specific reasons. Having quick conferences to check during the process of publishing the final piece would have helped Nebus and the teacher to identify which key language features were missing and how Nebus explained his use of evidence in his argument texts.

Shanelle composes and reflects on writing

Shanelle's final piece was about owning a pet. She showcases a clear thesis statement and previews three reasons in her introduction:

> *Owning a pet from the pound or Animal Rescue League has tremondas (tremendous) advatages (advantages). Child will feel great Adopting a pet. Adopting a pet is a lot of Responsibility. Adopting a pet from the pound cost less money.*

Although she has clear reasons and a thesis statement in her introduction, she forms body paragraphs for only two of those reasons: feeling great after adopting a pet and making a child feel responsible. Furthermore, the evidence for these reasons comes from personal experience rather than text or internet resources.

Language features in Shanelle's final piece indicate variation in register. The argument text contains evidence that is written in second person, which is in contrast to the reasons that are presented in third person. For example, in her final paragraph, Shanelle switches from third to second person in her first two statements. *Adopting a pet will make a child responsibility. You will have to take of it like wakeing (waking) it.* Similar to her shifts in person, Shanelle relies on *will* as a modal verb to highlight her reasons and evidence. Shanelle incorporates evaluative vocabulary and graduation in her writing, such as *happy, calm, less, tremendous, great* and *a lot*. As an entire text, Shanelle's argument text has a cohesive structure with an introduction as well as different reasons presented at the beginning of each body paragraph.

Shanelle's packet of drafts and graphic organizers that were written between the production of the first and final argument pieces demonstrate her continuous effort to take a stance on an issue supported by reasons. In her drafts and graphic organizers, Shanelle has at least two reasons to support her thesis statement. However, most graphic organizers were incomplete with a lack of presentation of reasons and/or evidence. Specifically, Shanelle's graphic organizer for her final piece about adopting a pet from a pound does not contain evidence for the three reasons she presents.

Shanelle's drafts present evidence for her three reasons about the merits of owning a pet from the pound. Compared to her final piece, Shanelle includes in her draft more evidence for her reasons for adopting a pet making a child feel great. She writes that *If you adop (adopt) a dog, cat, fish, or turtle <u>it will make you happy</u>. All these animals will <u>calm you down</u>*. However, in her final piece, Shanelle omits the clause about making a child happy and writes *If y (you) adop (adopt) a dog, cat, fish, or turtle <u>it will make will calm you down</u>*. Additionally, Shanelle's draft indicates that she did not refer to other resources or texts in her evidence. As such, her drafts reveal that she did not include evidence in her final piece nor did she refer to other sources or texts in her student work during the argument unit.

Shanelle's review and discussion of her packet of argument writing helped clarify omissions and inconsistencies that were displayed throughout her drafts, graphic organizers and final pieces. Consistent with her inclusion of a thesis statement and reasons in her work, Shanelle explains the stages and purpose of an argument piece, 'I had a thesis and then reasons there are many advantages and then the examples.' Shanelle also disclosed that she was frequently absent during the argument unit, which resulted in incomplete graphic organizers and drafts. For her argument piece on owning pets from the pound, she recalls using her personal experiences for evidence, 'Yeah we had three turtles in the room and two were babies but we used to have an adult. We had to take care of them and train them.'

When looking over her drafts and graphic organizers, Shanelle consistently justifies her linguistic choices throughout her text. When pointing to her inclusion of evaluative vocabulary and words of gradation, Shanelle states the need to have specific language to emphasize and accomplish the purpose of the argument genre, 'Like more specific language, like good words, because it didn't have a lot so we need to add more. It is important to the essay because it makes it better and you don't have to like say you forgot to do something.' Although she did not mention her intended audience, Shanelle disclosed that it is important to make language choices that convince the reader of her stance, 'It helps you understand a lot of things that you don't understand if you are too shy to ask like me. It's to help the reader so you explain and give the reason why that happens.' As such, Shanelle emphasizes the importance of being transparent about her stance on her topic to her audience through her writing.

Shanelle explains her views on the writing process, her abilities as a writer and the role of her teacher as she looked at her packet of argument texts. She believes she is a slow writer who needs extra time to write her ideas. She mentions that she thinks her writing is messy and she views writing as an arduous process, 'I am basically just taking my time writing everything. I don't like writing … too much work and I write not neat.' However, she acknowledges the constant support from her teacher throughout the argument unit. She notes how she would review paragraphs for her drafts with him before publishing her final piece, 'Because every time you write a sentence or a paragraph we go to him and he searches it. He would help fix it or help add another sentence or words or not.' Conferences with her teacher served as mini-teaching moments when he would offer suggestions for language structures and forms. Although Shanelle views writing as a challenge, she strives to be aware of her instructional context and the choices asked of her to make in her writing of a specific genre.

Josh composes and reflects on writing

Josh starts his final piece with good background information for the thesis, which he actually fails to state (inserted in brackets):

In march 2011, the Americans with Disabilities Act (ADA) made rules- the rules state that only dogs and miniature horses, should be service animals out in public. The rules are absolutely absurd. [Capuchin monkeys and dolphins should be approved as official service animals because] *Capuchin monkey make great animal helpers, so do dolphins!*

The reasons and evidence are not that strong because he only states one per animal. The language features are appropriate given the register. He uses generalized participants, mostly statements except for the exclamation in the introduction. He consistently writes in third person and has some use of evaluative language and graduation to enhance the argument: *good, amazing, life savers, serious*. As most children often do, he overuses the modal *can* and has in the Theme position the same participant he is writing about, although he varies the terms he uses. For example,

<u>Capuchin monkeys</u> **can** *operate microwaves and DVD players. <u>These animals</u>* **can** *turn lights off and on for their owners. <u>They</u>* **can** *open bottles and Flip pages Of a book for their owner. <u>Capuchins</u>* **can** *even scratch an annoying itch.*

Review of the packet with work that preceded writing the final piece reveals that Josh understood that arguments include a thesis statement supported by reasons and evidence. All the planners he created for the various projects included these stages. The challenge his plans and drafts show is that he had difficulty making these three components align to make sense. The three reasons supporting the presidential candidate made sense but only one piece of evidence clearly related to the reason. The other two were in the general theme but not directly supportive. The graphic organizers of the two projects that followed were incomplete but they always included a thesis statement. There were, however, partial drafts of these arguments showing that he did not always write based on a planner.

In the graphic organizer for his next to last piece, he wrote under the thesis: *I disagree that only dogs and miniature horses should be service animals*, which was changed to *I disagree with the rule* in his draft essay. However, the reasons and evidence were related to a different thesis: *capuchin monkeys make great service animals*, which he also included in the initial paragraph. In the planner and draft essay, he developed three reasons backed with evidence supporting well 'the capuchin monkeys make great service animals' thesis. As shown earlier, his final essay, however, includes only one reason and evidence related to capuchin monkeys but added the idea that dolphins should also be included (in bold). He gave one example related to dolphins as being helpful which he inserted in the middle of the evidence about the monkeys.

> *Capuchins can do lots of chores for a human with Disabilities.*
> **There is a girl who is a part of a special program, to help children with serious physical and learning difficulties. Swimming with dolphins help Children relax.**
> *Capuchin monkeys can operate microwaves and DVD players. These animals can turn lights off ...*

Thus, his final piece is less strong with respect to reasons and evidence and overall organization than his next to last draft, which, with some editing of the thesis, would have made a strong argument. In the conclusion he tried to connect the animal helpers with the legislation but his sentence was unclear. In reaction to the teacher's question 'What do you mean?' he added one more sentence about the monkeys rather than trying to fix the sentence in question, showing that he was unclear about the meaning of the teacher's question.

Josh's various drafts in his packet included numerous words crossed over with alternatives written above. For example, above *temporary* he wrote *short-term*, above *volatile* he wrote *tense*, above *they* he wrote *fifth graders*; in one of the essays he also wrote *verb*, *adjective* above such parts of speech. In the sentence *I disagree with this rule because capuchin monkeys make great animal helpers*. He crossed out *I disagree with this rule because*. His edits were always at the word or sentence level.

Reviewing his packet of work and reflecting on it clarify some contradictory evidence that his final written work presents. Josh started to work on writing arguments with a good idea of the purpose of arguments. He mentioned 'taking a stand', 'having an opinion' and 'finding reasons in the web'. Given that he had already worked with his teacher and that in fourth grade they had written arguments, it is not surprising. However, he admitted that when doing research 'I was having trouble finding reasons and evidence' and asked the teacher for help. As his plans and essays show, he had some difficulty with aligning reasons and evidence with the thesis.

When asked about the difference between his final draft and final essay, he explained that after writing his draft essay he went back to the research sources to make sure he had enough information in the evidence. In doing so, he came across some information on dolphins so he decided to add it, drastically changing a well-developed essay that only needed a coherent thesis.

In his interview Josh comes across as a thoughtful writer who is aware of his audience. He talked about reviewing his writing by 'looking for synonyms' of difficult words 'to make sure each sentence made sense and told the reader what it is supposed to say'. For example, he changed *volatile region* to *tense region* because 'there are some words that other readers might not know'. Other times he had an adult audience in mind when he changed *do* to *perform* to 'show adults how intelligent I am'.

In his early drafts, Josh started the essay with *I disagree*. In the final draft he eliminated the phrase because the teacher told them to do the essay in third person. As many children do, Josh had the subject of the sentence in the Theme position, often repeating the subject. He mentioned that in several occasions, following the teacher's directions, he 'changed to other nouns so that it wouldn't seem so boring', showing no understanding of the function of the language in the Theme position but eager to follow his teacher's directions. As shown earlier in the paragraph about capuchin monkeys, he used *capuchin monkeys, they, these animals* and *capuchins*. Following the teacher's instruction on the use of 'persuasive' language, Josh used the resources of evaluation and graduation: <u>violent</u> video, <u>amazing</u> country, <u>great</u> animal helpers.

To follow the teacher's directions, he would make the changes even if he was not quite sure why. For example, he changed *they* to *fifth graders* 'because we have to keep it in third person'. When a researcher noted that *they* is also third person, he responded: 'Yeah but our teacher told us to do that.' Teachers' instructions have a power influence on students' decisions signalling the need to be clear of the reasons why children are encouraged to make certain choices.

Given his discussion of his writing, Josh is a very conscientious writer eager to write well by being aware of his audience and eager to follow his teacher's instructions. He is able to write a relatively coherent argument as the next to last piece showed but his final piece was derailed by checking the sources for more information and adding information outside of his original essay. A short conference with the teacher about the thesis of his final draft would have been the only edit he needed to make it a good final piece that reflected all his efforts on writing well.

Ashley composes and reflects on writing

The three levels of data sources created different pictures of Ashley's ability to construct arguments. Analysis of her final product with respect to purpose, stages and elements of language given the register revealed that she does not know how to write an argument since her final piece is a report on capuchin monkeys and their features as service animals. Her language would have been appropriate for an argument for a general audience. She used declarative sentences, third person, generalized participants, and evaluative language and graduation to enhance the qualities of these monkeys, such as *extremely, amazing, very* and *more*.

The packet of work that preceded this final piece, however, reveals her knowledge and challenges with argument writing. The documents included partial work on three arguments. These included graphic organizers with places for the thesis, reasons, evidence and a conclusion. In the case of one topic she had a graphic organizer supporting the need for bedtime for children and the other against it. Yet another draft on the topic that video games lead to violent behaviour was written without a graphic organizer. Her work includes a full graphic organizer and draft on the final topic related to the law that determines that only dogs and small horses are considered service animals and can be taken to public places. Ashley's work demonstrates her difficulty in formulating a thesis statement. The first attempt in the graphic organizer reads: *Some animals should be able to go to public*. In the draft she writes: *Some animals should be able to go to public places*. The intended statement, however, would have been 'Some animals should be added to the list of service animals so that they can go to public places with their owner.' The final product introduces capuchin monkeys in order to report about them: *Capuchin monkeys are very good at helping people with there (their) needs*.

The reasons and evidence in the graphic organizer for her draft on service animals are not completely the same as those appearing in the draft. In the graphic organizer she includes capuchin monkeys and dogs as good service animals; the third reason is actually in support for not allowing other animals as service animals: *The changes were needed to protect people from diseases*. The draft includes a paragraph that is not only about dogs but also about birds, as well as two paragraphs about capuchin monkeys, with information different from that included in the graphic organizer. The counter-evidence was not developed in the final draft.

Included in the packet of plans and drafts were the source articles that Ashley had used for her research. Comparing them with her final product shows that she had copied chunks of the article verbatim. For example, Ashley's paragraph is a composite of chunks of a paragraph in the source text,

Ashley: *Capuchin monKeys are extremely Smart. In the wild, they have Shown the ability to picK up tools. This maKes it easier for them to handle modern items such as remotes and cell phones.*

Capuchin monkeys are very small. Some weigh less than eight pounds, even when fully grown. They **are** also **extremely smart. In the wild, they have shown the ability to pick up tools** and use them to solve problems. Their hands can easily carry small tools. **This makes it easier for them to handle modern items such as remotes and cell phones.** (MyANET, 2016).

The interview with Ashley helped put together the puzzle of her struggles. Ashley was aware that they 'were supposed to just write an opinion piece' and defined arguments as: 'is where you like when you are fighting for a reason why basically you want this to happen.' She showed understanding of the process of finding evidence for her reasons. She wrote questions on a topic in order to 'research something like some evidence'.

A number of circumstances prevented students from finishing the first few argument projects. When asked about it, Ashley explained, 'I didn't get to finish' but did not remember the reasons why. The first few unfinished pieces were produced with a partner with whom she had the opportunity to discuss them. She admitted that in the case of the argument related to children's bedtime, they changed their position because when doing research for reasons on having a bedtime 'I kept coming up with reasons for why they shouldn't have a bedtime'. This is the first piece of evidence of Ashley's major priority: to have enough information in her papers. When producing the draft on service animals, which was the project she got to complete and that she produced by herself, she admitted that after producing the graphic organizer she consulted again the research resources provided by the teacher because 'I didn't think I wrote down enough information [in the graphic organizer]'. Analysing the graphic organizer's entries, it seems that there was not enough information or the information was not clearly understood by Ashley. For example, for the reason of dogs being helpers, she only had one piece of evidence: *hearing dogs help people who are deaf or hard-of-hearing*. When consulting the article again, she came across information on birds, so she added: *Birds can also alert people with stuff as well ...* to her paragraph about dogs. She came across more information on capuchin monkeys, the source of her two last paragraphs in the draft. Thus, her concern for the amount of information led her to further consult sources after she had done the planning. Instead of improving her plan, she went ahead and wrote the draft losing some of the coherence of the original plan. The results left her dissatisfied so she went back to the sources and wrote a completely new piece just about the capuchin monkeys for which there was the most information in the research resources provided by the teacher. When asked why she had done that, she responded, 'I didn't really like how I wrote the other one.' This constant dissatisfaction with her writing led Ashley not only to keep consulting the sources but also to copy directly the language of the sources.

After all this effort to improve on her piece, Ashley was very disconcerted when her teacher told her that 'I was writing a report'. 'I think I was writing an argument,' declared Ashley. Looking just at Ashley's final product yielded very little information about Ashley's knowledge of the argument genre. The various plans and drafts showed her knowledge of the stages of an argument and her struggles in putting together a thesis with a coherent set of reasons and evidence. Only the interview, however, revealed her sincere efforts to write the best possible piece with lots of information as well as the strategy of disregarding the original plans in favour of the additional information that repeated reviewing of the source articles provided her.

Discussion

As a lens to understanding students' products over the course of a unit, interviews reveal students' knowledge about and challenges with argument writing. Persuasive writing can be difficult for fifth graders (Christie, 2012; Crowhurst, 1990; McCann, 1989). Yet, students in this study demonstrated that they had internalized what their teachers had taught with respect to purpose, stages and language features important for arguments and the need to be aware of audience. Their drafts and interviews reflected their learning and reasons for making choices. Occasionally, they were not completely sure why they had to do it, though. Students would explain what they did but would justify their decisions based on specific commentary from the teacher during lessons.

Both teachers and students faced challenges throughout the argument unit. The well-planned sequence of a report unit where students would gather the evidence they needed for their arguments did not work because the topic and language of the report unit were difficult for these fifth graders, thus disrupting the timing of both units and the content of the argument unit. The time constraint of the argument unit became a real challenge for students, resulting in a number of incomplete argument drafts on various topics, and feeling rushed when creating the last version of their final complete argument. Having incomplete versions of several topics took away the opportunity to deeply practise thinking through an argument to ensure that the stages made sense together. As Martin repeatedly expresses, language as a resource for making meaning goes beyond the sentence level to include the discourse level (Martin & Rose, 2007). The students often talked about changes and additions they made at the sentence or word level but neglected the text level. Making coherent arguments was also influenced by the difficulty of the topic. For Josh and Ashley, they struggled to make the connection between legislation related to legally permitted animal helpers and information about capuchin monkeys.

Students were aware that they were writing for an audience and that audience impacts language choices they make. However, without a specific audience (except for Nebus), students' choices about language were not always consistent with their intentions to persuade their audience about a specific position. During the student interviews, students would indicate decisions based on multiple potential audiences.

Specific language features important in argumentation, such as grammatical person, evaluative language and graduation and use of modals were appropriately used when creating drafts. Some aspects such as use of person were more difficult for some of the students while others were able to revise their work to show consistency of voice. Nebus attributed the teacher's reminders to his consistent use of voice.

There was a breakdown in the process of producing their final piece. The students worked very hard researching, planning and drafting their pieces but the final piece was never of the quality expected from analysing the next to last drafts. These were consistently better written and more complete than what they turned in as their final piece. These students expressed their dissatisfaction with their final pieces and were reflective about revisions and additions they would make if they were to work on their arguments. Furthermore, the process revealed that many of these students judged their writing abilities throughout the writing process, which led them to make drastic decisions and changes to drafts that completely deterred the purpose of the piece. They went back to the sources and added ideas that confused rather than improved their writing, or chose to include only parts of the final draft in their published piece, or dismissed completely the final draft and started brand new, which in the case of one student resulted in writing a different genre. Without analysing the work that preceded the final pieces and listening to what the students had to say about producing the final piece, evaluation of their writing capacity would have been greatly underestimated.

Implications for instruction

Student work as well as their commentary over the various plans and drafts reveal that students learnt a lot about the purpose, stages and aspects of language connected with argument writing through the activities carried out over the six-week unit. The data also show what they were still struggling with this challenging genre, while also concerned with producing good writing. There are several lessons learnt that can enhance instruction for writing in multiple genres:

- Familiarize students with the genre by reading and deconstructing texts and having discussions throughout the year before carrying out the argument writing unit.
- Establish with students a specific audience for each project.
- Have students plan in the form of graphic organizers with space to elaborate on the various stages of the genre, noting language features.
- Have individual and group conferences to ensure coherence of content and stages in the graphic organizers before students start drafting.
- Have students write a draft based on the plans without further consulting the research resources.
- Have conferences about why students made the choices that they made for content and language.
- Conference with students to revise the existing draft with the purpose of improving specific points.
- Have students produce a final piece that is a clean copy of the revised draft and not a new piece altogether.
- Balance the number of products with the length of time allotted for the unit.

Conclusion

Jim Martin's support to educators using genre pedagogy has had an everlasting impact on schools across the globe. Different educators, district leaders and researchers have strived to apply genre pedagogy and SFL in a variety of contexts, using different perspectives informed by their respective backgrounds and experiences. Although Martin goes on to explore new theories, leaving many of us behind, he continues to support the various innovative and progressive changes researchers and teachers bring to the education system. The impact of SFL and genre pedagogy in the way schools teach writing is unquestionable. Writing instruction in the United States is a neglected aspect in the literacy development of students. Most writing produced in schools does not have a clear goal and is used as a way of measuring reading comprehension or as a form to develop fictional stories. Martin (1993) challenged schools by suggesting that 'there is more to writing than story writing and that a broader range of types of writing, reflecting the needs of both schools and communities, needs to be introduced' (p. 119). Education reforms such as the Common Core State Standards (2010) in the United States recognize the importance of teaching genres, or text types as they call them. However, these text types are not well defined and not connected to forms of language and relevant purposes for students. Applying SFL informed genre theory and pedagogy has helped teachers negotiate the goals of educational reforms to meet the needs, experiences and desires of their students (Brisk, 2015).

References

Anderson, D. D. (2008). The elementary persuasive letter: Two cases of situated competence, strategy, & agency. *Research in the Teaching of English*, 42(3), 270–314.

Brisk, M. (2015). *Engaging Students in Academic Literacies: Genre-Based Pedagogy for k-5 Classrooms*. New York: Routledge.

Brisk, M. E., & Kaveh, Y. M. (2020). Mainstream teachers for successful multilingual classrooms: The case of a school that embraced a genre-based pedagogy to teach writing. In S. Hammer, K. M. Viesca, & N. L. Commins (Eds.), *Teaching Content and Language in the Multilingual Classroom: International Research on Policy, Perspectives, Preparation and Practice* (145–67). New York: Routledge.

Brisk, M. E., & Parra, M. O. (2018). Mainstream classrooms as engaging spaces for emergent bilinguals: SFL theory, catalyst for change. In R. Harman (Ed.), *Bilingual Learners and Social Equity* (pp. 127–51). New York, NY: Springer.

Brisk, M. E., Nelson, D., & O'Connor, C. (2016). Bilingual fourth graders develop a central character for their narratives. In L. de Oliveira & T. Silva (Eds.), *L2 Writing in Elementary Classrooms* (pp. 88–105). New York: Palgrave Macmillan.

Brisk, M. E., Kaveh, Y. M., Scialoia, P., & Timothy, B. (2016). Writing arguments: The experience of two mainstream teachers working with multilingual students. In C. P. Proctor, A. G. Boardman, & E. Hiebert (Eds.), *English Learners and Emergent Bilingualism in the Common Core Era* (pp. 138–56). New York: Guilford.

Brisk, M. E., Alvarado, J., Timothy, B., & Scialoia, P. (2018). Breaking the linguistic ceiling: Bilingual students appropriate academic English. In Sharkey, J. (Ed.), *Transforming Practices for the Elementary Classroom* (pp. 85–98). Alexandria, VA: TESOL International Organization.

Callaghan, M., & Rothery, J. (1988). *Teaching Factual Writing: A Genre-Based Approach*. Sydney, Australia: Metropolitan East Disadvantaged Schools Program.

Christie, F. (2012). *Language Education throughout the School Years: A Functional Perspective*. Chichester, West Sussex: Wiley-Blackwell.

Common Core State Standards Initiative: Preparing America's Students for College and Career. Retrieved from http://www.corestandards.org. Last accessed 15 April 2020.

Cope B., & Kalantzis, M. (1993). Introduction: How a genre approach to literacy can transform the way writing is taught. In B. Cope & M. Kalantzis (Eds.), *The Powers of Literacy: A Genre Approach to Teaching Writing* (pp. 1–21). Pittsburgh, PA: University of Pittsburgh Press.

Crowhurst, M. (1990). Teaching and learning the writing of persuasive/argumentative discourse. *Journal of Education*, 15(4), 348–60.

Derewianka, B. (2011). *A New Grammar Companion for Teachers*. Marickville, NSW: Primary English Teaching Association.

Derewianka, B. M., & Jones, P. T. (2016). *Teaching Language in Context* (2nd ed.). Melbourne, VIC: Oxford University Press.

Ferretti, R. P., & Lewis, W. (2013). Best practices in teaching argumentative writing. In S. Graham, C. MacArthur, & J. Fitzgerald (Eds.), *Best Practices in Writing Instruction* (2nd ed., pp. 113–40). New York, NY: Guilford.

Gillespie, A., Olinghouse, N. G., & Graham, S. (2013). Fifth-grade students' knowledge about writing process and writing genres. *The Elementary School Journal*, 113(4), 565–88.

Gutierrez, K., Rymes, B., & Larson, J. (1995). Script, counterscript, and underlife in the classroom: James Brown versus Brown v. Board of Education. *Harvard Educational Review*, 65(3), 445–72.

Halliday, M. A. K., & Matthiessen, C. M. I. M. (2004). *An Introduction to Functional Grammar* (3rd ed.). London: Hodder Arnold.

Hodgson-Drysdale, T., & Rosa, H. (2015). Go with the flow: Fifth grade students write about the flow of energy and matter through an ecosystem. *Science and Children*, 52(6), 32–7.

Humphrey, S., & Macnaught, L. (2015). Functional language instruction and the writing growth of English language learners in the Middle Years. *TESOL Quarterly*, 50, 792–816.
Humphrey, S., Droga, L., & Feez, S. (2012). *Grammar and Meaning*. Newton: Primary English Teaching Association Australia.
Kinloch, V. (2008). Innovative writing instruction: Writing in the midst of change. *The English Journal*, 98(1), 85–9.
Knoeller, C. P. (2004). Narratives of rethinking: The inner dialogue of classroom discourse and student writing. In A. F. Ball & S. W. Freedman (Eds.), *Bakhtinian Perspective on Language, Literacy, and Learning* (pp. 148–71). New York: Cambridge University Press.
Landay, E. (2004). Performance as the foundation for a secondary school literacy program. In A. Ball & S. Freedman (Eds.), *Bakhtinian Perspectives on Language, Literacy, and Learning* (pp. 107–28). New York: Cambridge University Press.
Martin, J. (1993). A contextual theory of language. In B. Cope & M. Kalantizis (Eds.), *The Powers of Literacy: A Genre Approach to Teaching Writing* (pp. 116–36). Pittsburgh, PA: University of Pittsburgh Press.
Martin, J. (2009). Genre and language learning: A social semiotic perspective. *Linguistics and Education*, 20(1), 10–21.
Martin, J. R., & Rose, D. (2007). *Working with Discourse: Meaning beyond the Clause*. New York: Continuum.
Martin, J. R., & Rose, D. (2008). *Genre Relations: Mapping Culture*. London: Equinox.
Martin, J. R., & White, P. R. R. (2005). *The Language of Evaluation: Appraisal in English*. New York: Palgrave Macmillan.
McCann, T. M. (1989). Student argumentative writing knowledge and ability at three grade levels. *Research in the Teaching of English*, 23, 63–77.
Nippold, M. A., Ward- Lonergan, J. M., & Fanning, J. L. (2005). Persuasive writing in children, adolescents, and adults: Study of syntactic, semantic, and pragmatic development. *Language, Speech, and Hearing Services in Schools*, 36, 125–38.
O'Connor, M. (2017). *Everybody Knows Everybody? Investigating Rural Secondary Students' Language Choices in Response to Audience across Argument Writing Experiences*. PhD dissertation, Boston College.
Ossa Parra, M., Wagner, C. J., Proctor, C. P., Leighton, C., Robertson, D. A., Paratore, J., & Ford-Connors, E. (2016). Dialogic reasoning. Supporting emergent bilingual students' language and literacy development. In C. P. Proctor, A. Boardman, & E. Hiebert (Eds.), *Teaching Emergent Bilingual Students: Flexible Approaches in an Era of New Standards* (pp. 119–37). New York: Guilford.
Rose, D., & Martin, J. R. (2012). *Learning to Write, Reading to Learn: Genre, Knowledge and Pedagogy in the Sydney School*. Sheffield: Equinox.
Rothery, J. (1996). Making changes: Developing an educational linguistics. In R. Hasan & G. Williams (Eds.), *Literacy in Society* (pp. 86–123). New York: Longman.
Schleppegrell, M., & Christie, F. (2018). Linguistic features of writing development: A functional perspective. In C. Bazerman, A. Applebee, V. Berninger, D. Brandt, S. Graham, J. Jeffrey, P. K. Matsuda, S. Murphy, D. Rowe, M. Schleppegrell, & K. Wilcox (Eds.), *The Lifespan Development of Writing* (pp. 111–50). Urbana, IL: NCTE (National Council of Teachers of English).

10

We are all one: Shifting reference in reconciliation talk

Lise Fontaine and Katy Jones
Cardiff University

Introduction

It is a great pleasure for us to contribute to this festschrift honouring Professor Jim Martin. His work has been inspiring in many ways but, in particular, we want to highlight two key areas – one more theoretical in the study of identification and participant tracking and one that is perhaps more personal: Jim's work on reconciliation. Our study examines a text that offers some insight into reconciliation discourse. Reconciliation in Canada can, to some extent, be viewed as quite similar to reconciliation in Australia (Borsa, 2016), for example, in setting up a kind of inquiry into the treatment of Aboriginal[1] peoples. However, one aspect that differentiates it from all others is that 'it did not have the kind of national and international attention that feeds into a broad public will to overcome a legacy of state sponsored harm' (Niezen, 2017, p. 3). Setting up the Truth and Reconciliation Commission (TRC) in Canada was not a response to any kind of public outcry; it was mandated by the Indian Residential Schools Settlement Agreement, the outcome of civil litigation. According to Borsa (2016), it is the only reconciliation process to have been initiated this way. Consequently, The Truth and Reconciliation Commission in Canada faced 'the challenge of persuasion' (Niezen, 2017, p. 4). What we might glean from this is that, in Canada, the reconciliation processes needed authentic voices to carry this persuasion through language so that all Canadians can 'find a way to belong to this time and place together' (Chief Joseph, 2018).

In Canada the word *Namwayut*, 'we are all one', has been adopted to embody the meaning of reconciliation. *Namwayut* captures a message of hope but in public truth sharing[2], there are still clearly shifting boundaries. Indeed, group reference poses particular challenges since referential boundaries may be fluid, in particular through the group deictic *we* (Fontaine, 2006). This is particularly relevant in reconciliation discourse, which has to cope with historical *us vs them* groupings while attempting to move, to some extent at least, towards a position of inclusion. This movement involves many challenges and it will take time. As Murray Sinclair (2011), the Truth and

Reconciliation Commissioner, explains, there are no quick and easy fixes; it will take time. He explains that given that it took generations to get to this point, that is, to the stage where Canada has reconciliation as an aim, it will take years to see improvements. It is argued that the education system plays a very important role. As Sinclair explains, 'It was the educational system that has contributed to this problem in this country and it is the educational system, we believe that is going to help us to get away from it' (2011, 1:25 min). One thing seems clear, reconciliation involves the language we use and in particular the language we use to talk about ourselves and each other. For Aboriginal peoples, it is also about the language used both by Aboriginal peoples and by non-Aboriginal peoples. As Martin (2004b, pp. 341–2) has said, 'Common sense tells us one text can change the world. Theoretically speaking, every text does.' We feel the text under study in this chapter offers a very good example of this point.

In this chapter we examine the use of reference in a narrative account from a residential school survivor and how it contributes to our understanding of reconciliation. The residential schools in Canada were developed out of a colonialist drive to assimilate Aboriginal children by placing the children in boarding schools. These boarding schools were run by the Church and children were often removed by force from their families. Many children were treated very badly, being denied their language and culture, and in many cases, this involved abuse and death. In Section 2, we provide more detail about reconciliation in Canada. The narrative we analyse presents simultaneously an individual and a voice for a speech fellowship and as such it plays a role in redress that affects many who have not been heard. The way in which a representative voice manages the various participants is revealing. In this paper, we analyse uses of reference which contribute to a shared feeling while also signalling aspects of the reconciliation process for the individual. Here we provide an overview of reconciliation in Canada, outlining a brief historical background to the work carried out by the Truth and Reconciliation Commission.

In Section 3, we provide some detail about our choice of text for this study, a spoken text by Chief Robert Joseph, and we outline the approach we have taken to the analysis, including an introduction to Martin's (1992) concept of reference chains, which we use to examine how participants are identified and tracked through the narrative. Following this in Section 4, we first introduce the IDENTIFICATION system as presented in Martin (1992) and then we consider the features of this system found in the text. In Section 5, we follow Chief Joseph's reconciliation discourse in detail, showing how he maps out how Aboriginal and non-Aboriginal Canadians can 'belong to this time and place together'. The chapter ends with some concluding remarks and directions for further research.

Reconciliation in Canada

On 11 June 2008, Stephen Harper, the Canadian prime minster at the time, formally apologized to the survivors of the Canadian residential school system on behalf of all Canadians. Harper referred to this enforced schooling as a 'sad chapter in our history'. This chapter was a particularly long one, in which, for well over 100 years, more than 150,000 First Nations, Métis and Inuit children were forced to attend residential schools run by the federal government and churches. These schools, which were used 'as a tool of assimilation' (National Centre for Truth and Reconciliation, n.d.), were underfunded and overcrowded and those running the schools were often untrained and unqualified to do so. Children were separated from their families and communities and forbidden to speak their own languages, interact with siblings and other children of the opposite sex. They were told that their cultures were worthless and uncivilized, and many were subjected to physical and sexual abuse. Many children did not survive: the mortality rate at these schools is estimated at between 35 per cent and 60 per cent (Bryce, 1922).

Those who did return to their home communities reported feeling cut off from their families and their culture. They had lost their language, had not developed traditional skills or learnt about cultural and spiritual traditions and practices, all of which are crucial to cultural identity (Truth and Reconciliation Commission of Canada, 2012, p. 1). At the same time, they had not been provided with the skills needed to succeed in the Euro-Canadian economy. On top of that, they did not have any experience of family life or parenting (Truth and Reconciliation Commission of Canada, 2015a, p. X). In addition, according to the Truth and Reconciliation Commission of Canada (2012, p. 1),

> These were not the side-effects of a well-intentioned system: the purpose of the residential school system was to separate children from the influences of their parents and their community, so as to destroy their culture.

The mandate to 'assimilate' Aboriginal people turned out to be nothing more than a devastating failure to provide children with the education they needed and the care they deserved, ultimately resulting in cultural genocide (Bennett & Blackstock, 2002).

The last federally supported residential schools remained in operation until the late 1990s and their legacy continues to have an impact on Aboriginal people to this day. Due to years of abuse and neglect, family and individual dysfunction increased as survivors had families of their own, 'until eventually, the legacy of the schools became joblessness, poverty, family violence, drug and alcohol abuse, family breakdown, sexual abuse, prostitution, homelessness, high rates of imprisonment and early death' (Truth and Reconciliation Commission of Canada, 2012, pp. 77–8). The Canadian government and churches had destroyed generations of Aboriginal families and communities.

A re-assessment of the impact of residential schools began in the 1980s, starting with Canadian churches issuing apologies for imposing European culture and values on Aboriginal people (Truth and Reconciliation Commission of Canada, 2015a, p. XI). Residential school survivors then started to speak out about their experiences, leading to criminal charges against some sexual abusers and the launching of class-action lawsuits against the churches and the federal government (Truth and Reconciliation Commission of Canada, 2012, p. XI). In 2006, the Indian Residential Schools Settlement Agreement was established, which included financial compensation for former residential school students (Truth and Reconciliation Commission of Canada,

2015a, p. VI). The settlement agreement also established a commemoration initiative, and the Indian Residential Schools Truth and Reconciliation Commission, to facilitate reconciliation among former students, their families, their communities and all Canadians.

In 2009, the Truth and Reconciliation Commission of Canada began the process of documenting the experiences of school survivors, communities and others affected by the residential school system, and heard from more than 6,500 witnesses (Government of Canada, 2019). The TRC also hosted seven national events to engage and educate Canadian people about the history and legacy of the residential school system and share the experiences of former students and their families. The TRC has published this history as a part of its mandate to educate the Canadian public about residential schools and their place in Canadian history, as a first step towards reconciliation.

In 2015, the TRC released an Executive Summary of its findings along with ninety-four calls to action and a set of guiding principles for truth and reconciliation between Aboriginal and non-Aboriginal Canadians. These principles emphasize that the rights of First Nations, Inuit and Métis peoples must be recognized and respected. They define reconciliation as an ongoing process of establishing and maintaining mutually respectful relationships. This involves restoring damaged trust by offering apologies, providing individual and collective reparations, and following through with concrete actions that demonstrate real societal change, as well as a revitalization of Indigenous law and legal traditions (TRC, 2015b, pp. 3–4).

The final report by the TRC acknowledges that it is the 'the courage and determination of former students – the Survivors of Canada's residential school system' (TRC, 2015b, p. 1) which allowed for the establishment of the TRC. It goes on to say that as part of the ongoing reconciliation process, all Canadians must now show 'the same level of courage and determination' (TRC, 2015b, p. 1). For reconciliation to become a reality, there needs to be an awareness and acknowledgement of the 'harm that has been inflicted, atonement for the causes, and action to change behaviour' (TRC, 2015b, p. 113).

However, as the TRC admits, 'We are not there yet. The relationship between Aboriginal and non-Aboriginal peoples is not a mutually respectful one' (TRC, 2015b, p. 113). Many Canadians are not aware of these historical atrocities nor of the contribution that Aboriginal peoples have made to Canadian history. In public spheres, this ignorance means that racist attitudes are reinforced and distrust between Aboriginal peoples and other Canadians is deepened (TRC, 2015b, p. 114). In the government, this ignorance could lead to poor policymaking. The TRC admits that some of the harm inflicted by residential schools on Aboriginal families, communities, languages, education and health may in fact be exacerbated by current government policies, because they are based on a lack of understanding of Aboriginal people (TRC, 2015b, p. 111).

So, despite the findings and calls to action of the TRC, the reform efforts of the Canadian government and the work of many other organizations dedicated to truth and reconciliation, there are still significant barriers to reconciliation. Many of these barriers are cultural, but others are systemic and institutional. For instance, a disproportionate number of Aboriginal people come into contact with the law. In

2011/12, 28 per cent of all those sentenced to prison were Aboriginal, even though Aboriginal people make up only 4 per cent of the Canadian adult population (TRC, 2015b, p. 110).

The TRC emphasizes that genuine reconciliation will not be possible until the whole legacy of the schools is both understood and addressed, and measures are taken to abandon policies and approaches that currently continue to extend that hurtful legacy (2015b, p. 204). It is clear that reconciliation requires more than an acknowledgement of and apologies for the harms inflicted by past (and current) government policies. Relationships also need to change.

> By establishing a new and respectful relationship between Aboriginal and non-Aboriginal Canadians, we will restore what must be restored, repair what must be repaired, and return what must be returned. (TRC, 2015b, p. 1)

New relationships of respect and understanding need to be built and sustained. As Chief Dr Robert Joseph states, 'Our future, and the well-being of all our children rests with the kind of relationships we build today' (Reconciliation Canada, n.d.). And these relationships, according to the Reverend Stan McKay of the United Church, another residential school survivor, need to foster mutual understanding and respect:

> [There must be] a change in perspective about the way in which Aboriginal peoples would be engaged with Canadian society in the quest for reconciliation .... [We cannot] perpetuate the paternalistic concept that only Aboriginal peoples are in need of healing .... The perpetrators are wounded and marked by history in ways that are different from the victims, but both groups require healing .... How can a conversation about reconciliation take place if all involved do not adopt an attitude of humility and respect? ... We all have stories to tell and in order to grow in tolerance and understanding we must listen to the stories of others. (TRC, 2015b, pp. 115–16)

Method and approach

In this section, we explain our choice of text and the approach we have taken to the analysis.

In the voice of Chief Joseph

In Martin's work on reconciliation in Australia, he rightly puts forward the following idea:

> for reconciliation to succeed ... we have to turn all of this around and complement the voicing I've been exploring here with discourse from the other – Indigenous discourse ... For this we need contexts in which Indigenous people design, produce and distribute discourse ... Without a handover of this kind, the reconciliation process as a whole is fraught with problems of paternalism. (2004a)

As discussed above, one important feature of the TRC is the way in which it has given a voice to residential school survivors and all Aboriginal peoples. In the spirit of Martin's ideas, then, we have selected one key voice from the TRC to study. *Namwayut: we are all one. Truth and reconciliation in Canada* is a video narrative by Chief Dr Robert Joseph, a hereditary chief of the Gwawaenuk First Nation and a residential school survivor. The video is part of the *Canada is …* online series, which showcases the different facets of Canadian identity. In this series, prominent Canadian figures explore how their area relates to Canadian culture and what it means to be Canadian. *Namwayut: we are all one* has 83,072 views on YouTube (as of 2nd April 2020) and has been played on the Canadian Broadcasting Corporation (CBC). This text was selected because the narrative represents the full journey to reconciliation: from the first day Chief Robert Joseph was taken to the residential school, to the impact of these actions on the residential school children, to the formal apology and, finally, the importance of truth and reconciliation today. As such, the voices of all participants are present in the reference chains, which will be explained in the next section. The full text, which is 550 words in length, is provided in the Appendix as a transcript of the video along with its URL.

Reference chains

As suggested above, there are various key participants in Canada's reconciliation process and Chief Joseph's text was selected because it includes them through his own voice. For Martin (1992, p. 140), 'a reference chain consists of two items, one presuming, one presumed' (cf. identity chains Hasan, 1984; Halliday & Hasan, 1985). The principle of reference chains is to 'take each phoric item back once to the item which last realized or presumed the information that needs to be recovered' (Martin, 1992, p. 140).

We identified ten reference chains in the text. These are listed in Table 10.1 along with the corresponding referent. The name of the chain, or its label, is indicated with #. For example, the chain of references to Chief Robert Joseph was labelled #ChiefJoseph.

Table 10.1 List of reference chains and associated referents.

Reference chains	Referent
#ChiefJoseph	Chief Robert Joseph
#Church	People of authority related to the Church
#ResidentialSchool	Residential schools
#Aboriginalchildren	Aboriginal children
#Aboriginalpeople	Aboriginal people
#Canadians	Non-Aboriginal Canadians
#Canada	Canada (country)
#ALL	Aboriginal and non-Aboriginal Canadians
#JusticeMurraySinclair	Justice Murray Sinclair
#PoliticallyResponsible	People of authority related to the government

The claim we are making then is that each chain contains all references to the given referent, including both explicit and implicit references.

SACR Annotation Software

The software we used to code the reference chains was SACR (Oberle, 2018), which is an initialism for 'Script d'Annotation des Chaînes de Référence' (annotation script for reference chains). SACR is a simple web-based tool for annotating co-reference chains, or indeed any relational features in text. It is similar to the UAM CorpusTool (O'Donnell, 2008) in that the annotation scheme is user defined and the annotation itself is guided by the user. The main difference is the ease of maintaining chains, which, while not impossible within the CorpusTool, is simpler. However, this simplicity means that, unlike the CorpusTool, it cannot autocode features, nor can it manage multiple levels of analysis. In SACR, all references to a given referent are then tagged and coded to create a chain using the drag-and-drop feature. Each chain is visually identified with a different colour and a user-defined label (by default, each distinct chain is simply given a number, e.g. M1 and M2). The annotation scheme includes the various features of interest for a given study. In this study, each reference in a given chain was coded for the following features. Firstly, we considered type of referring expression (e.g. personal pronoun and proper name) and the type of phoricity involved (e.g. anaphor, exophor and homophor), which would allow us to relate to Martin's (1992) IDENTIFICATION system (see below). We were also interested in coding the grammatical (interpersonal) role (e.g. Subject and Complement) as well as the experiential role of the expression (e.g. Actor and Senser), following Halliday and Matthiessen (2014). Finally, we also kept track of whether the unit in which the reference was contained was ranking clause, embedded clause or hypotactic. While in this case, we analysed one text, there is no limit to the number of texts which can be imported to SACR, nor is there a limit to the number of features that can be included in the coding scheme. See Sarda and Carter-Thomas (in press) for a much more elaborate use of SACR where twenty news articles were analysed for reference chains, contrasting referring strategies in English and French.

Reference chains in the text

As shown in Table 10.2, there was considerable variability in the lengths of the ten reference chains we analysed. Chief Joseph himself and Aboriginal peoples have the greatest number of references. We could also reasonably include reference to Aboriginal children, since Chief Joseph is a member of all three referent groups. In contrast, the only major referent outside this group is found in the #Church chain, which has twelve members. For Martin (1992, p. 140), 'dependency relations in the chain are worked out in accordance with the principle that anaphoric items are related backwards once to the item last realising or presuming the information they presume'. Concerning our text, we did find instances where referents and chains seemed to coincide (cf. conjoining or splitting chains in Martin (1992)) as will be discussed below, but we have kept the chains distinct. For example, as shown in (1) below, Chief Joseph is an individual person in the #ChiefJoseph chain but is also included in the #Aboriginalchildren

Table 10.2 Chain length for each chain (number of references), in order of length.

Chain	Chain length
#Aboriginalpeople	21
#ChiefJoseph	20
#Church	12
#Aboriginalchildren	9
#ResidentialSchool	8
#ALL	7
PoliticallyResponsible	6
#Canada	5
#Canadians	5
JusticeMurraySinclair	4

chain. Here the expressions referring to Chief Joseph are highlighted in bold and the expressions used to refer to the Aboriginal children are underscored. The main reason for this is that they are not fundamentally distinct participants and they do not come together in any experiential way, unlike the example provided by Martin (1992, p. 140) where we find, as shown in (2), that two distinct participants (i.e. the boy and the dog) conjoin in the expression 'they'. Here as with (1), one participant is highlighted in grey, the other is underscored, and the conjoined expression, 'they', is both highlighted and underscored. Each distinct participant can carry on in the discourse without presuming the other. However, in our text, when Chief Joseph is referring to himself as a child, he is not referring to all Aboriginal children; however, reference to all Aboriginal children includes Chief Joseph as an instance of that group.

(1) I remember the day walking toward that school with **my** mother and it was a silent walk and **I** was so afraid. <u>**Twenty or thirty little kids**</u> herded into the showers (lines 1–3[3]).

(2) **The boy** and <u>the dog</u> woke up and saw that the frog was missing. With **the boy** leading the way <u>**they**</u> headed off for the woods. (source: Martin, 1992, p. 142)

Identification

One of the main distinctions made is whether, in referring to a participant, the speaker anticipates that the addressee will or will not be able to successfully identify the referent. As Martin explains (1992, p. 98), 'Every time a participant is mentioned, English codes the identity of that participant as explicitly recoverable from the context or not.' This will be an important distinction to call upon in the analysis of participants in the TRC statement under analysis. This distinction is captured in Martin's (1992) IDENTIFICATION system, where we find, as shown in Figure 10.1, a principle distinction between 'presenting' and 'presuming', where the identifiability of the participant is

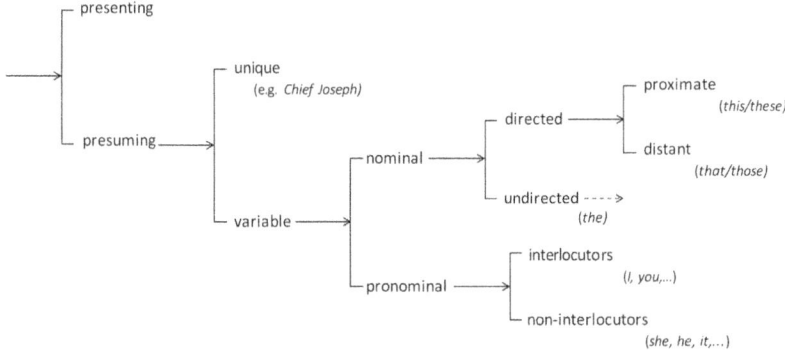

Figure 10.1 Martin's IDENTIFICATION System (adapted from Martin, 1992, p. 112).

seen as either recoverable ('presuming') or not recoverable, that is, new ('presenting'). Recoverability, or what Martin calls phoricity, involves relating 'phoric items to their context by way of presumed information' (Martin, 1992, p. 121). As we will see in the discussion below, the vast majority of referring expressions in the text under study in this chapter are presuming, even in those instances when a referent is brought into the discourse for the first time. Clearly, in these instances, the speaker has presumed that the addressee has the information to identify the intended participant. This is an important point that we will return to below.

The entry point to this system is 'participant', which Martin defines as 'a person, place or thing, abstract or concrete, capable of functioning as Agent or Medium in transitivity' (1992, p. 129). This use of 'participant' as a term comes, as Martin explains, from a stratificational framework (e.g. Gleason, 1968), and it does share some overlap with Halliday's term 'participant' or 'participating entity' (see Halliday, 1969, p. 160). For Martin (1992, p. 129) 'all participants are realized through nominal groups but not all nominal groups realize participants and some nominal groups realize more than one'. This suggests that the term captures what would be referred to as a (discourse) referent in many other theoretical frameworks. Some nominal groups do not have reference (e.g. 'it's raining', if we consider 'it' as a nominal group) and some nominal groups realize more than one participant, for example, 'John's son', given that this nominal expression refers to both 'John' and another participant 'son'. For Halliday, the term participant is typically used in relation to process in the TRANSITIVITY system. Participants are typically realized by nominal groups but even when a nominal group encodes two different discourse referents, the nominal group would be said to be realizing one participant at clause rank. For example, in 'John's son is kind', the nominal group 'John's son' is represented as Carrier in an attributive relational process (see Halliday & Matthiessen, 2014 for more detail on TRANSITIVITY). Martin and Halliday are not saying very different things, but rather they are using the term 'participant' in slightly different ways and to different purposes.

The use of proper names such as 'Chief Joseph', however, is quite different from both pronoun use and the use of nominal group resources. For example, names have no experiential content but, as Martin points out (1992, p. 121), 'referring to participants by name opens up an important set of interpersonal resources particularly sensitive to tenor'. In terms of reference, names are well established in all approaches to referring expressions as being uniquely identifying. Therefore, the use of a proper name suggests that the speaker presumes the referent is identifiable. There is no scope here for a thorough discussion of proper names but see Klassen (2018) for a very detailed account which challenges some of the existing assumptions underlying the referential status of proper names. For our purposes, it suffices at this point to simply consider how the use of proper names is seen as 'presuming' and 'unique' as opposed to 'variable'.

In Martin's framework, proper names are a type of homophoric reference. For Martin (1992, p. 122) homophora involves a 'presuming' identification which is due to 'interlocutors' membership in a particular community'. Proper names fall into this category as do referents such as 'the sun' or 'the dog', as in 'have you fed the dog?' (see Martin, 1992, for further details). There is an assumption made here about the use of proper names and that is that there is a given and established reference between the use of the proper name and a unique and identifiable referent. However, as we will show below, proper names are functionally versatile and allow for some degree of reference shift, that is, a referent other than its homophorically typical referent.

It is important to keep in mind that Martin's use of 'participant' is the entry point or condition for the IDENTIFICATION system and that this system is situated within discourse semantics, that is, part of the semantics stratum, whereas the nominal group is part of the lexicogrammatical stratum. As Martin (1992, p. 129) explains, IDENTIFICATION and nominal group structure operate on different strata; 'the IDENTIFICATION system has been stratified with respect to nominal group structure.' It is through this system that we are able to explore 'reference as semantic choice' (Martin, 1992, p. 93).

As mentioned above, the first distinction made in the IDENTIFICATION system relates to phoricity and whether or not the speaker considers the participant being referred to as explicitly recoverable or not. Of the ninety-seven expressions analysed in the ten reference chains, only four were presenting, as shown in Table 10.3, and illustrated in examples (3)–(6). Only two chains in total, #ResidentialSchool and #JusticeMurraySinclair, followed what we might consider a typical presenting identification followed by anaphoric reference, and both of these are relatively minor chains in the text. It is important to note here that implicit reference (e.g. agentless passives) was counted in the chain and coded as anaphoric, although this involves almost exclusively the #Church reference chain. Of the twelve instances where the reference was implicit, that is, inferred, eight occurred in the #Church chain. An example of this is shown in (7) below.

(3) a residential school (line 1)
(4) Twenty or thirty little kids (lines 2–3)
(5) Indigenous people, aboriginal people (line 9)
(6) Justice Murray Sinclair, the chair of the Commission denounced Canada (line 25)
(7) and then your body would be painted in white liquid of some kind (lines 3–4)

Among the instances of presuming identification, the use of unique reference through naming was relatively infrequent, with only seven instances overall and the majority of these ($N = 3$) were references to Canada, as illustrated in example (8).

(8) and the last school that closed in Canada was in 1996 in Saskatchewan (lines 19–20)

With respect to variable reference, there is a clear dominance of pronominal reference in the text. Pronominal reference occurred in 70 per cent of instances as compared to 30 per cent nominal reference. Most of the pronominal referring expressions are exophoric, where most frequently we find speaker interlocutor reference (e.g. *I, we*), as illustrated in examples (9) and (10). What is strikingly absent from the text is any instance of addressee interlocutor reference (e.g. *you*); in other words, the addressee is not represented in this discourse, at least not directly. Assuming Chief Joseph was addressing Aboriginal people and non-Aboriginal people in Canada, the addressee is included in some of the instances of the first-person plural interlocutor reference, but there is no evidence of any attempts to identify the addressee.

(9) and then I couldn't see because my eyes were just flowing with tears (line 30)
(10) so we're trying to look through a new lens (line 32)

Before moving on to a discussion of the use of reference throughout the text, we will consider the experiential representation of all instances of reference. Table 10.4 presents the frequency of the various experiential functions identified in the Chief Joseph text. Given that there were ninety-seven instances in total, the raw frequencies correspond quite close to a normalized percentage (e.g. the percentage frequency for Actor was 23.7 per cent). The roles of Actor, Carrier and Senser make up 60 per cent of the instances.

Table 10.3 Types of phoricity in all reference chains.

	Presenting	Homophoric	Exophoric	Anaphoric
#ChiefJoseph	0	0	19	1
#Church	0	1	0	11
#ResidentialSchool	1	0	0	7
#aboriginalchildren	1	0	4	4
#aboriginalpeople	1	0	14	6
#Canadians	0	4	0	1
#Canada	0	3	0	2
#ALL	0	0	5	2
#JusticeMurraySinclair	1	0	0	3
#PoliticallyResponsible	0	2	3	1
Totals	4	10	45	38

Table 10.4 Frequency of experiential roles in the Chief Joseph text.

Actor	Carrier	Senser	Goal	Location	Sayer	Identified	Deictic	Beneficiary	Existent
23	19	16	13	8	6	5	4	2	1

In order to gain a better appreciation of how these roles mapped onto individual reference chains, we will take a look at the three longest chains, that is, the chains with the highest number of references. As noted in Table 10.2, #ChiefJoseph ($N = 20$), #Church ($N = 12$) and #Aboriginalpeople ($N = 21$) were the dominant chains in the text. All others had fewer than ten. A comparison of the three main chains is presented in Figure 10.2, where we can see contrasting representations. It is clear to see here that the #Church chain holds the majority of Actor functions, suggesting that people of authority related to the Church, those responsible for the way Aboriginal children were treated, were more active and more responsible for carrying out actions than any other referent. While the frequencies are too low, and the text too short, to draw any significant conclusions, we can suggest that, as a reference chain, reference to people who held authority related to the Church signals them out contrastively in a very different way to the other two dominant chains. This might be expected in reconciliation discourse since it is an explicit aim of reconciliation to establish new relationships, new perspectives and to eliminate the divisive former ways of referring to *them* vs *us*. As we will see in the next section, Chief Joseph is very careful with his language, and while the majority of references in the #Church chain express an Actor function, the majority of these are left implicit. The other instances of Actor in the experiential analysis that are worth mentioning here include the instances in the #Aboriginalpeople chain and the #ALL chain, each with three instances of Actor. This is a point we will return to in the discussion in the next section since they make an important contribution to the reconciliation discourse. What is also evident in Figure 10.2 is how Chief Joseph is represented in a wide variety of experiential roles. How this unfolds in his text is discussed in the next section.

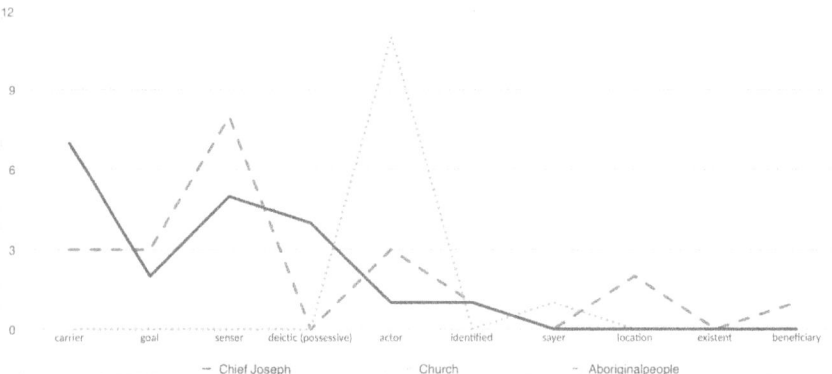

Figure 10.2 Experiential representation for the three main reference chains: #ChiefJoseph, #Church and #aboriginalpeople.

Namwayut, 'We are all one'

Our main interest in this chapter is how the words of Chief Joseph are able to capture both the experience of the Aboriginal peoples in Canada, in terms of the effects of their treatment by the system imposed by the officials of the Church and the Government of Canada, and the experience of reconciliation. These two perspectives seem entirely opposing and contrasting. It is clear from the opening of Chief Joseph's narrative that his self-reference is used to ground what he is saying in his own experience, as shown in example (11), where we also gain a sense of the *us* vs *them* positioning, evidenced in the quote by Hector Langevin at the beginning of this chapter. This division is not maintained in the text and in what follows, where the treatment of children is detailed, those responsible are not explicitly named, that is, there is no 'they' linguistically present. Chief Joseph's specific experience is generalized to other children, as we can see in example (12).

(11) I was 6 years old when they took me to a residential school. I remember the day walking toward that school with my mother and it was a silent walk and I was so afraid. (lines 1–2)

(12) Twenty or thirty little kids herded into the showers, and then your body would be painted in white liquid of some kind, your hair cropped and then doused in kerosene. That was pretty traumatising. The school held roughly 220 people, half boys and half girls and we were segregated. If I was caught waving at my sister, there'd be a punishment for it and so as a result of that segregation, I never really learned any social skills that young people should be learning as they grow up. (lines 2–8)

Despite the absence of an explicit reference, it is clear that 'they' herded the children into the showers, 'they' painted the children's bodies, 'they' cropped the children's hair and 'they' doused the children in kerosene; it is also clear that 'they' traumatized the children, 'they' segregated the children and 'they' punished the children. Furthermore, 'they' did not teach the children the social skills that young people should be learning. However, through this section of the text, the focus is on the children and their experience, without explicitly laying blame. The shift in reference from nominal ('Twenty or thirty little kids') to pronominal interlocutor ('your') in (12), while still clearly co-referential, is very interesting, bringing the addressee into the experience and perhaps suggesting that the addressee could imagine what that must have been like.

While 'they' is introduced as a first mention in (11), clarity about the referent is not provided until line 8 as shown in example (13), when Chief Joseph explicitly refers to people of authority related to the church, metonymically referred to by the homophoric nominal expression 'the churches'. Where 'they' are explicitly encoded, as given in the underscored expressions in (13), they are either represented as Sayer (a) or as Actor (b) with an abstract Goal (language and knowledge). There are also implicit references to their active role in converting Aboriginal people and eliminating their identity and knowledge.

(13) From a religious and spiritual perspective, of course the churches lobbied hard to convert Indigenous people, Aboriginal people. They_a said that we were heathens, pagan. They_b targeted language and those things that we had learned through all of millennia, to know where we came from, to know who we were as something that had to be eliminated. (lines 8–11)

The text then shifts again and uses self-reference (pronominal interlocutor) to bridge past and present: life before the residential schools and life following the residential schools, as illustrated in example (14). Here again, the trauma and devastation to both individual Aboriginal people and the Aboriginal communities is presented but without mention of an explicit Agent, without blame. The contrast of before and after seems to be more effective, allowing an agreement in the contrast and without the need to take sides.

(14) Before that time, I lived in a place called Kwikwasut'inuxw Haxawa'mis. They call it Gilford Island now. We harvested from the forest all of the animals that we needed to provide us with sustenance and from the ocean in front of us as well all of the species of whales and mink and fish and I had this connection to the environment around us and so after having spent years in those schools by the time we were ready to leave most of us were pretty broken. Many of us, including myself, descended into addictions, alcoholism, and violence and it was pretty … pretty difficult.

Having established the far-reaching effects of the residential school system, Chief Joseph presents facts about the residential schools. As shown in (15), the schools lasted for over a hundred years, over 150,000 children were affected directly, and one cannot even imagine the wider scale of all affected by this, family members and entire communities. And yet, non-Aboriginal Canadians did not know about this. Here we find again a type of blame-distancing/-avoiding strategy with the use of 'nobody' (instances are underscored in in (15)). As an indefinite pronoun, 'nobody' should not construe any phoricity. However, it seems reasonable to consider that in this case, 'nobody' actually refers to non-Aboriginal Canadians (#canadians).[4] It is clear that the 'we' of those who were affected by the residential school legacy, that is, #aboriginalpeople, is different from the 'we' who are responsible for the shared history, that is, #ALL. This is a real turning point in the text; here we begin to see evidence of what reconciliation might mean. It can mean a shared history and a shared responsibility.

(15) Those schools lasted for over a hundred years. There were over 150000 little children and the last school that closed in Canada was in 1996 in Saskatchewan. There was a history on this land that had been absolutely ignored. Nobody knew about the residential school legacy. Nobody knew about the Intent of the Indian Act, the chronic challenges now facing Aboriginals and we're starting to accept the idea that we have this shared history for which **we all** are responsible for.

Canada is a country that is now home to Aboriginal peoples and non-Aboriginal people and these people must reconcile. Chief Joseph manages to present simultaneously an individual voice and a collective voice for a speech fellowship. In the last section of the text, Chief Joseph demonstrates explicitly the reconciliatory use of 'we', highlighted in bold in (16). He does this by making very clear that he is able to speak both as a member of the Aboriginal peoples, as shown in (16) in the double underscored examples (*we*), contrasted with the reference to non-Aboriginal Canadians (*Canadians* highlighted in grey), and as a member of #ALL Canadians (**we**). In fact, the first 'we' used in (16) is arguably ambiguous, blurring the boundaries of the reference. The ambiguity appears to be picked up in the next use of 'we', where Chief Joseph makes clear that 'we and Canadians' refers to two groups and then clearly these two distinct participants conjoin to form part of the #ALL reference chain.

(16) Canada by the way is the only western country that has had a Truth and Reconciliation Commission, so **we**'re trying to look through a new lens. **We** and Canadians, **we** as an Aboriginal, **we** celebrate each other, everybody cheering each other up as **we** move toward a more equal prosperous future for all of **us**. (ines 31–34)

Concluding remarks

As discussed above, Martin (2004a, p.115) has made the point that 'we need contexts in which Indigenous people design, produce and distribute discourse' and this is precisely what this chapter has endeavoured to explore. By examining the reference chains in a key reconciliation text, we have shown how reconciliation discourse offers all Canadians a way 'to belong to this time and place together' (Chief Joseph, 2018).

This notion of 'togetherness' is highly salient in Chief Joseph's text. He weaves his own personal experience through a general and more widely shared experience and ultimately, using his voice as a representative of many voices, to show how reconciliation discourse can be transcendental. While this is a perspective gleaned from the analysis of one relatively short text, it is one that is supported Borsa's (2017) study of how Indigenous community newspapers reported on reconciliation. One of his main research questions was to discover how these newspapers reported on the process of reconciliation framed (p. 12). His corpus consisted of over 340 articles from five different Indigenous newspapers from across Canada over the period 2010-15. One particularly relevant conclusion from Borsa's study is as follows:

> In describing the expected outcomes of the formal process of reconciliation, the bulk of articles expressed optimism toward the potentially transformative impacts of intergenerational and community-level healing (52.2%) or individual healing and catharsis (44.0%). That the former eclipsed the latter as the most-cited outcome is an encouraging finding, and is an indication of the privileging of conceptions of health and well-being informed by syncretic re-imagination of traditional Indigenous epistemologies. (2016, p. 29)

Our analysis, when viewed in the larger context of media reports, such as that provided by Borsa's important work, supports the case Martin was making in 2004 (Martin, 2004a, b, c) and has been making since. Not only is it the case that for reconciliation to work we all must include Indigenous discourse and Indigenous perspectives on reconciliation, but we also need to evaluate how we engage with these discourses. While Borsa (2016, p. 34) suggests that critical discourse analysis (CDA) would be a fruitful methodology for furthering research into reconciliation discourse (as reported in Indigenous media), this may well be counterproductive. As Martin (2004c, p. 197) has explained:

> We do need to move beyond a preoccupation with demonology, beyond a singular focus on semiosis in the service of abusive power – and reconsider power communally as well, as it circulates through communities, as they re-align around values, and renovate discourses that enact a better world.

As concerns discourses of reconciliation, we would be better to focus on communal power or rather communal empowerment. Our work on the Chief Joseph text suggests that if we want to see reconciliation succeed, then we must (re-)evaluate our preoccupations.

Notes

1. In Canada the terms Aboriginal people and Indigenous people are frequently used interchangeably to refer to First Nations, Métis and Inuit people.
2. Public truth sharing refers to discourse acts where survivors share the truth of their experience in a public forum. In this case, this refers to the sharing of survivors' experiences of the residential school system in Canada. Truth sharing is generally seen as an important stage in reconciliation.
3. All line numbers, for examples, refer to the Appendix, where the full co-text can be found.
4. See Jones (2014, 2018) for a detailed account of indefinite expressions being used as identifying reference.

References

Bennett, M., & Blackstock, C. (2002). *A Literature Review and Annotated Bibliography Focusing on Aspects of Aboriginal Child Welfare in Canada*. Ottawa: First Nations Research Site of the Centre of Excellence for Child Welfare.

Borsa, T. (2016). *Truth on Trial: Indigenous News Media and the Truth and Reconciliation Commission of Canada*. MSc dissertation. London School of Economics.

Bryce, P. H. (1922). *The Story of a National Crime. Record of the Health Conditions of the Indians of Canada from 1904 to 1921*. Retrieved from https://archive.org/stream/storyofnationalc00brycuoft/storyofnationalc00brycuoft_djvu.txt. Last accessed 15 April 2020.

Fontaine, L. (2006). Where do 'we' fit in? Linguistic inclusion and exclusion in a virtual community. In K. Bührig & J. D. Ten Thije (Eds.), *Beyond Misunderstanding, the Linguistic Reconstruction of Intercultural Communication* (pp. 319–56). Amsterdam: John Benjamins Publishing Company.

Gleason, H. A., Jr. (1968). *Contrastive Analysis in Discourse Structure, 19*, 39–63. Washington: Georgetown University Roundtable.

Government of Canada. (2019). *Truth and Reconciliation Commission of Canada*. Retrieved from https://www.rcaanc-cirnac.gc.ca/eng/1450124405592/1529106060525. Last accessed 15 April 2020.

Halliday, M. A. K. (1969/1976). Types of process. In G. Kress (Ed.), *Halliday: System and Function in Language* (pp. 159–73). London: Oxford University Press.

Halliday, M. A. K., & Hasan, R. (1976). *Cohesion in English*. London: Longman.

Halliday, M. A. K., & Hasan, R. (1985). *Language, Context and Text: Aspects of Language in a Social-Semiotic Perspective*. Oxford: Oxford University Press.

Halliday, M. A. K., & Matthiessen, C. M. I. M. (2014). *An Introduction to Functional Grammar*. London: Routledge.

Hasan, R. (1984). Coherence and cohesive harmony. In J. Flood (Ed.), *Understanding Reading Comprehension: Cognition, Language, and the Structure of Prose* (pp. 181–219). Newark, Delaware: International Reading Association.

Jones, K. (2014). *Towards an Understanding of the Use of Indefinite Expressions for Definite Reference in English Discourse*. PhD thesis, Cardiff University.

Jones, K. (2018). 'A man who revels in his own ignorance, racism and misogyny': Identifiable referents trump indefinite grammar. *Functional Linguistics*, 5(1), 11.

Klassen, K. (2018). *Investigating the Lexical Load of Proper Names for L2 English Readers*. PhD thesis, Cardiff University.

Martin, J. R. (1992), *English Text: System and Structure*. Amsterdam: Benjamins.

Martin, J. R. (2002). Blessed are the peacemakers: Reconciliation and evaluation. In C. N. Candlin (Ed.), *Research and Practice in Professional Discourse* (pp. 187–227). Tat Chee Avenue, Kowloon, Hong Kong: City University of Hong Kong Press.

Martin, J. R. (2004a). Negotiating difference: Ideology and reconciliation. In M. Putz, J. Neff-van Aertselaer & T. A. van Dijk (Eds.), *Communicating Ideologies: Multidisciplinary Perspectives on Language, Discourse and Social Practice* (pp. 85–177). Frankfurt: Peter Lang Publishing.

Martin, J. R. (2004b). Mourning: how we get aligned. *Discourse & Society*, 15(2–3), 321–44.

Martin, J. R. (2004c). Positive discourse analysis: Solidarity and change. *Revista Canaria de Estudios Ingleses*, 49, 179–200.

Martin, J. R. (2008). Innocence: Realisation, instantiation and individuation in a Botswanan town. In A. Mahboob & N. Knight (Eds.), *Questioning Linguistics* (pp. 32–76). Newcastle upon Tyne, UK: Cambridge Scholars Publishing.

Martin, J. R., Zappavigna, M., Dwyer, P., & Cléirigh, C. (2013). Users in uses of language: Embodied identity in Youth Justice Conferencing, *Text and Talk*, 33, 467–96.

National Centre for Truth and Reconciliation (n.d.). University of Manitoba. Retrieved 5 September 2019, from http://nctr.ca/about-new.php

Niezen, R. (2017). *Truth and Indignation: Canada's Truth and Reconciliation Commission on Indian Residential Schools* (2nd ed.). Toronto: University of Toronto Press.

O'Donnell, M. (2008). The UAM CorpusTool: Software for corpus annotation and exploration. In C. M. Bretones Callejas et al. (Eds.), *Applied Linguistics Now:*

Understanding Language and Mind/La Lingüística Aplicada Hoy: Comprendiendo el Lenguaje y la Mente (pp. 1433–47). Almería: Universidad de Almería.

Oberlé B. (2018), SACR: A Drag-and-Drop based tool for coreference annotation. *Proceedings of the 11th Edition of the Language Resources and Evaluation Conference (LREC 2018)*. Miyazaki, Japan.

Reconciliation Canada. (28 August 2017), 'Partners.' *Reconciliation Canada – A New Way Forward Society*. Retrieved 5 September 2019, from http://reconciliationcanada.ca/about/partners/

Rogers, S. (28 June 2011), TRC meeting produces call for better Arctic mental health services. *Nunatsiaq News*. Retrieved 5 September 2019, from https://nunatsiaq.com/stories/article/28778_trc_meeting_brings_call_for_better_mental_health_in_the_arctic/

Sarda, L., & Carter-Thomas, S. (in press). Référence, qualification et distribution de l'information: approche contrastive français/anglaise. *Revue de sémantique et pragmatique*.

Sinclair, M. (2011). What is reconciliation? Truth and reconciliation Canada. Retrieved 15 June 2019, from https://vimeo.com/25389165

Truth and Reconciliation Commission of Canada Report (2012), They Came for the Children. Ottawa, Ontario.

Truth and Reconciliation Commission of Canada Report (2015a), The Survivors Speak, Ottawa, Ontario.

Truth and Reconciliation Commission of Canada Report (2015b), What We Have Learned: Principles of Truth and Reconciliation, Ottawa, Ontario.

Zifonun, G., Hoffmann, L., & Strecker, B. (1997). *Grammatik der deutschen Sprache 3*. Berlin: Mouton de Gruyter.

Appendix

Namwayut: we are all one. Truth and reconciliation in Canada
   Chief Robert Joseph
   (Transcribed from https://www.youtube.com/watch?v=2zuRQmwaREY. Last accessed: 14 June 2019)

I was 6 years old when they took me to a residential school. I remember the day walking toward that school with my mother and it was a silent walk and I was so afraid. Twenty or thirty little kids herded into the showers, and then your body would be painted in white liquid of some kind, your hair cropped and then doused in kerosene. That was pretty traumatising. The school held roughly 220 people, half boys and half girls and we were segregated. If I was caught waving at my sister, there'd be a punishment for it and so as a result of that segregation, I never really learned any social skills that young people should be learning as they grow up. From a religious and spiritual perspective, of course the churches lobbied hard to convert indigenous people, aboriginal people. They said that we were heathens, pagan. They targeted language and those things that we had learned through all of millennia, to know where we came from, to know who we were as something that had to be eliminated. Before that time, I lived in a place called Kwikwasut'inuxw Haxawa'mis. They call it Gilford

Island now. We harvested from the forest all of the animals that we needed to provide us with sustenance and from the ocean in front of us as well all of the species of whales and mink and fish and I had this connection to the environment around us and so after having spent years in those schools by the time we were ready to leave most of us were pretty broken. Many of us, including myself, descended into addictions, alcoholism, and violence and it was pretty … pretty difficult. Those schools lasted for over a hundred years. There were over 150000 little children and the last school that closed in Canada was in 1996 in Saskatchewan. There was a history on this land that had been absolutely ignored. Nobody knew about the residential school legacy. Nobody knew about the Intent of the Indian Act, the chronic challenges now facing aboriginals and we're starting to accept the idea that we have this shared history for which we all are responsible for.

When the Truth and Reconciliation Commission report was submitted, I was in a room when Justice Murray Sinclair, the chair of the Commission denounced Canada. He had just recited a litany of intensive harms against aboriginal people and when he said 'Canada you have committed cultural genocide' there was just a silence in that room and all of a sudden it erupted in euphoria and he said survivors want an apology from the prime minister in the House of Commons and I was there and I heard the words 'I'm sorry' and then I couldn't see because my eyes were just flowing with tears I was just so happy that somebody had said I'm sorry. Canada by the way is the only western country that has had a Truth and Reconciliation Commission, so we're trying to look through a new lens. We and Canadians, we as an aboriginal, we celebrate each other, everybody cheering each other up as we move toward a more equal prosperous future for all of us.

My name is Chief Robert Joseph and I believe that truth and reconciliation is Canada.

11

A nation remembers: Discourses of change, mourning and reconciliation on Australia Day

Helen Caple and Monika Bednarek
University of New South Wales and University of Sydney

Introduction

As a national public holiday, Australia Day falls annually on 26 January (since 1994). The Australia Day Council (2018) defines it as a 'day to reflect on what it means to be Australian, to celebrate contemporary Australia and to acknowledge our history'. January 26 marks the arrival in 1788 of the First Fleet of British ships and with this the beginning of the colonization of Australia. To many Aboriginal and Torres Strait Islander people, it marks the invasion of their lands by the British and the beginnings of the oppression of Australia's First Nations peoples. Hence, it is also known as 'Invasion Day' or 'Survival Day', and for some, it is a day of mourning. There are both celebrations and protests on the day itself, including campaigns for the date to be changed. Discourses on how the nation commemorates this day have shifted considerably in recent years, and the resulting divisions in how it is remembered have become more pronounced.

In this chapter we analyse the discourses around this national holiday across two sites of public discourse: newspapers and social media (Instagram). We focus on publicly mediated, mass communicated multimodal forms of communication. Both are media that represent the world in language and image and are thus engaged in the social construction of reality. Both have the potential to form communities around shared values. The analogue print news media was the focus of early genre work, for example, in the Disadvantaged Schools Program (DSP) Write-it-Right project that resulted in the contributions of Iedema, Feez and White (1994) to media literacy. The news media have historically offered the most tangible means of assessing audience values and beliefs, working with a target audience that was localized and sometimes known to journalists. At the other end of the scale sit the digital social media broadcasting their messages to the world and engaging with audiences that remain mostly unknowable. Thus, we get the formation of ambient communities, where users align around shared values (e.g. Zappavigna & Martin, 2018). This chapter explores competing discursive positions in relation to Australia's national holiday that are established in these two types of public discourse.

Nation and national holidays

A national holiday invokes reflection on both nationhood and national identity, and on their formation throughout history, with such reflection taking place discursively (Anderson, 2006, p. 122, as cited in Stanojević & Šarić, 2019). For Hall (1996, p. 613), the discursive construction of national identity is contained in the stories, memories and images that we share about 'nation'. National holidays belong to the 'nationhood projects' or 'national identity projects' that allow members of a nation to 'reconcile the distinct features of the different regions and ethnic groups that constitute a nation' (Stanojević & Šarić, 2019, p. 6). Both print and electronic media play an important role in what Anderson (2006) calls the 'imagining' of national communities (Stanojević & Šarić, 2019, p. 6). The realization of national holiday celebrations can be observed in both material practices (e.g. flag waving, parades and picnics) and through national holiday texts (e.g. speeches, advertisements and press releases), which are often sources for subsequent news reporting on the day (ben-Aaron, 2003, p. 78).

National holidays are also a site of tension. As ben-Aaron (2003, p. 77) notes, national holidays, as a manifestation of 'applied nationalism', may 'have a political subtext, such as mobilising for war, promoting a policy or platform, or reconstituting the nation in minority inclusive or exclusive terms'. She finds, however, that news reporting on national holidays is mostly a 'manifestation of politeness' (p. 97). For example, in her analysis of news reporting on the July 4 national holiday in the United States, the focus is on the 'nation's face'. Historically, this has resulted in reporting on 'duties citizens owe the nation', thus falling on the 'expected, consonant, positive side of the news value scales' (ben-Aaron 2003, pp. 98–9; see also ben-Aaron, 2005; Ting, 2017). She further suggests that 'considerable machinery' is needed for citizens to turn the focus onto 'the duties the nation owes its citizens' (p. 98). We suggest that such machinery now comes in the form of social media. It is here that citizens are able to highlight other facets of the Australian national holiday, and it is here that we can find discourses of change, mourning and reconciliation.

Reconciliation and change

Traces of celebration, reconciliation, mourning and change along with community building, the sharing of values, affiliation, iconization and bonding can be found throughout the body of work of Jim Martin. Sometimes this work has taken on issues and events concerning the First Nations people of Australia (Martin, 2004). In this chapter, we concern ourselves with the emerging discourses around Australia's national holiday (such as celebration, reconciliation and change). These discourses are important for all Australians, given the community-building function of national holidays and the contested nature of the event. They are realized both verbally and visually in our data, in particular through the use of alternative labels for 'Australia Day' and in the visual depiction of the official flags of Australia (displayed in Figure 11.1). With flags being, we would argue, the quintessential image of the day, we focus our visual analysis on photographs that depict flags.

In our analysis, we draw on Martin's concepts of APPRAISAL, iconization and bonding. As outlined in Martin and White (2005), APPRAISAL is a discourse semantic system which relates to how writers adopt stances (positive/negative ATTITUDE, with subsystems AFFECT, JUDGEMENT and APPRECIATION). It includes both how meanings are upscaled or downscaled (GRADUATION), and how writers present their propositions within a network of dialogistic alternatives (ENGAGEMENT). For reasons of scope, in this chapter we focus on selected APPRAISAL options, mainly ENGAGEMENT, and will introduce these options where they become relevant in the analysis. APPRAISAL resources play an important role in both iconization and bonding (see Martin, 2010).

Iconization, in Martin's (2010, p. 21) terms, refers to the process of instantiation whereby ideational meaning is discharged and interpersonal meaning is charged. He suggests that iconization is easiest to bring to consciousness in the context of images, artefacts and people (peace symbols, flags, statues, team colours, famous leaders and so on), which are a canonized form of bonds (2010, p. 26). As such, they become symbols around which communities rally or against which they rebel (Martin & Stenglin, 2007; Stenglin, 2009). Stenglin refers to bonds of this order as bonding icons, or bondicons for short (Martin & Stenglin, 2007; see also Tann, 2010, 2013).

Three bondicons are prevalent in the data sets we examine in this study: the national flag of Australia, the Aboriginal flag (shown in Figure 11.1) and the hashtag *invasionday*. (The Torres Strait Islander flag appears very rarely in our analysed data.)

As canonized forms of bonds, the flags carry a range of meanings. Briefly, the national flag is a 'defaced British blue ensign' and includes the Union Flag, five white stars representing the Southern Cross, a constellation of stars only visible in the Southern hemisphere and the Federation Star representing the federation of the colonies of Australia on 1 January 1901 (Ausflag, 2019). To some, the combination and incorporation of these elements into the Australian flag represent pride in Australia's history and achievements as tied to the British colonization of this Southern continent.

Figure 11.1 The national flag of Australia and the Aboriginal flag (used in conjunction with ©Commonwealth of Australia 2006 protocols).

To others, this flag signifies the forced dispossession of lands by the British and the genocide of First Nations people.

The Aboriginal flag, designed by Harold Thomas, a Luritja man of Central Australia, is viewed as a uniting symbol among Aboriginal people (Croft, 2006). It consists of two horizonal stripes – the upper black stripe represents the Aboriginal people of Australia, the lower red stripe represents the colour of the earth and the spiritual relation to the land (Croft, 2006). In the centre is a yellow circle symbolizing the sun, the giver of life and protector. The flag was first flown in Adelaide in 1971. In 1995 both the Aboriginal and Torres Strait Islander flags were recognized by the Australian government as official flags of Australia under the *Flags Act 1953*.

Each year, as 26 January draws near, we see a burgeoning of merchandise on the shelves of major retail stores plastered with the Australian flag. This includes footwear, hats, T-shirts and singlets. We do not see the same happening with the Aboriginal or the Torres Strait Islander flags, although such merchandise is available at specialized events such as the Yabun Festival (yabun.org.au).[1]

The third bondicon is the hashtag '#invasionday'. Hashtags are important as they allow social media users to bond around shared values (see Zappavigna, 2011; Zappavigna & Martin, 2018; see contributions to Lee, 2018 for linguistic analysis of hashtags). More specifically, #invasionday seems to function as a bondicon, as it is a highly interpersonally charged label that is used to enhance social affiliation around shared values about Australia's national holiday. This is confirmed by the fact that none of the social media posts we analysed attempted to distance themselves from this hashtag. Rather, this particular hashtag seems to be used as a means of rallying people around a particular attitude towards the national day.

Data/Methodology

To explore both print news and social media discourse, we collected data from two Australian newspapers, *The Australian* and *The Sydney Morning Herald*, as well as the social media platform Instagram. *The Australian* is a national daily newspaper (News Corp Australia, established in 1964), with a total monthly (print) 'reach' of 1.9 million (Australian, 2018). In terms of political stance, it tends to be sympathetic to right-leaning governments. Its target audience is middle to upper class with high (A) socio-economic status and includes business owners/leaders and managers (Australian, 2018).[2] *The Sydney Morning Herald* (Fairfax Media, established in 1841) is the largest metropolitan newspaper in Australia. It claims a monthly total readership (in both print and digital formats) of more than 7.6 million (Adcentre, 2019). It is sympathetic to left-leaning governments, and its target audience comprises tertiary-educated, middle-class readers, with high (AB) socio-economic status (Adcentre, 2019). In 2019, Fairfax Media was sold to Nine Entertainment, a commercial television and entertainment organization.

From these two newspapers we collected articles that were published between 19 January and 1 February in both 2016 and 2017, that is, a one-week span either side of the national holiday (on 26 January). To do so, we surveyed the print copies of these two newspapers and identified news about the national day. We scanned the images that were published with these articles to obtain a digital copy for analysis, and we collected the relevant verbal text from an online database (Factiva). Articles include news stories about the national day as well as associated awards (Australia Day honours, Australian of the Year). The resulting corpus consists of 136 articles (62,330 words),[3] with 158 images. Sixty-seven of these articles appeared in *The Australian* (34,027 words), while sixty-nine articles were published in *The Sydney Morning Herald* (28,303 words). We will refer to this data set as the AusDay corpus.

In addition, we collected data from the photo-sharing social media application, Instagram (established in October 2010). We chose Instagram specifically because it was established around the sharing of photography. All posts must include a visual of some sort, which is still overwhelmingly a still photograph, despite the fact that users may now post video (Siever & Siever, 2020). This may be accompanied by verbiage in the form of a caption, including metadata such as hashtags, and comments and replies between users (all of which are optional). The 'visual' may additionally have filters applied to it, or may consist of language, or a combination of image and language.

Instagram posts (the image, verbiage in the caption space) and metadata (such as username, bio notes, likes, number of posts) were collected over a five-day period (24–28 January) in 2017 only. During 2016 we noticed a shift in public discourse about Australia Day, along with calls to change the date. Thus, Instagram was added to the data collection for 2017 in order to capture discussion of this day by members of the public.

The hashtag #invasionday was used as a search term to collect the data, as we were specifically interested in how this interpersonally charged hashtag may function as a bondicon (see 'Reconciliation and change' above). Hashtags are discourse coordinators that serve many functions including to signal the topic of the post, to create humour, to signal the target of evaluation and to convene with other social media users, often emotionally, around a theme or event (Zappavigna, 2011; Bruns & Burgess, 2015; Lee, 2018; Caple, 2019). As metadata, or an information-organizing tool, the hashtag symbol, #, when attached to a string of letters/words (e.g. #aflw, #invasionday) can also be used to retrieve all instances of that combination of hashtag + words from a social media platform. Therefore, the use of the hashtag as a search term to compile a social media data set has become a popular research method (Page et al., 2014); however, hashtag-based sampling does have limitations in that it may not necessarily capture all relevant communication (e.g. Zappavigna, 2018, p. 7). Thus, it is important to acknowledge that this method does not produce a fully exhaustive data set. Our search of Instagram over five days, using #invasionday as the search term, retrieved 4,290 posts.

As Figure 11.2 shows, the overwhelming majority of posts (83 per cent) using this hashtag were made on the contested national day, 26 January, which suggests that #invasionday functions here as a form of direct dissent against the national day. We did not examine alternative hashtags such as #survivalday or #noprideingenocide separately, as these hashtags are often listed all together in the same post; thus, much of our analysis would have been repetitive. It is also important to note that our Instagram data set does not cover all reactions to Australia Day, which would include news sources, businesses, 'ordinary Australians', politicians, etc., posting to Instagram using the hashtag #australiaday or other hashtags. Space precludes a fuller analysis and comparison.

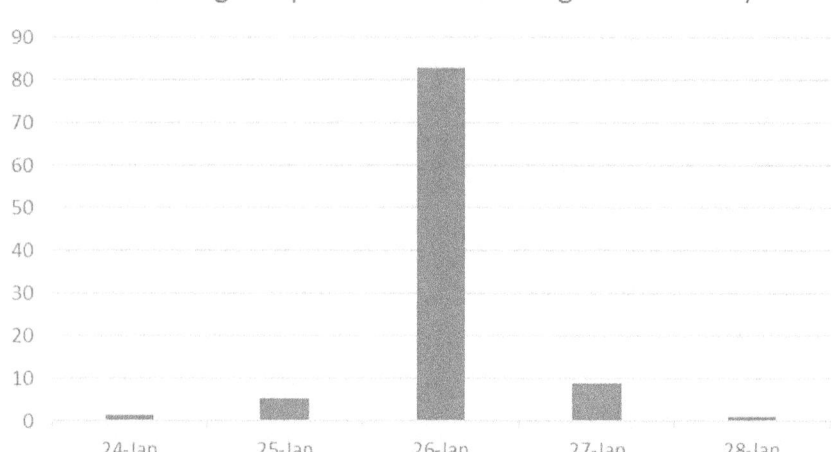

Figure 11.2 Instagram posts using #invasionday, collected over five days between 24 to 28 January 2017.

To analyse the two data sets (news/Instagram posts), we used a form of *corpus-assisted multimodal discourse analysis* (CAMDA; Bednarek & Caple, 2014), i.e. combining corpus linguistic techniques to analyse the verbiage with analysis of the visuals (images). Most often, corpus linguistic analysis focuses on *either* newspaper data *or* social media (typically, Twitter), rather than comparing the two (with the exception of McEnery et al.'s 2015 case study on press and Twitter reactions to Lee Rigby's murder in London in 2013). Here we analyse both newspaper data and social media, with Instagram constituting a different platform to Twitter (with its important dialogic function of retweeting; see McEnery et al. 2015, pp. 256–7), with different affordances, and one where images play a central role (Caple, 2020).

We therefore analysed the images in both newspaper data and the social media data, with a focus on depictions of flags (bondicons). For the social media data set (over 4,000 posts) we used automatic image recognition software (https://cloud.google.com/automl/) to identify all images that likely contained a depiction of the Aboriginal flag. The software was first trained using 253 images of flags (including thirty-eight from the #invasionday data set), and then all images were classified according to this model. In the first round, 1,245 images were classified as containing an Aboriginal flag, and 3,045 as not containing one. The images were then manually scanned, mistakes were removed, and missing images were added. The final total of images containing an Aboriginal or Torres Strait Islander flag was 1,764 or 44 per cent of the total data set. We then also manually extracted posts including the national flag (155 or 3.8 per cent).

To analyse the verbal data, we used the corpus linguistic program WordSmith (Scott, 2018), which enables identification of word forms and their frequency in and across texts in a data set. The program includes a Concordancer which allows manual inspection of each word form for qualitative analysis, for example, to ascertain how a particular word is used in its co-text. It thus becomes possible to combine quantitative and qualitative analysis. Rather than using methodologies such as keywords analysis to compare the newspaper and social media data in an inductive, corpus-driven way (see McEnery et al., 2015), we focus on exploring specific aspects of the data that we are interested in, given what we already know about the controversy around the national day. This means analysing potential references to Aboriginal or Torres Strait Islander people or matters and labels used to refer to the national holiday.

Findings

Newspapers

As canonized bonding icons, we first investigated how flags were incorporated into the photographs in our newspaper data set. Two different patterns of use were detected, with the Aboriginal flag associated with protests/marches and the Australian flag associated with celebratory events, neither of which was unexpected. Alignment with the newspapers' ideological tendencies can also be detected. The Aboriginal flag appears in only five photographs (6 per cent of the total), and all instances are connected to Invasion Day marches that were taking place on the day. The use of the Aboriginal flag in the context of Invasion Day marches can be viewed as signifying survival and resilience in the face of colonization. Affiliation with Aboriginal people is also depicted in a photograph showing a group of Muslim women holding up an Aboriginal flag at a march (published in *The Sydney Morning Herald*). The Torres Strait Islander flag does not appear in any of the photographs. The reporting of Invasion Day marches only occurs in the 2017 data sets (and has increased still further in 2018 and 2019).

The Australian flag appears in fifteen photographs (19 per cent of the total) and acts as a symbol of nation-building and of shared identity. In three instances, the national flag appears in the background at official events (e.g. with politicians standing at a podium with the flag behind them), but most often, it is shown being waved or worn at various celebratory cultural events such as the Ute Parade in Darwin, hung around the shoulders of new Australian citizens and of youngsters at the beach (all published in *The Australian*). Two photographs, also published in *The Australian*, show young Muslim women (one a new Australian citizen) wearing the Australian flag around their shoulders, giving both the impression of a diverse Australia and that they embrace the values encapsulated in the flag and the day (which is also repeated in the verbal text accompanying these photographs). In the 2017 data set, there are no instances of such celebratory flag-waving images in *The Sydney Morning Herald*.

The low presence of the Aboriginal flag in the newspaper data is mirrored in the low frequency of potential references to Aboriginal or Torres Strait Islander people or matters in the verbal text. Table 11.1 compares word forms that appear in WordSmith's word list.[4]

Table 11.1 Frequency and distribution of word forms (separately).

	The Australian		The Sydney Morning Herald		AusDay corpus	
Word form	Raw (n. f.)	No of texts	Raw (n. f.)	No of texts	Raw (n. f.)	No of texts
Aboriginal	22 (6.47)	11/67	16 (5.65)	6/69	38 (6.10)	17/136
Aborigines	2 (0.59)	2/67	0	0/69	2 (0.32)	2/136
Indigenous	43 (12.64)	19/67	23 (8.13)	12/69	66 (10.59)	31/136

Note that the form *Aborigine/s* is dispreferred by some: '… the terms "Aborigine/s" or "Aboriginals" have negative connotations and are highly offensive to many. Historically, these have been used in racist contexts as a derogatory term to belittle or objectify Indigenous people' (Reporting on Aboriginal and Torres Strait Islander Peoples and Issues, 2018, p. 5). Interestingly, both instances of this problematic form in *The Australian* are attributed to Aboriginal speakers via reporting statements (i.e. indirect speech):

(Ex 1) … activist Robbie Thorpe told the crowd Australia Day was a shameful reminder of the oppression of **Aborigines**.
(Ex 2) She [Linda Burney] said Australia Day better reflected the place of **Aborigines** in Australian history than it did a decade ago …

Since both are indirect quotations, without a transcript it remains unclear if these speakers actually did use the word *Aborigines* – but other news reports of the same event that cite Robbie Thorpe do *not* paraphrase him as using this word form (sbs.com.au; https://www.heraldsun.com.au; https://www.news.com.au).

In any case, it is readily apparent that the forms *Aboriginal* and *Indigenous* are both rare and not well distributed across the AusDay corpus. In fact, the distribution is even lower than Table 11.1 suggests, because the forms *Aboriginal* and *Indigenous* often co-occur in the same text, as identified by a search for instances of *Aboriginal* OR *Aborigines* OR *Indigenous* (not case-sensitive and again excluding *non-*). As Table 11.2 shows, one or more of these terms occur in 21 of 67 texts in *The Australian* (31 per cent of data) and in 15 of 69 texts in *The Sydney Morning Herald* (22 per cent of data) – together in a total of 36 out of 136 texts (26 per cent of the AusDay corpus). In other words, only a quarter of the texts about Australia Day refer to Aboriginal or Torres Strait Islander peoples or matters using these forms.

As noted, our analysis of Instagram posts focuses on #invasionday, which is infrequent in the newspaper corpus where the following labels for the national holiday are used: *Australia Day* (249 instances in 111 texts), *Invasion Day* (14 instances in ten texts), *national day* (ten instances in seven texts), *Oz Day* (three instances in three texts), *Survival Day* (two instances in one text). The expression *day of mourning* also occurs (three instances in three texts, once modified by *national*). Table 11.3 shows the frequencies and distribution of these different forms per newspaper.

Table 11.2 Frequency and distribution of word forms (combined).

	The Australian		The Sydney Morning Herald		AusDay corpus	
	Raw (n. f.)	No of texts	Raw (n. f.)	No of texts	Raw (n. f.)	No of texts
Aboriginal*/ Aborigines/ Indigenous*	67 (19.69)	21/67	39 (13.78)	15/69	106 (17.01)	36/136

Table 11.3 Competing labels, their frequencies and distribution.

	The Australian			The Sydney Morning Herald		
	Raw f	N.f.	No of texts	Raw f	N.f.	No of texts
Australia Day*	125	36.74	59	124	43.81	52
Invasion Day*	8	2.35	7	6	2.12	3
national day*	6	1.76	5	4	1.41	2
Oz Day*	2	0.59	2	1	0.35	1
Survival Day*	2	0.59	1	0	0	0
Day of mourning	2	0.59	2	1	0.35	1

As evident, *Australia Day* is the common label that is widely used in both newspapers, with competing labels such as *Invasion Day* or *Survival Day* comparatively rare. None of the latter are preceded by a hashtag; in other words, the newspapers do not appear to refer to the discussion on social media.

In terms of discourse semantics (APPRAISAL), the 'alternative' labels (*Invasion Day, Survival Day, day of mourning*) are identified as **not** originating in the institutional voice of the newspaper (through [attribution], an ENGAGEMENT option under [heterogloss] and [expand] in Martin & White, 2005), and are most often accompanied by quotation marks (see Figure 11.3) or other means of indicating projection.

Such formulations 'disassociate the proposition from the text's internal authorial voice by attributing it to some external source' (Martin & White, 2005, p. 111). In some cases, there appears to be no explicit indication as to the stance of the authorial voice with respect to the label – the formulation is neutral in this respect [attribution: acknowledge], for example:

(Ex 3) Elsewhere across the country, however, thousands of their new compatriots marched in solidarity with **indigenous Australians who consider January 26 to be a day of mourning.**

(Ex 4) **Kali Bellear**, whose father Bob Bellear was deeply involved in the civil rights movement and then became the first Aboriginal judge, **said** growing up watching parents and uncles being arrested at protests "made me realise that

N	Concordance
1	ahead," he said. Asked about those who regarded the day as "Invasion Day", Mr Wilson said: "There'll always be detractors , but like
2	Melbourne chanting "no pride in genocide" while the words "Happy Invasion Day" were spray-painted on a train station wall. Amid a heavy
3	Australians who consider January 26 to be a day of mourning . "Invasion Day" protests were held peacefully in Brisbane and
4	a schism in Australia's society" Protesters took to the streets for "Invasion Day" rallies in every capital city except Darwin . despite
5	'Invasion day and survival day' Kali Bellear , whose father Bob Bellear
6	people had to fight every step of the way for their rights ... today is invasion day but also survival day". Speaking at the Yabun Festival in
7	26, marking the 1788 arrival of the First Fleet at Port Jackson , as "Invasion Day". But fireworks were still due to go off above the port's
8	States and territories agree to all celebrate on January 26; first official "Invasion Day" marked in Sydney 1994: January 26 formally becomes
9	Premier Gladys Berejiklian says she was disappointed by the "invasion day" protesters who burned the national flag and clashed
10	In Sydney, Melbourne , Brisbane and Canberra , hundreds of people at "invasion day" rallies chanted "always was, always will be Aboriginal
11	Day since 1994 but is not embraced by many Australians who call it "Invasion Day". Mr Joyce told Sydney radio station 2GB he gets "sick of
12	'Invasion Day' suspect linked to Greens A man arrested for allegedly
13	for allegedly assaulting police during the flag-burning melee at the "invasion day" march through Sydney is a Greens campaign manager
14	its right to exist within the Greens . Mr Shoebridge addressed the invasion day rally , demanding the date of Australia Day be changed .

Figure 11.3 *Invasion Day* in the AusDay corpus.

Aboriginal people had to fight every step of the way for their rights ... today is **invasion day** but also **survival day**".

(Ex 5) 1938 First official **"national day of mourning"** marked by Aboriginal leaders.

In the vast majority of cases, quotation marks are only enclosing the label (e.g. lines 1, 3–4, 7–13 in Figure 11.3), with a common pattern linking it with protests ('invasion day' + *protests/protesters, rally/rallies, march*). In certain uses, this graphological choice can realize 'an explicit distancing of the authorial voice from the attributed material' (Martin & White, 2005, p. 113), that is, [attribution: distance]. Bednarek (2006, p. 182) refers to these uses as *hearsay hedges* – a category that also includes *so-called* and WH-structures such as *what X call(s) Y*. Hearsay hedges are evaluative in that they express the writer's evaluation (e.g. distance, scepticism or disapproval) towards content that is explicitly identified as hearsay in terms of evidentiality (Bednarek, 2006, p. 182). Stubbs calls such hedges markers of 'detachment' (Stubbs, 1986, p. 13). They indicate that the meaning of the modified item is somehow problematic and convey the speaker's group membership or his/her attitude towards the referent (Stubbs, 1986, p. 13).

For analytical purposes, quotation marks around labels are problematic. They can signal that the label is not the writer's own and can additionally imply criticism of or sarcasm towards either the source and/or the linguistic expression that is quoted (Haiman, 1989; Weizman, 1984). They are then sometimes described as 'scare' or 'snigger' quotes. However, it can be difficult to tell whether quotation marks around labels just indicate that the label is not the writer's own ([attribution: acknowledge] in Martin & White's terms) or whether there is an explicit distancing from the label ([attribution: distance] in Martin & White's terms). The co-text can provide some clues, but how these quotation marks are read also depends on the reader's attitude, and the evaluative strength of distancing uses can vary (Bednarek, 2006, p. 182). Rather than trying to quantify here which of the quotation marks should be analysed as 'acknowledge' and which as 'distance', we want to emphasize what all uses have in common: namely, that the alternative labels are never 'endorsed' by the newspapers.[5]

They are always treated as labels used by others – unnamed Australians, protestors or Aboriginal Australians, although there are clear differences between texts in terms of the attitude that is implied towards these others (e.g. ... *is not embraced by many Australians who call it 'invasion day'* [line 11] vs *'invasion day' protesters who burned the national flag* [line 9]). In contrast, the common, sanctioned term is *Australia Day*. While there is clearly much more to explore with respect to these newspaper data, we will now move on to the social media data to offer insights into an alternative set of multimodal data, with personalized rather than institutionalized authorship.

Instagram

We will start by discussing a few salient points from the analysis of the verbiage as used in hashtags, bio notes and posts, before focusing on the use of flags. The most frequently occurring hashtag (excluding the search term #invasionday) in this data set is #changethedate, pointing to discourses of change and indicating that the current date is inappropriate as it is associated with colonization and survival (realized as #survivalday). Three other hashtags are also common: #noprideingenocide, #alwayswasalwayswillbe and #aboriginalland. These hashtags all co-occur with #invasionday and point to conflicting histories and ongoing differences in remembering how 'Australia' came into being.

Interestingly, we were also able to examine more closely how the people making these posts identified themselves through their bio notes (which can be included with user accounts). A corpus linguistic *keywords* analysis of the language used in the bio notes shows that the people posting to Instagram and using this particular hashtag self-identify as 'activists' (advocating for change, human/animal rights, equality, the environment), as belonging to non-mainstream groups (vegan), as 'creatives' (writers, artists, actors, film makers), but much less frequently as Aboriginal or Indigenous (less than 1 per cent).[6] This implies that non-Aboriginal people, by using #invasionday along with the hashtags noted above, were aligning themselves with Aboriginal and Torres Strait Islander people in their activism for change.

Since national days are meant to be celebrated, we examined the lemma CELEBRATE as used in the posts by these particular Instagram users. In APPRAISAL terms, its meaning potential is at least indirectly associated with positive AFFECT. As shown in Example 6, this lemma is co-textually associated with changing the date to a date that 'we can all celebrate':

(Ex 6) I'm choosing to remember tomorrow is not a day of celebration for our First People. Time to be respectful and seriously consider changing the date of Australia Day so we can all celebrate as one. As a nation we've achieved great things and we should celebrate, just not on a day with such a horrible history. #invasionday #saynoto26january

Most often, CELEBRATE is used in conjunction with negation and modality (e.g. *cannot/don't/do not/will not/won't/never celebrate, not a day to celebrate, no day to celebrate, nothing to celebrate, refuse to celebrate*), as in:

(Ex 7) I will not celebrate genocide, enslavement, rape and dehumanisation. White Australia has a shameful history. #changethedate #australiaday #invasionday #auspol #australia

With respect to APPRAISAL (ENGAGEMENT) choices, users make use of [disclaim: deny] options, where 'the textual voice positions itself as at odds with, or rejecting, some contrary position' (Martin & White, 2005, p. 97). Such problematizing of the idea of *celebrating* the national day (and of the associated positive AFFECT) is an important feature of the social media data set.

While a wide range of subjects appear in the photographs (including people, landscapes and animals), the most dominant visual theme is the Aboriginal flag, which appears in 44 per cent of the images in the #invasionday data set. The flag is mostly shown being carried at Invasion Day marches (in 38 per cent of flag images). A further 18 per cent of posts including the Aboriginal flag have verbal text overlaid onto the flag. This text reinforces how the national day is perceived by those who identify with the Aboriginal flag (as Invasion Day) and highlights issues of sovereignty of the land (Always was always will be Aboriginal land), alternative versions of history (White Australia has a Black History) and intertextual references to war discourses (1788: Lest We Forget) among others. Such visual depictions of the Aboriginal flag in #invasionday posts made on the day of the national holiday can be simultaneously viewed as a rejection of the status quo and as a uniting symbol among both Aboriginal people and those who support them.

It is interesting to note that the national flag also appears in posts made using #invasionday, both singly (in 3.8 per cent of all posts) and alongside the Aboriginal flag (in 1.4 per cent of all posts). How it is visually depicted differs from how the Aboriginal flag is photographed: at first blush, the national flag appears to be portrayed in largely patriotic ways (worn, waved, or flown), but is then rejected as a symbol of unity/patriotism in the accompanying verbal text. Thus, while initially seeming to act as a means of nation-building and creating a shared identity and sense of unity (Stanojević & Šarić, 2019), the national flag is also used to index a conflicted history and the need for change and reconciliation. This contrasts markedly with how the national flag is conceptualized in the newspaper data.

Among the 155 images that show the national flag, 9 per cent visually depict direct dissent against the flag, for example, including an expletive gesture (middle finger) directed at the flag, or showing a damaged flag where the Union Flag is cut out. The majority of images (55 per cent), however, show people wearing (clothing, tattoos), waving or standing in front of the national flag, and mostly smiling (positive AFFECT). Thus, they appear to be celebrating the national day. When read in conjunction with the accompanying verbal text, however, a more conflicted impression emerges. Some use the verbal text to encourage remembrance of what this day signifies for Aboriginal people. Many posts actively call for change, while some merely acknowledge the alternative label:

(Ex 8) Straya mate! #invasionday #australiaday

In Example 8, the use of the national flag in the visual alongside recognizably Australian verbiage (*Straya mate*) suggests a strong identification with 'Australianness' and implies national pride and celebration. At the same time, the #invasionday hashtag problematizes the national day, which could mean that 'Straya mate' is being used ironically here. It is difficult to interpret these types of post – are users just using both hashtags so their posts can be found by other media users or are they using the #invasionday hashtag to affiliate with those who regard the day as problematic?

A small number of images (fifty-five) depict both the Aboriginal and national flags (flying side by side, or in cartoon/drawn form), and very few of these include people. The verbal text accompanying these images contains messages that call for change and reconciliation, acknowledge Elders and custodianship of the lands, and also acknowledge the suffering, genocide and loss since colonization. The call for change and truth-telling is a clear message in these posts, and this comes from Instagrammers who do not explicitly self-identify as Aboriginal or Torres Strait Islander.

Conclusion

While our discussion in this chapter merely scratches the surface of the richness of these data sets, our analysis demonstrates various struggles with how the national holiday in Australia is referenced in public discourses. In their analysis of another form of social media, Twitter, McEnery et al. (2015) found that 'while porous, the direction of influence seems to be from the press to Twitter' and that 'the press appears largely deaf to the attempts to reframe the discussion on Twitter'. The same can be said for our findings. The news media analysed for this study did not mention hashtags or make use of images from Instagram. If the controversy was referred to, the focus was on activism on the street (Invasion Day marches/protests) rather than social media activism on Instagram. In addition, the *Australia Day* label is clearly the sanctioned label that newspapers align with, with *Invasion Day* being both rare and not endorsed. Results could be different if newspaper editorials and other opinion texts were also examined rather than focusing solely on news reporting. In any case, this study represents a baseline for future comparisons of the role of different types of activism and their interaction with news reporting. In addition, the focus on Instagram has allowed us to investigate bondicons that are realized both visually in such iconic iterations as flags and through hashtags that rally people around shared values and attitudes towards key issues facing Australians. Additional analysis is necessary to uncover the full range of meanings encoded in the combination of both verbiage and image in the multimodal communicative acts made on Instagram, as well as to compare different hashtags (including #australiaday).

In conclusion, our examination of the discursive construction of Australia Day in both the print and electronic media highlights the struggles Australia faces in imagining nationhood and any sense of unity or shared identity meant to come from that. The discursive struggle uncovered in our analysis around changing the date of this national holiday has more recently been superseded by calls to also 'change the nation' (Pearson, 2019). Legitimate recognition of Aboriginal and Torres Strait Islander peoples in mainstream discourses is an ongoing struggle in Australia (see Davis et al.,

2018 for discussion of the government's rejection of the Uluru Statement from the Heart), and social media sites such as Instagram may provide a space for alternative positionings to be heard and shared.

Acknowledgements

This research was supported by the Sydney Informatics Hub, a Core Research Facility of the University of Sydney. Funding assistance was provided through an ARC DECRA: Project ID DE160100120.

Notes

1. The company WAM Clothing, not owned by Indigenous Australians, currently has exclusive rights to use the flag on clothing (Alexander, 2019). However, the extent to which this impacts on the availability of merchandise is unclear.
2. A and AB are socio-economic grades originally developed by the UK's National Readership Survey to classify readers according to their income, occupation and education level. These grades are commonly used by newspapers to sell audience types to advertisers.
3. Tokens in text; settings: hyphens separate words; ' allowed within word.
4. Settings were adjusted so that the forms *non-Aboriginal* or *non-Indigenous* were excluded; raw = number of instances; n.f. = normalized frequency per 10,000 words.
5. Endorsements are 'formulations by which propositions sourced to external sources are construed by the authorial voice as correct, valid, undeniable or otherwise maximally warrantable' (Martin & White, 2005, p. 126).
6. Keywords analysis is a tool in WordSmith that automatically identifies words that are more frequent in a data set compared to a second data set (which acts as a reference norm), hence allowing the identification of salient or 'key' words.

References

Adcentre (2019). Brands: The Sydney Morning Herald. *Fairfax Media*. Retrieved from https://www.adcentre.com.au/brands/the-sydney-morning-herald/. Last accessed 15 April 2020.
Alexander, I. (2019). Explainer: Our copyright laws and the Australian Aboriginal flag. *The Conversation*. Retrieved from http://theconversation.com/explainer-our-copyright-laws-and-the-australian-aboriginal-flag-118687. Last accessed 15 April 2020.
Anderson, B. R. (2006). *Imagined Communities: Reflections on the Origin and Spread of Nationalism*. London: Verso.
Ausflag (2019). Australian National Flag. Retrieved from http://www.ausflag.com.au/national_flag.asp. Last accessed 15 April 2020.
Australian (2018). Brands: The Australian. *News Corp Australia*. Retrieved from https://www.newscorpaustralia.com/brand/australian/. Last accessed 15 April 2020.
Bednarek, M. (2006). *Evaluation in Media Discourse. Analysis of a Newspaper Corpus*. London/New York: Continuum.

Bednarek, M., & Caple, H. (2014). Why do news values matter? Towards a new methodological framework for analyzing news discourse in Critical Discourse Analysis and beyond. *Discourse & Society*, 25(2), 135–58.

ben-Aaron, D. (2003). When news isn't news: The case of national holidays. *Journal of Historical Pragmatics*, 4(1), 75–102.

ben-Aaron, D. (2005). Given and news: Evaluation in newspaper stories about national anniversaries. *Text*, 25(5), 691–718.

Bruns, A., & Burgess, J. (2015). Twitter hashtags: From ad hoc to calculated publics. In N. Rambukkana (Ed.), *Hashtag Publics: The Power and Politics of Discursive Networks* (pp. 13–28). New York: Peter Lang.

Caple, H. (2019). Lucy says today she is a Labordoodle: How the dogs-of-Instagram reveal voter preferences. *Social Semiotics*, 29(4), 427–47.

Caple, H. (2020). Image-centric practices on Instagram: Subtle shifts in footing. In H. Stöckl, H. Caple & J. Pflaeging (Eds.), *Shifts towards Image-Centricity in Contemporary Multimodal Practices* (pp. 153–76). London/New York: Routledge.

Croft, B. L. (2006). Account of Invasion Day, 26 January 1988, Cook's Sites exhibition, National Library of Australia, Canberra, 16 March to 18 June. Retrieved from https://aiatsis.gov.au/explore/articles/aboriginal-flag. Last accessed 15 April 2020.

Davis, M., Saunders, C., McKenna, M., Morris, S., Mayes, C., & Giannacopoulos, M. (2018). The Uluru Statement from Heart, one year on: Can a First Nations Voice yet be heard? *ABC Religion & Ethics*. Retrieved from https://www.abc.net.au/religion/the-uluru-statement-from-heart-one-year-on-can-a-first-nations-v/10094678. Last accessed 15 April 2020.

Haiman, J. (1989). Alienation in grammar. *Studies in Language*, 13(1), 129–70.

Hall, S. (1996). The question of cultural identity. In S. Hall, D. Held, D. Hubert & K. Thompson (Eds.), *Modernity: An Introduction to Modern Societies* (pp. 595–634). Oxford: Wiley.

Iedema, R., Feez, S., & White, P. R. R. (1994). *Stage Two: Media Literacy*. A report for the Write it Right Literacy in Industry Research Project by the Disadvantaged Schools Program, N.S.W. Department of School Education.

Lee, C. (Ed.) (2018). Discourse of social tagging. Special issue, *Discourse, Context & Media*, 22.

Martin, J. R. (2004). Positive Discourse Analysis: Solidarity and change. *Revista Canaria de Estudios Ingleses*, 49, 179–200.

Martin, J. R. (2010). Introduction: Semantic variation: Modelling system, text and affiliation in social semiosis. In M. Bednarek & J. R. Martin (Eds.), *New Discourse on Language: Functional Perspectives on Multimodality, Identity, and Affiliation* (pp. 163–94). London: Continuum.

Martin, J. R., & Stenglin, M. (2007). Materializing reconciliation: Negotiating difference in a post-colonial exhibition. In T. Royce and W. Bowcher (Eds.), *New Directions in the Analysis of Multimodal Discourse* (pp. 215–38). Hillsdale, NJ: Erlbaum.

Martin, J. R., & White, P. R. R. (2005). *The Language of Evaluation: Appraisal in English*. Basingstoke/New York: Palgrave Macmillan.

McEnery, T., McGlashan, M., & Love, R. (2015). Press and social media reaction to ideologically inspired murder: The case of Lee Rigby. *Discourse & Communication*, 9(2), 237–59.

Page, R., Barton, D., Unger, J. W., & Zappavigna, M. (2014). *Researching Language and Social Media: A Student Guide*. London: Routledge.

Pearson, L. (2019). I no longer support #ChangeTheDate. We must change Australia. *Guardian Australia*. Retrieved from https://www.theguardian.com/commentisfree/2019/jan/16/i-no-longer-support-changethedate-we-must-change-the-country. Last accessed 15 April 2020.

Reporting on Aboriginal and Torres Strait Islander Peoples and Issues: An introductory resource for the media (2018). *Media Diversity Australia in partnership with National Congress of Australia's First Peoples and with the Support of the Australian Broadcasting Corporation*. Retrieved from https://www.mediadiversityaustralia.org/indigenous/. Last accessed 15 April 2020.

Scott, M. (2018). *WordSmith Tools 7.0* Version 7.0.0.164 (3/9/2018).

Siever, C. M., & Siever, T. (2020). Emoji-text relations on Instagram. Empirical corpus studies on multimodal uses of the iconographetic mode. In H. Stöckl, H. Caple & J. Pflaeging (Eds.), *Image-Centric Practices in the Contemporary Media Sphere* (pp. 177–203). London/New York: Routledge.

Stanojević, M.-M. & Šarić, L. (2019). Metaphors in the discursive construction of nations. In L. Šarić & M-M. Stanojević (Eds.), *Metaphor, Nation and Discourse* (pp. 1–34). Amsterdam: John Benjamins.

Stenglin, M. (2009). Space odyssey: Towards a social semiotic model of 3D space. *Visual Communication*, 8(1), 35–64.

Stubbs, M. (1986). A matter of prolonged fieldwork: Notes towards a modal grammar of English. *Applied Linguistics*, 7, 1–25.

Tann, K. (2010). Imagining communities: A multifunctional approach to identity management in texts. In M. Bednarek & J. R. Martin (Eds.), *New Discourse on Language: Functional Perspectives on Multimodality, Identity and Affiliation* (pp. 163–94). London: Continuum.

Tann, K. (2013). The language of identity discourse: Introducing a framework for functional iconography. *Linguistics and the Human Sciences*, 8(3), 361–91.

Ting, S. H. (2017). An agenda-setting study of National Day coverage in State and National newspapers. *3L, Language, Linguistics, Literature*, 23(4), 41–55.

Weizman, E. (1984). Identifying implied referents: An interlingual study of linguistic, pragmatic, textual, and contextual factors in information processing. *Applied Linguistics*, 5, 266–74.

Zappavigna, M. (2011). Ambient affiliation: A linguistic perspective on Twitter. *New Media & Society*, 13(5), 788–806. doi: 10.1177/1461444810385097.

Zappavigna, M. (2018). *Searchable Talk: Hashtags and the Discourse of Social Tagging*. London: Bloomsbury.

Zappavigna, M., & Martin, J. R. (2018). #Communing affiliation: Social tagging as a resource for aligning around values in social media. *Discourse, Context & Media*, 22, 4–12. http://dx.doi.org/10.1016/j.dcm.2017.08.001. Last accessed 15 April 2020.

Name index

A
Alvarado, Jasmine 7, 182
Assange, Julian 31–3

B
Bakhtin 6, 12–13, 17, 37, 155, 164, 183
Bartlett, David 19, 82, 165
Barton, David 219
Bateman, John A. 39–40, 42, 47–8, 53, 133, 150
Bednarek, Monika 11–12, 15, 17, 19, 36–7, 128–9, 205, 210, 214, 218–20
Bellear, Bob 213
Ben-Aaron, Diana 206, 219
Bennardo, Giovanni 110, 127
Benson, James D 17, 54, 82
Bernstein, Basil 13, 17, 96, 106
Berry, Margaret 18, 82
Bezemer, Jeff 133, 150
Boonsawasd, Attasith 115, 128
Brisk, María Estela 167
Burney, Linda 212
Burns, Anne 126, 128–9
Butt, David 18, 82, 128

C
Caffarel, Alice 19, 57, 82
Caple, Helen 11, 205, 209–10, 219–20
Christie, Fran 18, 85, 91, 106, 165, 168, 179, 182–3
Coffin, Caroline 12, 129
Cruz, Prixie 8

D
Derewianka, Beverly 167, 182
Doran, Yaegan 1, 11, 17, 19, 58–9, 82–3, 86, 106, 108, 138, 150
Dreyfus, Shoshana 85, 91, 106, 151
Dwyer, Paul 11, 201

F
Feez, Susan 12, 36, 183, 205, 219
Firth, John Rupert 2, 6
Fontaine, Lise 15, 53–4, 185, 201
Fuller, Gillian 12

G
Gregory, Michael 3, 17

H
Halliday, Michael 2–4, 6, 8, 10, 13, 17–18, 54, 80–2, 85, 105–6, 150, 163–4, 193, 201
Hao, Jing 85–6, 91
Harper, Stephen 186
Hasan, Ruqaiya 3, 18, 128
Hjelsmlev, Louis 13, 41
Hood, Susan 19, 88–9, 91–2, 96, 107, 151, 154–5, 165
Humphrey, Sally 5, 7, 85, 106–8, 167, 183

I
Iedema, Rick 12, 27, 36, 205, 219

J
Joseph, Robert 185–6, 189–93, 195–9, 203

K
Knox, John S. 8, 17, 106, 109, 111, 128, 130
Kress, Gunther 2, 6, 11, 17–18, 39–40, 48–50, 54, 145, 150, 156, 158–9, 165

L
Labov, William 6, 12–13

M
Macken-Horarik, Mary 12, 27, 36
Macnaught, Lucy 183

Matthiessen, C.M.I.M. 2, 18–19, 54, 57, 82, 105–7, 150, 165, 182, 191, 201
McKay, Stan 189

O
Orwell, George 31

P
Page, Ruth 209, 219
Painter, Clare 19, 39–40, 49–52, 55, 101, 107, 133, 145, 151, 155, 157, 163, 165
Peirce, Charles Sanders 55
Poynton, C. 12, 109, 111–14, 118, 125–7

Q
Quiroz, Beatriz 8, 19, 81, 83

R
Ramos, Kent 8
Rigby, Lee 210, 219
Robert, Joseph 202
Rochester, Sherry 11, 20
Rose, David 85
Rothery, Joan 6, 12, 20, 167, 182–3

S
Sinclair, Murray 185–6, 190, 194, 202–3
Smethurst, Annika 21, 23, 29–32, 34–5

T
Thomas, Harold 208
Thorpe, Robbie 212

U
Unsworth, Len 11, 13, 19, 55, 86, 107–8, 131, 134, 151, 153, 165

V
van Leeuwen, Theo 2, 11, 18, 40, 47–50, 54–5, 134, 145, 150, 165
Ventola, Eija 42

W
Webster, Jonathan 17–18, 107, 165
Whorf, Benjamin Lee 82

Z
Zappavigna, Michele 11, 19–20, 22, 24–7, 30, 32–3, 38, 201, 205, 208–9, 219–20
Zang, DL 153–4
Zhenhua, Wang 20

Subject index

A
abduction 46, 49, 139, 141–2, 144–5
Aboriginal peoples 185–92, 194–200, 202–3, 208, 210–17
    Aboriginal English 130
    of Australia 205, 208, 212–13, 215, 217, 220
    of Canada 186–90, 197–8
    Child Welfare in Canada 200
    children 186, 190–2, 195–6
    land 215–16
    leaders 214
    national flag 207–8, 210–11, 216–17
actor 158, 191, 195, 197
address 20, 26, 90, 110–12, 114–15, 117–18, 125–6, 129, 133
addressee 26–8, 32, 35, 125, 192–3, 195, 197
affect 161, 163
affiliation 11–12, 17, 19, 22–4, 28, 36–7, 128–9, 206, 211, 217, 219–20
    ambient 22, 24–5, 38, 208, 220
    strategies 24
affordances 144, 210
agent 193, 198
agentless passives 194
aggregation 134, 148
alignment/dis-alignment 22, 27–8, 30, 43, 154, 211
analysis, multimodal 39–40, 128
applied linguistics 16, 22, 36
appraisal analysis 7, 9–13, 27–9, 35–7, 39, 41–2, 153–5, 164–5, 170, 207, 213, 215–16, 219
appreciation 183
argument texts 168–75, 179–80
articles, indefinite 93
assessment criteria 103
assessments 7, 22, 27–9, 35, 92, 170

attitude system 9, 22, 24, 27–8, 30, 33, 153–5, 159–63, 207, 214–15, 217
    attitudinal force 31
    attitudinal invocations 28–9, 164
    attitudinal proposition 26, 92
    attitudinal recontextualization 162
    attitudinal targets 28
    expressing explicit 92
    system of 7, 27
attitudinal alignment/dis-alignment 24–6, 30, 35
attribution 49, 213–14
audience 155, 168–9, 172–4, 176–7, 179–81, 205
    adult 177
    ambient 26
    intended 23, 172–4
    language choices in response to 169, 183
audience awareness 169
audience types 218
Australia Day 205–6, 209, 212–13, 215, 217
Australian curriculum 150
Australian educators 167
Australian English 8, 20, 109, 117, 129
    spoken 117
Australian newspapers 208
Authorial stance 37, 165
authorial voice 213–14, 218
    internal 213
axial argumentation 58
axial perspective 10
Axial Relations 83
axiology 34

B
beliefs 26, 36, 91, 205
bilingual students 167–83
bonding icons / bondicons 31–2, 207–11, 217

bonds 22, 134, 207–8
    deferred 36

C
chains, cohesive 52
change, social 15, 188
children's picture books 11, 19, 55, 107, 151, 165
China
    curriculum reform in 165
    curriculum standards 153
Chinese language
    classification system of 76
    nominal groups in 57–83
    qualification system of 79
    quantification system of 77
classification networks 48
classifier 62–5, 67–9, 74, 76–7, 80, 117, 120, 141–2
classroom practice 165
clause
    embedded 73–4, 191
    expanding 94
    minor 35
    ranking 191
    relational 91
clause grammar 3
code theory 13, 19
cohesion 3, 41, 55
    lexical 42
cohesion analysis 3
cohesion in Literary Texts 17
cohesive harmony 201
commentary 170, 179–80
commitment 4, 16, 46, 109, 126, 133–4, 147, 160
communing affiliation 25, 38, 220
communities, adversarial 27, 33
community 10, 14–15, 22, 24, 32, 36, 105, 113, 118, 181, 187–8, 198, 200
    ambient 205
comparison/contrast relations 50
complementarities 11, 58
composition
    intermodal construal of 144, 149
    taxonomy 138, 141
    visual 159
compositional relations 132, 138–9, 141–2, 144, 147–9

abductions of 141–2
concurrence 144, 147–8
conjunctive relations 8, 10, 41–5, 47, 55, 64, 94, 105
connexion 94, 103, 105
    causal 95
    logical 94
    position 96
convoke system 25
coupling 22, 25, 28
coverbal phrase 74, 80–1
    embedded 73–4
coverbs 81
critical discourse analysis (CDA) 1, 14–15, 200, 219
curriculum
    elementary 168
    genres 6–7, 96–7, 101, 105
    knowledge 97, 105
    registers 85
    standards 153, 159, 161, 164–5
    values 105
curriculum reform 153, 165

D
deixis 51, 71–5, 78–80, 93, 112
dependency 8, 69
detailed reading 104
dialogic affiliation 24, 26–7
dialogistic positioning 27
dialogue 42, 102, 156, 160
dialogue balloons 156–7, 160–1, 163–4
Disadvantaged Schools Program (DSP) 12, 205
dis-affiliation 24
dis-alignment 24–5, 32, 35
discourse semantics
    stratum of 39–41, 48, 60, 69, 88
    and multimodality 47

E
educational levels 162
EFL
    education 154, 161–2
    pedagogic materials 153
    textbooks 155–8, 159, 163–4
emotion 154, 159, 163

expressed 160
negative 28
positive 154, 161
sharing 163
energy 171–2, 182
engagement 7–8, 12, 27, 91–3, 102, 153–5, 207, 216
English kinship terms 119
entities 60–3, 65–6, 69–71, 73, 75–7, 80–1, 92–3
epithet 63–7, 69, 71–2, 76–81
evaluative stance 154, 161
explanation genres 131–2
    effective infographic 148
    unabbreviated canonical 148
    verbal 131

F
factorial explanations 132
factual genres 7
field 58–61, 63, 88, 92–3, 97, 100, 102, 104, 131–2, 134–5, 138–9, 148–9, 155
finesse system 25
focalization 50
function and class analysis 67, 74
functional language instruction 183

G
genre analysis 108
genre-based pedagogy 4, 16, 85–6, 90, 97, 101–6, 164, 168, 170, 181–2
genres
    argument 85, 170–1, 173–4, 179
    canonical 134
    chronological 168
    constituent 97
    narrative 12, 69
    report 134
gesture 11, 106, 159–60
graduation 12–13, 25, 104, 154–5, 165, 168, 170, 172, 174–5, 177, 180
group class 61–5, 67–8, 70–2, 74, 78

H
hashtags 25, 207–9, 213, 215, 217
heterogloss 213

heteroglossia 30, 155–6
hypotaxis 8, 67, 69, 73

I
iconization 134, 206–7
ideation systems 86
identification 41–2, 51, 58, 60, 69, 104, 185, 192, 194, 210
    presenting 194
    presuming 194
    system 69, 186, 191–2, 194
identity 1, 11, 22, 51, 85, 169
ideology 10, 211
Indigenous discourse 189, 200
Indigenous law 188
Indigenous people 15, 189, 194, 198–200, 202, 212–13, 215, 218
individuation 10, 12, 19, 37, 85, 109, 129, 201
    individuation hierarchy 22, 113
infographics 11, 132–5, 138–49
information flow 95
inscriptions, attitudinal 28, 151, 161, 164
Instagram 205, 208–10, 212, 215, 217–20
instantiation 14, 101–2, 133, 149, 207
intermodality 132–4, 138, 148–9
Invasion Day 205, 208–17
investigation report 86, 89–90, 92, 94, 96–7
invocation (of attitude) 28, 161

J
joint rewriting 97–8, 102
jointly constructed text 6–7, 97–8, 104–5, 164
journalism 21, 35
Journalistic Commentary 21–35
judgement 7, 27–30, 154–5, 161–3, 207

K
keywords analysis 211, 215, 218
kinship terms 109–12, 114–15, 117–26, 128–30
knowledge, scientific 149
knowledge genres 89–90, 96–7

L
language typology 19, 57, 82
LCT (Legitimation Code Theory) 13–14, 131
learning cycles 98–101, 105
Legitimation Code Theory. *See* LCT
literacy development 181
literacy pedagogy 4, 7, 131
logogenesis 5, 41, 52
logogenetic recontextualisation 161–2

M
macro-explanation 133
macro-genres 133
   complex multimodal 131
macro-theme 46
mass 13–14, 131–2, 134, 145, 148
Measurer 63, 66–9, 71–5, 77–81
metafunctions 51
modality 95, 168, 170, 172, 215
momenting 138–9, 145, 148
moments (of activity) 134, 139, 145–8
monoglossic 29, 36
monologic 24, 35, 58
multimodality 1, 10, 39–40, 47–8, 52, 85, 153, 158–9, 164, 217

N
naming 12, 25, 76, 122, 142, 194
nationhood 206
negotiation 10, 41, 110
newspapers 48, 199, 205, 208, 211–14, 217–18
nominal group 8, 57–8, 60–2, 64–8, 69–73, 75–81, 193–4
   embedded 72–3, 78
   structure 73, 75–8, 81, 194
   systems 75, 80

O
ontogenesis 5, 163

P
paradigmatic meanings 10, 43, 111, 115
paralanguage 11
pedagogy 1, 4–7, 16, 82, 97, 102, 108, 181
periodicity 10, 41–2, 95–6

persona 21–2, 113
phases 89, 95, 99, 101, 104
phoricity 51, 191, 193–5, 198
phylogenesis 5, 120, 126
picture books 49–52
positioning (of figures) 94, 101–2, 104, 126, 141–2, 197
Positive Discourse Analysis 1, 14–16
power 15, 109, 111–13, 124, 127, 169, 200
prefixes 111, 125
presence 13–14
pronouns 51–2, 60, 70, 75–6, 78, 80, 82, 110, 125
proper names 70, 191, 193–4
protests 36, 205, 211, 213–14
prototypicality 155
putative reader 28–30, 161

Q
qualification 72–5, 79–81
quantification 66–7, 73, 77, 80–1

R
ranks 8, 10, 13–14, 74, 127
reader positioning 7
realization
   hierarchy 14
   statements 49, 51, 76, 80
reconciliation 185–6, 188–9, 206
reference 10, 51, 191–7, 199
reference chains 186, 190–1, 194–6, 199
referent 190–4, 196–7, 214, 220
register 1, 3, 6, 10, 12, 41, 58, 85–6, 88–90, 95–7, 105, 171, 173, 175, 177
restorative justice 11
Rhetorical Structure Theory 46

S
sayer 156, 197
scaffolding 98, 168
school education 4, 6, 11, 85–6, 88–90, 97, 103, 105, 155–6, 164–5, 167–8, 170–2, 181, 187, 189
school science textbooks 134, 138
science explanations 131

Segmented Discourse Representation Theory (SDRT) 44–7
self-reference 198
semantic density 13, 131
semantic gravity 13, 131
semiotic modes 39–40, 47–9, 52–3
senser 191, 195
shared values 22, 24, 27, 30–3, 163, 205, 208, 217
  community of 28, 32, 35
SLATE Project 91
social media 24, 205–6, 210, 213, 217
solidarity 22, 127
spurning 26–7, 32–5
stages 4, 6, 47, 89, 136, 148
status 111–13, 125, 127
story genres 7, 12, 58
stratification 3, 10, 49–53, 59
Survival Day 205, 209, 212–15
Sydney School Genre pedagogy 4–5, 7, 12, 85, 97
system networks 42–3, 50, 75, 111, 122

T
Tagalog 1, 8–10, 57
Teaching Learning Cycle (TLC) 6, 167–8, 170
technicality 134, 148
tenor 12, 58, 88, 104, 109, 111–13, 124–6, 169, 194
Teochew 8, 109–11, 114–18, 122–6
textbooks 134–5, 138, 150, 154, 163

primary 155, 161, 163
secondary 154–5, 163
text linguistics 7
text types 6, 168, 181
Thai 8, 109–11, 114–18, 121–2, 125–6, 130
thesis statement 170–3, 175, 178
tier (of activity) 9, 134, 139–40, 145, 147–8
tiering (of activity) 139, 144–5, 148–9
Torres Strait Islander peoples 205, 211–12, 215, 217
transitivity 8, 193
Truth and Reconciliation Commission of Canada 185, 187–8, 203
Twitter 22, 24–5, 210, 217
typology 1, 10, 101

U
UAM Corpus Tool 191

V
valeur, 117 126
value positions 22, 26–8, 31–2, 34–6
vectors 48, 133–4, 145, 158, 161
vocatives 112

W
Write-it-Right project 205

Y
Youth Justice Conferencing 11

www.ingramcontent.com/pod-product-compliance
ghtning Source LLC
ambersburg PA
HW072107010526
111CB00037B/2024